A generation ago, the Joint Commission on the Mental Health of Children concluded that "there is not a single community in this country which provides an acceptable standard of services for its mentally ill children." Since then, many states have acknowledged the need to develop a system of care for such children, yet few adequate solutions have been implemented. Parents and other decision makers often face two unsatisfactory choices: coping as well as they can by themselves or turning the child over to someone else.

This book surveys issues related to the care and civil commitment of children with emotional disturbance. The authors examine research on the residential treatment system for children and youths, then analyze the prevailing legal framework for the commitment of minors to such treatment. They systematically address the question of what child mental health policy should be and conclude by proposing a policy that emphasizes privacy, autonomy, and family integrity. *No Place to Go* is both a major scholarly statement on the treatment of children with emotional disturbance and a rallying cry for principled change.

Gary B. Melton is the director of the Institute for Families in Society and a professor of neuropsychiatry and behavioral science, and adjunct professor of law, pediatrics, and psychology at the University of South Carolina. Phillip M. Lyons Jr. is an assistant professor at the College of Criminal Justice, Sam Houston State University. Willis J. Spaulding is an attorney in Charlottesville, Virginia.

CHILDREN AND
THE LAW

General Editor

GARY B. MELTON

University of South Carolina

Editorial Board

THOMAS GRISSO

University of Massachusetts Medical School

in Worcester

GERALD P. KOOCHER

Harvard Medical School

ROBERT J. MNOOKIN

Harvard Law School

W. J. WADLINGTON

University of Virginia

LOIS A. WEITHORN

San Francisco

No Place to Go

The Civil Commitment of Minors

•

GARY B. MELTON
PHILLIP M. LYONS JR.
AND WILLIS J. SPAULDING

University of Nebraska Press

Lincoln & London

⊖ The paper in this book meets the minimum requirements of

American National Standard for Information Sciences —

Permanence of Paper for Printed Library Materials,

ANSI Z39.48-1984.

Library of Congress Cataloging-in-Publication Data

Melton, Gary B.

No place to go : the civil commitment of minors / Gary B. Melton,

Phillip M. Lyons, Jr., and Willis J. Spaulding.

p   cm. — (Children and the law)

Includes bibliographical references and index.

ISBN 0-8032-3095-8 (cl : alk. paper)

1. Insane — Commitment and detention — United States.   2. Mentally
ill children — Legal status, laws, etc. — United States.   3. Mental
health laws — United States.   I. Lyons, Phillip M.   II. Spaulding,
Willis J., 1948–   .   III. Title.   IV. Series.

KF3828.M434   1998

362.2′1′083 — dc21   97-28085

CIP

Contents

Contents

CHAPTER 6

Toward Respect for Children, Youth,
and Families: Framework for a "New" Mental Health Policy

148

APPENDIX A

A Model Act for the Mental
Health Treatment of Minors

163

APPENDIX B

Division 37 Position Statement: Revised
Resolution on Advertising by Inpatient Programs

181

NOTES

183

REFERENCES

189

INDEX

225

NO PLACE TO GO

•
Rethinking Child Mental Health Policy

Nearly three decades ago, the Joint Commission on the Mental Health of Children concluded that it was "an undeniable fact that there is not a single community in this country which provides an acceptable standard of services for its mentally ill children, running a spectrum from early therapeutic intervention to social restoration in the home, in the school, and in the community" (Joint Commission, 1969, pp. 6–7).

The Joint Commission was especially outraged by the de facto policy of institutional treatment of troubled and troubling youth and the poor quality and intrusiveness of such treatment:

> The admission of teenagers to the state hospitals has risen something like 150% in the last decade. . . . Instead of being helped, the vast majority are the worse for the experience. The usual picture is one of untrained people working with outmoded facilities within the framework of long abandoned theory (where there is any consistent theory), attempting to deal with a wide variety of complex and seriously sick youngsters and produc-

ing results that are more easily measured by a recidivism rate that is often 30 to 50%, and occasionally higher.

    What we have, in effect, is a state of quiet emergency, unheralded and unsung, silently building up its rate of failure and disability and seemingly allowed to go its way with an absolute minimum of attention from the public, the legislators, or the clinical professionals. Nor is it difficult to understand why this state of affairs obtains — no one likes a delinquent youth, a bad actor, and when he is sent away the chief wish is just that, that he "go away." Out of sight. Out of mind. (Joint Commission, 1969, p. 6)

The unfortunate reality is that the conclusions the Joint Commission reached are still largely valid. In her landmark report for the Children's Defense Fund, Knitzer (1982) pointed out that no state had developed a true continuum of care for children and adolescents. Few states had even begun to create alternatives for care.

Although some progress has been made, the options that are available far too often boil down to counseling (30 or 50 minutes weekly or biweekly) and residential treatment. Without a continuum of care,[1] parents of children with serious emotional disturbance are confronted with only two alternatives: cope with their problems as well as they can largely by themselves, or turn the child over completely to someone else. Many children and families remain confronted with a choice of being underserved or overserved. Sometimes overservice is not an option; although the situation continues to improve, there remains a shortage of residential care for many children and adolescents, especially the latter.

Various initiatives at the state level have narrowed the gaps but without the full development of less intrusive services. The federal Child and Adolescent Service System Program (CASSP)[2] provided some impetus for development of alternative services. Most states now at least have an official with primary responsibility for development of child and family mental health services, and there are exemplary programs of "wraparound services" in some communities (see, e.g., Clark & Clarke, 1996; Evans, Armstrong, et al., 1994) — although still typically as demonstration programs or special programs for particular populations. Few communities offer a full range of mental health services for children, youth, and their families.

Perhaps the most salutary development is that state mental health agencies have approached a consensus about "what the *ideal* system of care should be" (Duchnowski & Friedman, 1990, p. 4, emphasis added) — an ideal typified by a wide range of alternatives. Nonetheless, that ideal remains far from realization. Unfortunately, the de facto mental health policy for children and youth, to the extent that there is *any* policy, often remains hospitalization or other residential treatment (see, e.g., Kiesler, 1982b, 1994; Wells, 1991). The biggest change has been in the players, as private hospitals absorb, often for profit, much of the continuing increase in inpatient treatment of children and youth.

Unfortunately, attention to this perverse policy has focused less on *what* we do to and for children in the mental health system than the secondary question of *who* does it. The emphasis on the allocation of responsibility for decisions about mental health treatment of minors is reflected in a line of cases culminating in the Supreme Court's controversial decisions in *Parham v. J. R.* (1979) and its companion case, *Secretary of Public Welfare v. Institutionalized Juveniles* (1979), about the procedures constitutionally required for admission of minors to mental hospitals. *Parham* was a landmark case in mental health law, family law, and legal procedure. It has received substantial citation (Perry & Melton, 1984) and has attracted much scholarly attention (see, e.g., Annas, 1979; Herbsleb, 1980; Keiter, 1982; Melton, 1984b; Perlin, 1981; Richards, 1980; Rothman & Rothman, 1980; Schoenberger, 1981; Silverstein, 1980; Spaulding, 1979; Sutnick, 1993; Tiano, 1980–81; Watson, 1980; Weithorn, 1988; Wingo & Freytag, 1982). The problem of due process requirements for civil commitment of minors had been in the federal courts for several years (e.g., *Bartley v. Kremens*, 1975), and it had been the focus of much commentary even before *Parham* (see, e.g., Ellis, 1974; Szasz, 1977; Wilson, 1978).

As we describe in greater detail in Chapter 5, *Parham* involved a class-action lawsuit filed by the plaintiffs on behalf of themselves and about 200 other minors in Georgia's mental hospitals. The plaintiffs alleged, among other things, that Georgia's statutes authorizing the "voluntary" commitment of minors by their parents without the minors' assent violated the minors' constitutional right to freedom from restraint of their liberties. The Supreme Court rejected the minors' assertion and upheld the statutes.

3

The substantial attention scholars have paid to *Parham* and similar cases is probably the result of a couple of factors. First, as reflected in most of the commentary, psychiatric hospitalization of minors seems to raise starkly the question of the limits of family privacy—in this instance, parental autonomy—in conflict with the personal privacy and autonomy of minors. The Court recognized that "a child, in common with adults, has a substantial liberty interest in not being confined unnecessarily for medical treatment" (p. 600). Nonetheless, the Court held that, in view of the presumed congruence of parents' and children's interests, parents and guardians constitutionally could volunteer their children and wards for hospitalization. The only procedural protections necessary were (a) an informal but comprehensive,[3] pre-admission inquiry by a mental health professional[4] acting as "neutral factfinder" (p. 606) and (b) some form of post-admission review.[5] Contrary to the lower court's earlier holdings (*J. L. v. Parham*, 1976), no formal, adversary hearing is required under *Parham*. Indeed, the late Chief Justice Burger, writing for the majority, trivialized such procedures as mere "time-consuming . . . minuets" (p. 605).

Second, in order to justify its divergence from seemingly well-established trends in its decisions on mental health (e.g., *Lessard v. Schmidt*, 1972) and child/family law (e.g., *In re Gault*, 1967), the Court went to great length to construct a vision of mental hospitals and family life. Chief Justice Burger's reading of the "pages of human experience" was so divorced from empirical reality as to be characterized fairly as mythology (see chap. 5 for discussion). *Parham* in fact helped to stimulate a psycholegal approach to family law that has largely refuted assumptions of adolescents' incompetence (see generally Davidson, 1991; Melton, Koocher, & Saks, 1983; Redding, 1993; Reppucci, Woolard, & Redding, 1996; Weithorn, 1982; Weithorn & Campbell, 1982).

The question of proper allocation of control over decisions of great personal significance to minors is an important one. Indeed, concern over this problem and the Supreme Court's rather jaundiced approach to it led the American Psychological Association's Division of Child, Youth, and Family Services (Division 37) to appoint a committee to consider the issue. This book and the model statute we present in Appendix A emanated from it. Although we take full responsibility for the opinions expressed in this book (the model statute, however, was endorsed by the Division 37 executive committee), we wish to acknowledge the helpful comments of the other committee members (Lenore Behar, Jane Knitzer, Gerald Koocher, Kerby Neill, Herbert Quay, and Lois Weithorn), as well as outside reviewers.

To show our colors from the beginning, we are convinced on both deontological and utilitarian grounds that minors deserve respect for privacy and autonomy (see chap. 6; also Melton, 1983e, 1987b, 1989). Moreover, as most of the Supreme Court justices in fact recognized in *Parham*, allocating control over decisions among child, family, and state has great constitutional significance (see generally Melton, 1996; Mnookin, 1978; Wadlington, Whitebread, & Davis, 1983). How much weight to give to parents' and children's interests and the degree of congruence between them is an important question for defining the legal and moral status of childhood (see generally Melton, 1983a, 1987b, 1989). Nonetheless, we have become convinced that it is the wrong question with which to begin an analysis of child mental health policy.

As we discuss in detail in Chapter 1, questions about allocating decisional control are more often than not moot. Children and adolescents who are admitted to psychiatric facilities are often already wards of the state. Even when patients come from families that are intact, their parents also often are reluctant volunteers who have placed their children because less intrusive alternatives are unavailable, unaffordable, or simply not offered. Sometimes, for example, hospitalization may be presented to parents as the only realistic opportunity for diversion of their child from incarceration in a juvenile correctional facility. The image that the Supreme Court and some mental health professionals have presented of parents and children in full-fledged legal combat in adversary hearings is an illusion.

For commitment law to have a real impact on the level of intrusion into minors' lives and the quality of care they receive, it must not divorce mental hospitals from the larger system of residential care for youth (e.g., Sutnick, 1993). As we show in Chapter 1, most children and youth in psychiatric facilities are troublesome and perhaps troubled, but they do not have classical mental illnesses. Moreover, they often are unable to return home even if they are not admitted. In the current service system, some kind of out-of-home placement often is inevitable, but the specific system (e.g., juvenile justice; child welfare) may vary. If procedures for admission and retention in psychiatric facilities are tightened without attention to the rest of the system of residential services, there is a substantial risk of merely "transinstitutionalizing" (see Warren, 1981) children and youth into treatment in group care, residential schools, or juvenile correctional facilities that may be even more intrusive than the hospitals from which they are being diverted (see Pandiani, Maynard, & Schacht, 1994 for a mathematical modeling technique to predict movement of children and youth among various placements).

Therefore, the central policy problem is not how to allocate decision control, although that problem must be considered. Rather, the key task is the design of procedures and standards that will ensure children access to reasonably good care while avoiding unnecessary intrusion into their lives and those of their parents. The problem in a nutshell is matching legal structures to the empirical reality of how the mental health system functions and the normative principle of respect for the personhood of children and youth. This task is formidable but achievable. In this book, we seek to provide a realistic but ethically and legally coherent approach to the formulation of child mental health policy, particularly as it regulates or encourages treatment that is highly intrusive into personal and family privacy or restrictive of personal freedom.

To begin this task, in Part 1 we review research describing the residential treatment system for children and youth: who enters it, why they do, how they are treated, and how they experience what is done to and for them. Having discussed what actually happens in residential mental health services, we turn in Part 2 to the prevailing legal framework for commitment of minors to such treatment. That is, we describe what child mental health policy is. Part 3 comprises a systematic examination of the question of what child mental health policy should be. After analyzing *Parham* and related perspectives (e.g., American Psychiatric Association, 1982b; Burlingame & Amaya, 1985; Silverstein, 1980), we propose a policy that is more protective of the historic ethical and constitutional values of privacy, autonomy, and family integrity and more consistent with treatment goals. The outcome of that analysis is a model statute presented in Appendix A.

PART I

The Nature of the Child
Mental Health System

CHAPTER ONE

•

Residential Treatment

The departure here from the usual approach to correction, child welfare, and mental health as completely separate fields is necessary to make clear the available evidence on the general patterns, over time, of juvenile institutionalization. There have been significant reductions in long-term traditional correctional handling of many youths in trouble [a trend that itself now has been reversed], but it would be misleading to conclude that deinstitutionalization has been achieved; for there have been offsetting changes in the use of private correctional facilities, residential treatment associated with child welfare, and psychiatric units of general and state hospitals. *In effect, there has emerged in unplanned fashion a new youth-in-trouble institutional system* that includes old and new institutions from all three fields: juvenile correction, child welfare, and mental health.

Lerman, 1980, emphasis added

9

THE INTERLOCKING SYSTEMS
OF RESIDENTIAL TREATMENT

The youth-in-trouble institutional system to which Lerman referred is the focus of this chapter and, to a large extent, this book as a whole. Even a cursory examination of children's mental health needs requires consideration of multiple systems whose boundaries are often blurred. The traditional divisions among children's service systems reflect somewhat arbitrary regulatory and payment structures more than they do differences in purpose, type of service, clientele, or even source of referral. Indeed, it is common for a therapeutic school or group home to have children and youth in the same program with funds provided for different residents by each of the major public brokers of children's services: local school systems, departments of youth services (juvenile justice), departments of social services (public welfare), and, in those instances in which they have authority to purchase services from private providers, departments of mental health. Private insurance carriers, which are heavily state-regulated, also may be paying part of the tab.

In fact, the type of agency paying for each particular child may reflect ease of bureaucratic action at a specific time and place more than the child's particular characteristics and needs. Children in residential treatment tend to be, or have been, clients of all or most of the major children's service systems. And if they are not clients of several systems, they could have been. Just as a single residential treatment facility may be a special school, a juvenile correctional facility, a child welfare placement home, and a mental hospital or mental health group home, the same child may bounce from one system to another for treatment because the populations served by the various systems, as we shall see, are substantially interchangeable.

Indeed, any attempt to study precisely how the youth-in-trouble institutional system works is apt to be blocked by its complexity and lack of planned action. Thompson and Wilcox (1995) summarized this state of affairs as it relates to child protection:

> [R]esearchers know astonishingly little about how children fare once they have become identified by child protection caseworkers. Where are they placed when the caseworker decides to remove them from the home?

How many placements occur before a permanent home is found? How do these placements vary with the age of the child? What alternatives exist to foster care and what are their consequences for children? Although there are a few large-scale studies of the experience of children in foster care, states have moved slowly to compile and analyze federally mandated data concerning the outcomes of children in out-of-home placements, and a thorough analysis will probably require the collaborative support of behavioral scientists. (p. 792)

The concerns voiced by Thompson and Wilcox about the child welfare system are generally germane to the child mental health treatment system. Commentary about the unplanned nature of child mental health treatment policy and the corollary problem of even describing the system has been common for at least a decade. With some obvious frustration, investigators from the General Accounting Office (GAO, 1985a) indicated the difficulty in examining how and why children are placed outside their homes for treatment: "We would have liked to collect data through observation of the placement process in operation, but this was not possible. . . . [T]here is not one placement process but many. Furthermore, these processes are often complex, the decision points numerous, and many decision points (e.g., an informal meeting between a private physician and a child's parents) do not lend themselves easily to observation by outsiders" (pp. 6–7).

Mental Health and Juvenile Justice

The children's service systems interlock to such a degree that consideration of them as separate systems is an artificial (even if legally recognized) categorization that invites incomplete policy analysis and ineffective policy initiatives. A well-known example of this principle is the net-widening effect apparently engendered by the Juvenile Justice and Delinquency Prevention Act of 1974 (JJDPA). The JJDPA had explicit goals of deinstitutionalization and diversion of nonserious juvenile offenders. These goals applied most obviously to status offenders, whose offenses — for example, disobeying parents, truancy, frequenting undesirable places — would not have been crimes if committed by adults.

Laudable though they are, these goals have largely gone unrealized. Krisberg and colleagues (1993), for example, found in their study of incarcerated juveniles in 14 states that an average of 31% of these children could be placed in much less restrictive settings less expensively and without compromising public safety. Moreover, in many localities, programs to divert youth from the juvenile justice system simply provided a new resource to police and juvenile courts for treatment of troubling youngsters whom they formerly would have diverted from juvenile court action altogether (Kobrin & Klein, 1983). The same youngsters who would have been subject to juvenile court jurisdiction prior to the establishment of a policy of diversion remained so, but a new population of juveniles now were diverted to treatment programs at least nominally connected to the court (Schwartz, 1995).

Even more germane to our analysis is the *transinstitutionalization* (Krisberg et al., 1993; Pandiani et al., 1994; Warren, 1981) of youth who ostensibly had been deinstitutionalized and diverted from the juvenile justice system. Many status offenders simply were relabeled as emotionally disturbed and placed in mental hospitals. States have experienced large increases in mental health referrals when juvenile codes are revised to decriminalize status offenses (Costello & Worthington, 1981; Hinckley & Ellis, 1985; Schwartz, 1991; Van Dusen, 1981; Warren, 1981). Nationally, by 1981 almost 30% of institutionalized status offenders were in facilities in the health system (GAO, 1985a). A dramatic decline (37%) in admissions of females — usually status offenders — to juvenile training schools in the five years following enactment of the JJDPA was matched by an equally dramatic increase (36%) in female admissions to private residential treatment facilities under juvenile justice auspices (Krisberg & Schwartz, 1983).

Often the movement between systems is direct — not simply an offset as intake policies change. Rather, many youths who enter the juvenile justice system find that they are actually on the way to the mental health system. Indeed, court-referred juveniles comprise a large proportion of the minors in mental hospitals. For example, in the early 1980s, one-third of the youth in northern Ohio state hospitals were court-referred, and one-half of the youth in North Carolina state hospitals had histories of serious juvenile charges (Knitzer, 1982). Almost 43% of youth in Nebraska's state inpatient unit for adolescents in 1985–86 were referred by juvenile courts (Department of

Public Institutions, pers. comm., 2 January 1987). A recent Vermont study showed that children in detention centers are more likely to be transferred to a treatment center than any other institutional setting (Pandiani et al., 1994).

Mental Health and Special Education

The juvenile justice system is not the only juvenile system interlocked with the mental health system. As a result of the federal Individuals with Disabilities Education Act (IDEA) and analogous state legislation, responsibility for care of mentally disordered children is divided between the mental health system, including private third-party payers, and the public schools. Indeed, private mental hospitals for children are likely also to be therapeutic schools and thus eligible for funds from local school systems. Knitzer (1982) described this relationship aptly as "the confused mandate" (p. 68). The confusion emanates from the fact that IDEA and its implementing regulations are unclear not only about the nature of emotional disturbance that qualifies for special education placement but also the appropriate division of responsibility for payment of residential treatment.

IDEA requires that the public schools provide children with handicaps with a "free appropriate public education which emphasizes special education and related services to meet their unique needs" (§ 1401(a)(18)). Among the related services that may be provided are "psychological services" and "medical and counseling services," "except that such medical services shall be for diagnostic and evaluation purposes only" (§ 1401(a)(17)). IDEA limits related services to those that "may be required to assist a handicapped child to benefit from special education" (§ 1401(a)(17)). The Supreme Court has interpreted IDEA's mandate narrowly, despite the express congressional intent to provide children with educational services "to meet their unique needs" (§ 1401(a)(18)). The Court has held that the child's individual educational plan need only be "reasonably calculated to enable the child to receive educational benefits" (*Board of Education of Hendrick Hudson Central School District v. Rowley*, 1982, p. 177), with one measure of benefit for children in regular classrooms to be whether they are receiving passing marks and advancing from grade to grade. Even services that clearly are not educational in the usual sense of the word (e.g., catheterization of a child with spina bifida) are required, however, if they are necessary for the child to be able to attend school and receive *some* educational benefit (*Irving Independent School District v. Tatro*, 1984). Furthermore, some state appellate courts have read IDEA's guarantees, as incorporated into state law, more broadly. These more expansive constructions (e.g., *Geis v. Board of Education*, 1984, defining an appropriate education as one in which "the pupil can best achieve educational success") may be enforceable in federal court (e.g., *David D. v. Dartmouth School Committee*, 1985). Confusing matters further, the criteria for "serious emotional disturbance" as a cognizable educational handicap require an untenable differentiation between "disturbance" and "social maladjustment" (see, e.g., Forness & Knitzer, 1992)[1] and may require a definitive medical (rather than educational) diagnosis (e.g., Bateman, 1995).

The law is particularly confused about the use of IDEA as a funding mechanism for psychiatric hospitalization. Some courts have held that all costs of hospitalization or other therapeutic residential placement must be borne by the schools if the child could not be educated otherwise (e.g., *Manchester School District v. Charles M. F. and Ellen P.*, 1994). Others have viewed *psychiatric* hospital services as "medical services" excluded from related services under the IDEA and have required that schools pay only the costs of education per se (e.g., *Salley v. Saint Tammany Parish School Board*, 1994).

Given both the ambiguity of the IDEA mandate and the expense of private placement and treatment, conflict over precisely defining school systems' obligations for treatment of mentally disordered children and youth is hardly surprising. The proportion of children identified as disabled because of serious emotional disturbance varies markedly from state to state—0.12% to 2.82% of the total enrollment and 1.1% to 27.0% of the children provided special education services (Knitzer, 1982, app. D; see also "Numbers," 1985). More recent estimates suggest that over 850,000 children with disabilities could have qualified for services under the IDEA during the 1991–92 school year, but that well over 25% of them received no such services (Bowe, 1995).

Thus, despite its nationwide scope, IDEA has failed to achieve its goal of providing children and adolescents with access to treatment services because of variations in interpretation and a general tendency by the courts to interpret its mandates narrowly. Regardless, the special education and mental health systems are interlinked. Courts that construe IDEA broadly provide a ready funding mechanism for hospitalization and other forms of residential treatment. Those that take a narrow view may indirectly increase placement through other mechanisms, because they minimize the likelihood of community-based (more specifically, school-based) services that might enable children with serious emotional disturbance to remain at home. In short, both broad views of the service types that may be funded through IDEA and narrow views of the population eligible for such services may work to increase use of residential treatment.

Mental Health and Social Services

Perhaps the greatest entanglement occurs between the mental health and child welfare systems. As we will show, a very large proportion of children in mental hospitals and other residential treatment facilities are wards of the state. Hence, their social workers qua guardians have placed them voluntarily in residential treatment.[2] With the "decriminalization" of status offenders, jurisdiction over them frequently has been transferred from youth service (juvenile corrections) to social service agencies, which ironically often rely upon the same placements (Lerman, 1980; Pandiani et al., 1994). The GAO (1985a) found that half of the youths institutionalized in "health" facilities in the three states it examined (Florida, New Jersey, and Wisconsin) were referred by welfare authorities. Even if the children were not already wards of the state prior to placement, the state sometimes required parents to relinquish custody if the placement was to be state-funded. Unfortunately, this practice has changed little. The Second Circuit Court of Appeals held that the requirement to relinquish custody does not infringe parents' substantive due process right to family integrity, because they voluntarily choose to accept the state's service of residential care (*Joyner v. Dumpson*, 1983).

Once children are placed in state custody, a new set of problems emerge. Social service placements often are far from children's families and, therefore, promote an institutional climate (Knitzer, Allen, & McGowan, 1978; Lyman, Prentice-Dunn, Wilson, & Taylor, 1989). Children find themselves amid a slow bureaucracy in which they are stuck in restrictive settings for long periods of time without effective recourse (see Hoagwood & Cunningham, 1992, on the inverse relationship of length of stay and treatment efficacy).

Even if state welfare agencies do not place children directly in residential treatment, they typically serve as the indirect brokers of services through Medicaid funding. As Kiesler (1980) pointed out, Medicaid is the largest mental health program in the country. The low ceiling on outpatient care and the common lack of reimbursement for alternative care (treatment models other than hospitalization and office-based psychotherapy) have combined to establish substantial financial incentives for inpatient mental health services for children (Knitzer, 1984). States sometimes spend about *40 times* as much on inpatient care for children with emotional disturbance as they do for outpatient mental health services under Medicaid (Kiesler, 1994). Put in more general terms, the social service system determines in large part where and how mental health services will be delivered, at least for children who are wards of the state or from poor families.

Besides being a broker and regulator of residential mental health services, the social service system also is a major provider of such services. Both public and private child welfare agencies, including — perhaps especially including — group care facilities, have evolved to a clear mental health orientation (Friesen & Koroloff, 1990; GAO, 1985a; Maluccio & Marlow, 1972). Former homes for dependent and neglected children are now commonly residential treatment centers (Lerman, 1980). Group care facilities commonly provide services resembling those in child and adolescent units of mental hospitals, although typically on a somewhat smaller scale (Curry, 1991; GAO, 1985a).

Although it is questionable whether the image of child welfare authorities "saving" children through the mere provision of humane care, custody, and training was ever accurate (Sutton, 1985), it is quite archaic. Social services now are professional, bureaucratic, and therapeutic (see, e.g., Billingsley, 1964; Bush & Gordon, 1978; Melton, 1983a, chap. 6) — so much so that there may be ever greater obstacles to the provision of "ongoing support . . . to help families in dealing with everyday crises" (Melton, 1993b, p. 496). Although the development of family resource centers in some communities may be increasing the availability of "family-friendly" services, in the bigger picture private child welfare agencies are more likely to resemble private psychiatric programs than neighborhood settlement houses. Clearly, if the youth-in-trouble institutional system is to be understood and regulated, attention must be given to residential treatment programs administered by social service agencies, as well as those in juvenile justice, special education, and the specialty mental health system.

Can the Web Be Untangled?

Two broad conclusions seem obvious from the discussion thus far. First, the aegis under which children and youth are placed in residential treatment is, if not entirely accidental, certainly not established and organized to address children's needs most effectively. The youth-in-trouble institutional system is an unplanned web of historically entrenched bureaucracies with similar ideologies and tasks but somewhat different staffing patterns and categorical funding streams. The need for coordination among these bureaucracies has been a theme of long standing in children's services (see, e.g., Hobbs, 1975, chap. 7; Joint Commission, 1969). Bureaucratic rigidity and professional prerogatives inherently impede the design of services that offer help to families where they are, when they need it, and in a form that they can use easily and without stigma (Melton, 1993b).

Thus, there is a need for substantial reform in the structure of child and family services. The U.S. Advisory Board on Child Abuse and Neglect (ABCAN, 1993), for example, observed, "Human service programs, including health and mental health, juvenile services, substance abuse programs, education, and economic and social supports, must collaborate to provide prevention and early intervention services that offer practical solutions to problems faced by families in crisis" (p. 27).

The historical record does not bode well for such collaboration. Although some progress is being made, mental health agencies have been notoriously slow to coordinate their work with the other children's service systems or even to provide support for advocacy services for the children who fall between the cracks in the system (Knitzer, 1982; Melton, 1977). If an effective child mental health policy is to emerge, it must begin with the understanding that clear delineation of young clients according to the system in which they are placed at the moment may not be helpful.

Second, if policies about the delivery of services to the most troubled and troubling youth are to have any effect, they must take into account the entire youth-in-trouble institutional system. A child mental health policy (which still does not exist in a highly coherent fashion anyway) is doomed to failure if it does not reflect the functional roles and efficacy of juvenile justice, special education, and child welfare. Mental hospitals and mental health group homes for children and youth cannot be viewed in a vacuum apart from residential treatment programs under other auspices. Therefore, our formulation of policy recommendations embraces an approach that not only views youth within the context of the children's service systems but also views components of those systems within the same larger context.

The seemingly random nature of child mental health policy historically is not unique. Mental health policy in general (usually taken to be synonymous with *adult* mental health policy) has been formulated poorly. Actual practices have departed grossly from stated policy goals, with de facto policy driven by a combination of irrational, inefficient funding structures and erroneous beliefs (Andrulis & Mazade, 1983; Kiesler, 1980, 1982b; Mordock, 1990; Sutnick, 1993). John Talbott (1985), then president of the American Psychiatric Association, scathingly attacked the expenditure of 1.38% of the gross national product on an "antiquated, unresponsive, scandal-ridden, mental health 'non system'" (p. 46). Although Talbott enumerated a long list of ills in public mental health services, he concluded that the most basic problem is the unplanned diffusion of responsibility for service delivery:

> The most important systems problem is the continuing severe fragmentation of the psychiatric delivery non system. Despite our long-standing awareness of the problem . . . , we remain burdened by a plethora of federal, state, and city-county programs and services. We have federally funded Veterans Administration, Public Health Service, and Armed Forces hospitals and clinics; we have federally initiated community mental health centers; we have state hospitals, clinics, children's services, and alcoholism and drug treatment programs; we have city-county hospitals, clinics, and other programs; and we have community general hospitals, free-standing clinics, and psychosocial rehabilitation centers — all of which coexist without any comprehensive planning or coordination. . . .

18

While this statement has been made so many times before that we no longer hear it clearly, let me repeat it: we do not have a system that works as a system should, automatically responding to internal changes (that is, patient movement) or external changes (that is, shifts in funding) by shifting resources from one area to the other, without losing any. Rather, we empty some very inflexible concrete boxes and overfill others. Our crazy-quilt of services has absolutely no capacity to act as a system. (Talbott, 1985, p. 47)

The rather accidental and unwieldy evolution of child mental health policy thus reflects the vagaries of mental health policy generally, but the scale of the problem is much larger and more complex in children's services. The problem of coordinating services *within* the health/mental health system is present in children's mental health services, just as in adult programs. But, as we have shown, responsibility for residential treatment of children and youth is fragmented *across* systems. Child mental health, child welfare, and juvenile justice developed together (Fagan, 1995; Levine & Levine, 1992); these systems have long been fragmented and enmeshed in law and in practice. Indeed, the majority of referrals for inpatient psychiatric care do not come from health providers (Schwartz, 1989). These organizational realities must be considered when attempting, as we are here, to develop a legislative framework for regulation of restrictive and intrusive treatment (e.g., Dore, 1993).

THE DE FACTO POLICY OF RESTRICTIVE TREATMENT
Restrictiveness and Privatization

Child mental health policy historically has aped adult mental health policy in one other critical way: a de facto preference for unnecessarily restrictive and intrusive treatment. As Talbott summarized, "Current inefficient reimbursement practices favor funding of inpatient over outpatient treatment, hospitalization over prevention of hospitalization, direct over indirect services, acute treatment over chronic care, and more restrictive alternatives over less restrictive ones" (1985, p. 47). Despite the long-prevailing rhetoric about deinstitutionalization, the steady trend has been toward increasing use of inpatient care, albeit much less frequently in state and county hospitals (Kiesler, 1982b). Even looking at state facilities alone, though, *budgets* historically have not reflected movement toward deinstitutionalization (Leviton & Shuger, 1983). State hospitals continue to absorb a substantial portion of state mental health dollars (e.g., Lee, 1994). Frank and Kamlet (1985) reported that state hospitals consumed about 70% of all government funding for mental health services during the 1980s. Expenditures for mental retardation services also have shown an institutional bias, although not as markedly and persistently (Fernald, 1986; Weicker, 1987).

Perhaps most depressing is that, although mental health agencies are beginning to realize the steps that *must be* taken to improve mental health service delivery (e.g., Duchnowski & Friedman, 1990), the changes remain largely theoretical. In a survey of state mental health directors little more than a decade ago, Ahr and Holcomb (1985) asked the administrators to rank 62 priorities for public mental health services. Closing or consolidation of state hospitals ranked sixty-second! An unfortunate side effect of block grants to the states may be that state mental health agencies find it easy to do what state mental health authorities historically did before the federal government provided direct support to community mental health centers — provide essentially custodial care for adults with serious mental disabilities, to the exclusion of preventive and less restrictive mental health services for broad segments of the population (Andrulis & Mazade, 1983; Eamon, 1994; Hargrove & Melton, 1987).

The continued, indeed growing, use of residential treatment provides clear evidence of continued reliance on the most restrictive forms of treatment (Eamon, 1994; Frank & Dewa, 1992). Reliance on residential treatment has been increasing at a particularly marked rate for children and youth (Burns & Friedman, 1990; Kiesler, 1994; Lerman, 1980). In a survey of state mental health agencies, Knitzer (1982) found that when agencies were planning increases in children's services, the focus was almost exclusively on residential treatment, with little or no attention to the much-ballyhooed continuum of care. Kiesler (1993) reported that the number of children in some form of residential treatment rose from 33,000 in 1980 to 169,000 in 1985. This trend is being reflected quite clearly in the private mental health sector. As revealed in congressional hearings (House Select Committee, 1985), the number of adolescents admitted to private mental hospitals increased by *450%* from 1980 to 1984 ("Testimony Focuses," 1985). Television commercials, sometimes bordering on unethical scare advertising have become commonplace as private, often for-profit hospitals aggressively market inpatient mental health and substance abuse programs for adolescents (see Dawley, 1985; app. B).

Although reliance on residential treatment facilities in general has increased, private psychiatric hospitals in particular have experienced large increases in market share (Frank & Dewa, 1992). Indeed, the growth of for-profit mental hospitals is a remarkable business phenomenon. Gutkind (1993) reported that "[p]rivate psychiatric hospitals . . . have grown from 200 in 1984 to 440 in 1988" (p. 94). The membership records of the National Association of Private Psychiatric Hospitals showed 198 private free-standing mental hospitals in the United States in 1982 (Levenson, 1983). Of those, 86 (43%) were chain-owned (71 of them owned by just four chains), and 44 (22%) were for-profit independently owned facilities. Just two years earlier, only 41 (25% of the then-extant private mental hospitals) were owned by hospital chains. A dozen years before that, the for-profit chains did not exist at all.

Despite long-standing de jure policies of deinstitutionalization and family preservation, the dual trends toward privatization and residential placement are echoed in the other children's service systems. The number of children and adolescents placed in residential treatment centers rose from 16,735 in 1980 (Milazzo-Sayre, Benson, Rosenthal, & Manderscheid, 1986) to 35,000 in 1985 (Jackson-Beeck, Schwartz, & Rutherford, 1987b). Lerman (1980) noted a shift in the proportion of private placements among nondetention juvenile correctional admissions from 21% in 1950 to 48% in 1974, with a much larger proportion of child welfare placements being made in private facilities. He concluded that, despite moves to deinstitutionalize *public* mental health and juvenile justice facilities, the rate of confinement of children and youth actually grew between 1950 and 1975. This trend is continuing at an escalating rate. When private programs are included, the rate of custody in juvenile correctional facilities increased by 47% between 1979 and 1991; incarceration of juveniles in adult prisons also has increased (Howell, Krisberg, & Jones, 1995).

Two-Tier System

Krisberg and Schwartz (1983; Krisberg, Litsky, & Schwartz, 1984; Krisberg, Schwartz, Litsky, & Austin, 1986) documented still stronger trends toward confinement in private facilities, but with notable race differences. As already noted, the decline in female admissions to juvenile training schools in the first years after enactment of the JJDPA was offset by female admissions to private facilities. Nonetheless, the training school beds that females have vacated have not gone unfilled; admissions of black and Hispanic male youth have risen at a rate sufficient to keep the training schools overcrowded.

Indeed, there is some evidence to suggest that nothing short of closing the juvenile detention centers and training schools will result in substantial, lasting reduction of their population. The number of detention beds available for the juvenile population is the best predictor of the number of youth admitted to detention (e.g., Schwartz & Willis, 1994). Juvenile arrest rates and teenage unemployment are weak correlates with detention rates, but the number of detention beds accounts for 76.8% of the variance in the use of juvenile detention (Krisberg et al., 1984). More recent data suggest that "86% [of the variance in use of detention] is explained by bed rates alone" (Schwartz & Willis, 1994, p. 15). The relationship between availability of training school beds and admissions to training schools is much weaker, but bed rate is still by far the strongest correlate, accounting for 27% of the variance.

Since about 1980, apparently as a reflection of the "get tough" policy in juvenile justice, both admissions to and one-day counts (the latter also reflecting length of stay) of detention centers and training schools have been increasing (Krisberg et al., 1986), notwithstanding de jure policies ostensibly favoring less restrictive alternatives. "Juvenile court statistics reveal that a growing portion of delinquency referrals are handled via formal delinquency petition filings, increased use of pretrial detention, reduced use of probation, and increased out-of-home placements and transfers to adult court" (Howell et al., 1995, p. 15). This increase is accounted for almost exclusively by minority youth. The number of incarcerated African Americans is nearly four times that of whites, and the number of incarcerated Latinos is nearly twice that of whites (Howell et al., 1995). White youth also have been entering residential treatment at an increasing rate but in *private* facilities, often within the mental health system. In contrast to the rate of confinement of minority youth in juvenile detention centers and training schools, about two-thirds of the youth in private juvenile justice placements are white.

Other studies document the two-tier system of children's services that Krisberg et al.'s (1986) data suggest. In its three-state study of residential treatment, the GAO (1985a) found youth in private facilities and in the health stream to come from much more affluent families, on average, than youth confined in public facilities and within justice centers. Echoing Krisberg et al.'s (1986) national census data, 70% of youth in the health facilities in the GAO survey were white, but the majority of youth in juvenile correctional facilities were from minority groups. About one-half of youth in public facilities but only about one-fourth of the youth in private centers were not white.

Studies of the specialty mental health system have yielded similar results. For example, a study of utilization of public-sector mental health services by children and adolescents with severe emotional disturbances in San Francisco found that over 40% of treatment recipients were African American (Barber, Rosenblatt, Harris, & Attkisson, 1992). This figure contrasts with the actual representation of African Americans in the local population — just over 10%.

Examination of the placement data on a case-by-case basis suggests that discriminatory decisions are being made. In a study of mental hospital and training school admissions in a metropolitan area, Lewis and Shanok (1981) found that African American males were especially likely to be sent to juvenile training schools. Three-fifths of the juvenile correctional inmates but only one-ninth of the adolescent hospital patients were black. About 15% of the training school residents were female, compared with about 45% of the hospital patients. Most important for interpreting these discrepancies is the fact that the training school and hospital samples did not differ in histories of violent acts or notations of mental health problems in their medical charts. Accounting for 18.1% of the variance, race was the most powerful correlate of place of confinement. Lewis and Shanok's (1981) conclusion was succinct and damning: "In brief, violent, disturbed adolescent blacks were incarcer-

23

ated; violent, disturbed whites were hospitalized. Even when black children were initially considered to be psychiatrically disturbed and were hospitalized, they often subsequently were transferred to corrections" (p. 306).

More recent studies show that race continues to be a powerful factor in placement decisions. In essence, the deeper one looks into the various service systems, the more pronounced are the racial differences. Data from California, an ethnically diverse state, provide a striking example (see Austin, 1995):

> Disturbing racial disparities permeate California's juvenile justice system. Although incarceration of white youth *decreased* by ten percent between 1985 and 1989, incarceration of minority youth *increased* by about fifty percent. African-American youth, in particular, are grossly overrepresented. Comprising only nine percent of the overall youth population, they represent nineteen percent of juvenile arrests, and thirty-seven percent of the youth in custody. Among juveniles who were referred for violent felonies in 1989, almost two thirds of African Americans but fewer than one half of whites were detained, and 11.4% of African-American youth but only 3.4% of white youth were committed to the California Youth Authority ("cya"). In fact, placement rates for African-Americans were consistently higher than for other ethnic groups, regardless of offense class. (Melton, 1993a, p. 2008, footnotes omitted)

The somewhat chaotic entanglement of children's services systems likely is at least partly to blame for the disparities in juvenile court dispositions along racial and socioeconomic lines. Although there is some support for the notion that the juvenile justice system is becoming increasingly adult-like in its focus on punishment (see, e.g., Grisso, 1993; Melton, Petrila, Poythress, & Slobogin, 1997; Poulos & Orchowsky, 1994; Sherman, 1994), it theoretically has been oriented toward treatment and rehabilitation tailored to the individual child (e.g., Reppucci & Crosby, 1993). To the extent that juvenile courts rely on the treatment rationale, they must focus on the best treatment that is available to the particular youngster at issue in a specific case. Thus, their dispositions are likely to vary considerably as a function of such factors as parents' ability to pay for treatment, comprehensiveness of private insurance programs and so forth—all of which, arguably, are less appropriate factors on which to rely for adjudicatory dispositions than more offense- and offender-related criteria (e.g., seriousness of the charge, severity of psychopathology, etc.). Thus, the juvenile justice system, by design, engenders inconsistent entanglement with other systems, both public and private. This design necessarily leads to widespread inconsistencies in outcome that systematically produce less desirable consequences for poor children, who disproportionately are ethnic minorities — a troubling bottom line.

Support for the hypothesis that system enmeshment is partially to blame for dispositional disparities inheres in the fact that the two-tier system observed in juvenile justice is also clear within the mental health system itself, with nonwhites twice as likely to be hospitalized in state and county hospitals (Taube & Barrett, 1985; Thompson, Rosenstein, Milazzo-Sayre, & MacAskill, 1986). Private hospitals have been criticized for skimming through locations in affluent areas and providing services only if profitable and only to patients who can pay (Eisenberg, 1984). The profits that have fueled the growth of proprietary mental hospitals emanate not from economies of scale but from increased ancillary procedures and higher rates of collections relative to nonprofit and public facilities, which disproportionately serve ethnic minorities, those with inadequate insurance, and individuals with more chronic disorders (Minkin, Stoline, & Sharfstein, 1994; Pattison & Katz, 1983; Relman, 1983). The rise of proprietary mental hospitals can be expected to increase the disparity of services across classes and ethnic groups, escalate aggregate costs of mental health services, and provide further fuel to the trend toward increasing use of residential mental health treatment. These concerns have influenced our approach to child mental health policy recommendations.

The Growing Hidden System of Restrictive Treatment

Absent major changes in the political climate, the privatization of residential treatment is likely to continue, regardless of the specific service system involved. During the Reagan administration, the Office of Human Development Services (1985) solicited applications for grants to "franchise" innovations in child and family services — a request for proposals that read like a prospectus for Kentucky Fried Social Services. Congress and many state governments now appear to be moving further along the course charted by the Reagan administration more than a decade ago. In that regard, states increasingly are embracing managed-care companies and other proprietary corporations for juvenile justice (cf. American Bar Association, 1986; Shichor, 1993), child welfare, health, and mental health services previously provided by public employees.

The inequity and costliness of private residential treatment are disturbing enough, but the most basic problem with the trend toward privatization of residential treatment is that it *hides* unduly restrictive, intrusive, or costly treatment. Although private residential treatment centers receive about 80% of their funds from government sources (GAO, 1985a), few states have effective schemes for regulating growth, cost, or quality of private services (Lerman, 1980). State health authorities charged with reviewing certificates of need for new hospitals often have little basis for determining whether need has been demonstrated (e.g., Scalora, 1986). Prevalence data for child mental health problems are very soft (Gould, Wunsch-Hitzig, & Dohrenwend, 1981), and states often do not even have plans for how *public* child mental health services are to be developed (Knitzer, 1984). Even if reasonably good evidence can be gathered that *some* new private child mental health services are needed, health planning agencies may lack the expertise or the authority to consider the sorts of services that should be developed first.

Unless third-party payers, including public agencies, rebel, the dramatic increase in private treatment centers for children is likely to continue, simply because such enterprises are profitable and low risk. Mental health services thus far have escaped, to a large extent, the innovations in cost containment (e.g., prospective payment plans) that have restructured physical health care (Ruggie, 1990, noted little retrenchment in U.S. mental health policy), although managed mental health care is increasing.

Development of residential treatment facilities is attractive to investors because the capital construction and maintenance costs for mental hospitals, psychiatric wards, residential treatment centers, and mental health group homes (cf. Rosenblatt, Attkisson, & Fernandez, 1992) are much lower than for the medical wards of general hospitals. Less investment in equipment is necessary for psychiatric facilities, and the bricks and mortar for mental hospitals can easily be used to capitalize additional buildings. The relatively high proportion of budgets in personnel costs — without the civil service rules that constrain public administrators — gives corporate administrators of private mental health facilities considerable flexibility to respond to changes in market conditions and maximize profit accordingly. Children's treatment centers may be especially attractive to investors because of the relative scarcity of such facilities and the multiple sources of referrals and third-party payment. In short, private residential treatment centers are apt to continue to appear and to take increasing proportions of dollars spent for children's services, especially those delivered to children and youth from relatively privileged backgrounds. With minimal governmental constraints on establishment of new centers, this trend is likely to continue regardless of either the optimal mix of public and private services or the utility of residential treatment in comparison with less restrictive forms of children's services.

The regulatory vacuum does not end with the actual establishment of new centers. Except for whatever self-regulation a private facility develops (e.g., adherence to accreditation standards), it is apt to be without the detailed statements of resident rights and the procedures and structures (e.g., protection and advocacy staff) for vindicating them that are now common in public treatment centers. Moreover, because private facilities often rely on ostensibly voluntary admissions, courts may be reluctant to recognize rights for residents that are recognized almost universally, if not necessarily applied, in public treatment centers (e.g., *Milonas v. Williams*, 1982). Thus, although private residential treatment centers often may have more aesthetically pleasing facilities than their often aged public counterparts, the lack of effective oversight raises the potential for treatment that is even more intrusive and restrictive than in old-style state hospitals and training schools.

We do not mean to suggest that privatization is inherently pernicious or even inherently undesirable. State services may be hamstrung unduly, for example, by civil service strictures and existing physical plants that were much better suited to the days when large institutions were the settings of choice (Okin, 1985a; S. J. Schwartz, 1989/1990). Monitoring public children's mental health services also is woefully inadequate in most states (Kiesler,

1993; Knitzer, 1982). Privatization also can provide an avenue for *community* (rather than proprietary) development of services that are not constrained by bureaucratic categories and service units.

Absent effective regulation and planning, however, the growth of private residential treatment centers, especially proprietary private hospitals, is likely to continue to be accompanied by a disproportionate growth in the rate of residential placement of children and youth and perhaps greater restrictiveness and intrusiveness than within public facilities.

THE MARKET FOR RESIDENTIAL TREATMENT

In attempting to identify an appropriate balance of treatment approaches for youth by way of fashioning a more informed child mental health policy, we are careful to avoid being too quick to conclude that residential treatment is overutilized. To determine whether such treatment is "too much" for most child and adolescent recipients one must look at the characteristics of those youth. The results are telling.

Diagnosis

Whether public or private and regardless of the specific children's service system, residential treatment centers are most likely to receive children and youth whose most obvious characteristic is that they are "troubling" (e.g., Hobbs, 1982; Silver et al., 1992). The common perception may be that children and youth in residential treatment have disabilities, like schizophrenia, that the public consensually recognizes as mental illnesses, but the youth-in-trouble institutional system clearly is oriented toward male adolescents with conduct disorders. Even in most mental hospitals, few of the child and adolescent patients have psychotic disorders (Melton, 1993b). The common theme among youth admitted to residential treatment is a history of aggressive misbehavior. It is this behavior, not disordered thinking or disturbed mood, that typically results in the institutionalization of children and youth.

The general picture of youth in residential treatment is remarkably consistent in reports from diverse settings. Consider, for example, the demography of inpatient mental health units under various auspices across the country:

- A national study of mental health admissions of minors to general hospitals showed that one-half had primary diagnoses of adjustment reaction, behavior disorders, or neuroses; only one in eight had a diagnosis of schizophrenia (Jackson-Beeck et al., 1987a).

- In the adolescent inpatient mental health unit of a private general hospital in a large Midwestern city, Conduct Disorder and Problems with Feelings (e.g., resents authority, does not like self) accounted for 57% of target symptoms, in contrast with Problems with Thinking (e.g., hears voices that are not real, has strange thoughts and beliefs), which accounted for only 1% of target symptoms (Fineberg, Kettlewell, & Sowards, 1982).

- Only 8% of the children in the children's psychiatric unit of a California community general hospital were diagnosed as psychotic; by contrast, 73% were diagnosed as having a personality, reactive, or developmental disorder (Blinder, Young, Fineman, & Miller, 1978).

- In a California state hospital unit for children up to age 15, two-thirds had diagnoses of behavior or personality disorder (Schain, Bushi, Gardella, & Guthrie, 1980).

- Thirty-seven percent of the adolescent inpatients at the UCLA Neuropsychiatric Institute were diagnosed as having schizophrenic, schizoaffective, or major affective disorders; the majority were characterized as having conduct, personality, or attention-deficit disorders (Strober, Green, & Carlson, 1981).

- Most of the adolescents in a Virginia state hospital were diagnosed as having situational, behavior, or personality disorders (77.3%); only 14.7% were psychotic (Bloom & Hopewell, 1982).

- Similar data were reported in litigation concerning state hospitals in Georgia and Pennsylvania.

- In a university-based state hospital unit for elementary-school-age children in central Missouri (ages 7 to 12), the most common referral problems were incorrigibility, aggression, frequent fighting, and serious classroom problems (Kashani & Cantwell, 1983). Temper tantrums, hyperactivity, acting out, and enuresis were common symptoms; no child was diagnosed as psychotic.

- In a study of residential and community-based treatment programs in four states, over 75% of children in residential treatment and nearly 60% of children in community treatment programs had been diagnosed with Conduct Disorder (Silver et al., 1992).

The profile looks little different in residential treatment settings in other service systems. For example, Wurtele, Wilson, and Prentice-Dunn (1983) examined the population of 15 residential treatment centers through stipends paid by the Alabama Department of Pensions and Security (the state social service agency). The main referral problems were noncompliance, academic difficulties, immaturity, and aggression. Bizarre or psychotic behavior was reported infrequently. Of course, a history of antisocial behavior is universal among youth in juvenile justice placements. When one looks across systems, the relatively low proportion of children with the most severe disorders in residential treatment — the most intrusive treatment delivery modality — suggests strongly that such treatment is overutilized and that policy should be modified accordingly.

Age and Gender

Although younger children are more likely to benefit from residential treatment (Prentice-Dunn, Wilson, & Lyman, 1981), adolescents are much more likely to receive such treatment. For example, in Wurtele et al.'s (1983) survey of residential treatment centers for children and youth, about 70% of the residents were aged 13 or older. In the GAO's (1985a) three-state survey of residential treatment for children and youth, about 90% of the residents were found to be 12 or older.

Youth in residential care are usually male. The GAO (1985a) found three-fourths of all placements to be of boys. The proportion of males among residents of juvenile justice facilities was especially marked (91.6%). However, males also predominated in residential treatment centers within the welfare (69.0%) and health (70.5%) systems.

The distribution of age and gender in residential treatment centers coincides in general terms with the incidence of serious delinquent behavior (e.g., Henggeler, 1989; see Rutter & Giller, 1984, for a comprehensive review of the epidemiology of delinquency). The frequency of both violence and serious property offenses rises greatly in adolescence, and males are much more likely than females to engage in aggressive misconduct. Thus, as in the admitting diagnosis, the distribution of age and gender in residential treatment suggests that mental health treatment needs are not driving mental health treatment placement decisions. Modifications in social policy must take this inattention into account.

Academic Problems

Another pervasive characteristic of youth in residential treatment is academic delay. In Wurtele et al.'s (1983) survey of youth in child welfare facilities in Alabama, two-thirds were more than one grade level behind in achievement when they entered residential treatment. Academic skill deficits are a particularly strong correlate of delinquency (Dishion, Loeber, Stouthamer-Loeber, & Patterson, 1984; Thornberry, Lizotte, Krohn, Farnworth, & Jang, 1991; Thornberry, Lizotte, Krohn, Farnworth, & Jang, 1994), which remains statistically significant when other demographic variables are controlled (Rutter & Giller, 1984). A low level of academic competence also is a particularly strong predictor of reinstitutionalization (Bloom & Hopewell, 1982; Hobbs, 1982; Yoshikawa, 1994).

The actual characteristics of youth in residential treatment thus may depart substantially from the stereotype of troubled children and youth: "Regardless of the particular public service system for children and youth — child mental health, child welfare, juvenile justice, or the behavior disorders side of special education — the modal client is adolescent, male, conduct disordered, poor, educationally delayed, a resident of a "bad" neighborhood, and a member of a "multiproblem" family with serious problems in general" (Melton, 1993b, p. 513).

In that regard, the trend across systems toward a traditional "mental health" orientation is unfortunate. The problems that youth in residential treatment typically have are not in the strict sense mental health problems, but misconduct, deficits in educational and vocational skills, and, as we shall see, social disadvantage. Although these difficulties are serious for both so-

31

ciety and the youth themselves, they require interventions other than traditional mental health treatments (see, e.g., Lipsey, 1992; Melton & Pagliocca, 1992; Mulvey, Arthur, & Reppucci, 1993; Tate, Reppucci, & Mulvey, 1995). Michael Rutter, perhaps the most eminent psychiatric researcher on childhood disorders, has concluded flatly that such interventions are generally unhelpful in treating conduct disorders: "Counselling and psychotherapy are of no value as means of preventing delinquency, and as a mode of treating offenders it is likely that they are useful only in a minority of cases" (Rutter & Giller, 1984, p. 318).

We are not suggesting that difficult adolescents should go unserved or that the mental health system simply should dump them upon other children's services. Rather, our point is that the ubiquitous notion of adolescents as the most underserved population (see, e.g., President's Commission, 1978, p. 633) reflects the failure to shape treatment services to meet the needs of the population that in fact is placed in residential treatment. The sort of care traditionally provided by mental hospitals — and now by a range of public and private facilities — is not the answer (e.g., Eamon, 1994; Mirin & Sederer, 1994), a fact that we have known for some time (see Miller & Kenney, 1966). To a large extent, the existing youth-in-trouble institutional system serves merely to incapacitate the most troubling youth, not to effect lasting positive change in the youth themselves or their situation.

THE FAMILIES OF CHILDREN AND YOUTH
IN RESIDENTIAL TREATMENT
The Myth and the Reality

Much of the commentary on civil commitment of minors has focused on (a) whether the interests of parents of children being considered for hospitalization and the interests of the children themselves are congruent and (b) whether formal, adversary procedures will fractionate the family. We do not believe that adversary proceedings in fact will exacerbate conflict between parent and child. Regardless, examination of the characteristics of families of children and youth in residential treatment clearly indicates that the great emphasis placed on parental interests (and their relationship, whether positive or negative, to children's interests) in discussions of child mental health policy is misplaced. The rather idealized image of the family in *Ozzie and Harriet* (or fill in your favorite situation comedy from the 1950s) misrepresents American families generally (ABCAN, 1993; Barber et al., 1992; Conger, 1981; Edelman, 1981; Melton, 1993a), but it is especially distant from the families of children and youth in residential treatment (e.g., Parmelee et al., 1995). The image of concerned parents admitting their children to the hospital for mental health treatment just as parents do for surgery to alleviate physical conditions[3] is not realistic in the majority of cases.

First, admission of children to residential treatment rarely comes on their parents' initiative. Although mass-market advertising by private hospitals may lead to some change in this regard, parents rarely are the referral source for children in residential care. The GAO (1985a) survey found that just 8.5% of children in welfare facilities and 18.1% of children in health facilities had been referred by their families. The issue of potential parent-child conflict has been framed typically in terms of admission to public mental hospitals. However, the GAO found that, when parents did refer their children directly for residential treatment, it was almost eight times more likely to be to a private than a public facility.

Second, parents themselves often are reluctant volunteers — forced to place their children in residential care because of the apparent absence of alternatives. Some states require that parents placing children in residential treatment surrender custody (see, e.g., Cohen et al., 1993; *Joyner v. Dumpson*, 1983). Parents, like their children, may welcome less restrictive alternatives if they are presented (Hoagwood & Cunningham, 1992; Perlin, 1981). When the states fail to create less intrusive alternatives to residential treatment, force parents to surrender custody in order to access the only services available, and then place the children in residential treatment, it is improper to blame parents for the ultimate placement decision.

In a class action challenging the adequacy of Louisiana's out-of-state placements of children and youth for residential treatment (*Gary W. v. Louisiana*, 1976), the federal district court implicitly accepted the argument by the United States, as plaintiff-intervener, that parents' actions were only nominally voluntary. The parents did not have access to Louisiana institutions. They were beset by personal and financial problems as a result of having a child with unusual problems in their home and they were not able to care for and treat the children adequately. As the funder of services, the state usually supplied the only information the parents had about available facilities. In some instances, juvenile courts required that the parents place their child outside their home or risk the loss of custody.

The court emphasized the difficulty of the choices facing parents:

> No compassionate human being could fail to be moved by the plight of the children who are plaintiffs. Nor can that tragedy be viewed in isolation as the child's alone. For in many instances, the child's family is wrenched by the calamity. There is interaction between family and child, child and family, so intricately entwined that the family's disorder heightens the child's, and the child's plight rends the family. Unable to care for the child, parents are willing, sometimes eager, to have the child placed elsewhere if only to obtain the adequate custodial care that they no longer manage to provide. (p. 1217)

Third, when children enter residential treatment, they often *already* are wards of the state or otherwise separated from at least part of their families (e.g., Rosenblatt & Attkisson, 1992). The vast majority are not admitted from two-parent homes. Only 26% of the residents of treatment centers in the GAO (1985a) survey were admitted from two-parent homes; one-fourth of the youth had not been living with a family member at all. In Wurtele et al.'s (1983) Alabama survey, only 10% had been living with both natural parents, and 60% had been living with neither natural parent. The placement was the first for only 6% of the children. Olsen (1981) found that 42% of the adolescents on Massachusetts's adult state hospital wards and 60% of the children on the single pediatric state hospital ward had been admitted from a setting other than their families. Most of the children were clients of the state social service agency. In a California state hospital unit for children, most (84%) had several previous placements; only 17.7% had been living with both natural parents (Schain et al., 1980). In a state hospital unit limited to elementary-school-age children in Missouri, few (8%) had been living in foster care prior to admission, but almost as few (14%) had been living with both natural parents (Kashani & Cantwell, 1983). In Parmelee et al.'s (1995) study of two public hospitals in Virginia, 17% of children were from two-parent homes at the time of hospitalization. Sixty-five percent had been previously hospitalized in a psychiatric facility and 64% had received prior outpatient care. Clearly, it is improper to cast placement decisions in terms of conflict between the interests of parent and child when the state has eliminated parents from the placement decision-making process altogether.

Fourth, even when families are available, they commonly have multiple serious problems and are under substantial stress. The GAO (1985a) found that two-thirds of the children in placement came from families earning less than $15,000 annually. Fifty-seven percent of the inpatient children's parents in Kashani & Cantwell's (1983) sample had a history of mental disorders, most commonly alcoholism. This proportion was 2½ times greater than a matched sample of children in outpatient treatment. Bloom and Hopewell (1982) found that 50% of adolescents readmitted to a state hospital within six months had close relatives with a history of mental hospitalization, compared with 28% of those who had not recidivated. In view of the family variables known to correlate with children's behavior disorders (for reviews, see Hawkins & Catalano, 1992; Hetherington & Martin, 1979), family instability may be, as one research team pointedly stated, "almost a required factor for the development of conditions leading to admission of 'mentally disabled' children to Camarillo State Hospital" (Schain et al., 1980, p. 50). Truly informed policy must take account of the fact that families can be expected to endure only so much before their resources for coping are depleted entirely.

Fifth, parents and children sometimes *do* appear to have some conflicts of interest by the time placement is considered. These conflicts are typically not the sort of selfish expression of parental interest that sometimes is presumed in commentary by child libertarians. Parents do not place their children cavalierly because they are simply in the way, and placement is not apt to occur because of a mere difference in values or life style. Rather, parents may be concerned about the effects of the identified patient on siblings or the family as a whole.

These issues assume particular significance if the family is in fact on the verge of breaking up or the care and management of the child is especially taxing. Studies of children with mental retardation have shown, for example, that placement is more likely if parents perceive themselves as lacking adequate social support or if they are elderly, sickly, or single (Blacher, 1994). However, longitudinal research to show a causal linkage between placement and marital breakup has not been conducted.

Regardless, the evidence is clear that families welcome in-home services even when they are in periods of intense crisis (see generally Schwartz & AuClaire, 1995). When services are available to families when and where they need it, conflicts of interest evaporate. At that point, the family as a whole shares an interest in the preservation of the family and avoidance of more intrusive and restrictive strategies.

Similarly, when parents and siblings need occasional breaks to provide them with energy to cope, the provision of respite services *before* a crisis emerges and *before* family members are emotionally drained is in the interest of all family members. Such an approach is likely to serve their collective interest in family integrity and to meet the child's right to a stable family environment (see Melton, 1996).

This point was poignantly illustrated by the comments of a focus group of adolescents in a temporary shelter who were awaiting a longer-term placement, often *again* awaiting placement: "The children were unanimous in preferring foster care over group homes and other institutional arrangements (see also Bush, 1980), and they also agreed that the worst part of being in any kind of out-of-home care is the feeling of not really belonging *any* place" (Davis & Ellis-MacLeod, 1994, p. 123).

In short, the primary interest of all family members is in avoidance of a circumstance in which one of their members has no place to go. Given the multiple, often chronic, and sometimes intense needs of many of the families whose children ultimately are admitted to residential treatment, policy must be structured to make the resources available that would prevent the development of circumstances in which families are left with no real choices.

Implications

The evidence is clear that placement of children and youth rarely results from an objective judgment of need for residential treatment by concerned parents. Rather, whether action is formally taken by a parent or the state, placement of a child or adolescent in residential treatment is likely to occur only when it seems as though he or she has no other place to go. In combination with the bothersome behavior of most institutionalized children and adolescents, this fact explains both the relatively long stay common in residential treatment centers and the tendency for minors to remain in restrictive care when it is viewed consensually as unnecessary or even harmful.

Unfortunately, unnecessarily restrictive and intrusive treatment is the central reality of the institutionalized youth-in-trouble system. Summarizing from agency reports in several states, Knitzer (1982) concluded that at least 40% of children and youth in state hospitals could have been treated in less restrictive settings, *by the states' own admission*. This is true of residential treatment facilities as well. In their three-year study of 36 residential placements, Hoagwood and Cunningham (1992) found that, according to the facility personnel themselves, two-thirds of the children could have avoided hospitalization if community-based services had been available.

Not only are children and youth admitted unnecessarily, but they also remain for long periods of time—typically much longer than hospitalized adults. Hoagwood and Cunningham (1992) found a median length of stay of 15 months for children placed in residential facilities through educational referrals. In the three states studied by the GAO (1985a), average length of stay in health facilities was about a year and in welfare facilities about 7.5 months. These mean lengths of stay may be briefer than in residential treatment centers nationally (e.g., Marsden, McDermott, & Minor, 1977). For example, Wurtele et al. (1983) found that many (about half) of the youth then in residential treatment centers in Alabama already had been there between three months and a year. A substantial additional proportion (20%) had resided in the center for at least two years.

Whether lengthy residential treatment is desirable is a matter of controversy (see, e.g., Eamon, 1994; Henggeler, Schoenwald, Pickrel, Rowland, & Santos, 1994; Mirin & Sederer, 1994; Wolins, 1969). Probably it is preferable to being bounced from placement to placement, as had been the experience of many of the youth in Wurtele et al.'s (1983) sample. We are aware of no studies of residential treatment for children and youth that directly address the issue of youth treatment efficacy and length of stay in residential placements. However, studies of adult patients clearly show that less is better; longer hospitalization does not decrease, and in fact often increases, the probability of rehospitalization (Hoagwood & Cunningham, 1992). Regardless of whether some form of long-term treatment is desirable, the point is that youth frequently are kept in highly restrictive placements for much longer than even the programs' clinicians and administrators believe they need to be, simply because they lack a better place to go. Parmelee and colleagues (1995), for example, found that in the judgment of the attending clinician 56% of the children in their sample were discharged to a less-than-ideal placement. Child mental health policy must take this motivation for initial and continuing placement into account.

FAMILIES OF CHILDREN WITH MENTAL RETARDATION IN RESIDENTIAL PROGRAMS

Informed child mental health policy also must take into account the actual, rather than imagined, characteristics of the families involved in making decisions about treatment placement. The federal government has offered some financial incentives for deinstitutionalization of people with mental retardation (see GAO, 1977). States frequently have adopted stringent requirements for admission to state facilities for persons with mental retardation (e.g., Sherman, 1988; see also Sutnick, 1993), and the ideology of deinstitutionalization has met greater acceptance among mental retardation professionals than mental health professionals. This greater acceptance may have resulted from the fact that the movement toward deinstitutionalization of persons with mental retardation was entrenched over two decades ago. As Halpern, Sackett, Binner, and Mohr (1980) observed: "[T]he most important factor distinguishing programs for the mentally ill from programs for the mentally retarded was the existence of a set of well-organized advocacy groups. Advocacy groups . . . demonstrated their effectiveness in making the system respond to the client's views of his or her interests and needs. In the past, advocacy groups have also been very influential in demanding and monitoring the provision of community-based services and the rights of individuals residing in institutions" (p. 99). For these and other reasons, deinstitutionalization of people with mental retardation has occurred more successfully than attempts to develop alternatives to mental hospitals, although formidable barriers still stand in the way from time to time (e.g., Woodward, 1993).

Nonetheless, the factors leading to placement of minors with mental retardation tend to be similar to those resulting in placement of minors with behavior disorders. That is, placement is most likely when there is a combination of difficult behavior, multiple family stressors, and scarcity of alternative placements. This general conclusion has to be tempered by the fact that many of the studies of factors in placement decisions were conducted in the 1960s, before deinstitutionalization was well under way. However, the factors appearing in the older research may be even more important now that restrictions have been established on admission to training schools for persons with mental retardation (e.g., Sherman, 1988).

In a comprehensive review of the literature on placement decisions, Sherman and Cocozza (1984) noted that the level of disability is the most important factor. Not surprisingly, residents of institutions for people with mental retardation most commonly have a severe or profound mental disability often with accompanying physical disabilities. The trend is toward increasingly higher proportions of persons with profound retardation in the populations of state institutions (see, e.g., Eyman, Borthwick, & Tarjan, 1984). However, client characteristics do not account for a large proportion of the variance in placement decisions. Many minors with severe or profound mental retardation remain at home, and some minors with mild or moderate mental retardation still are institutionalized (Scheerenberger, 1978).

The characteristics of families who institutionalize their children with mental retardation are similar to those of families who hospitalize their children with behavior disorders. Specifically, the existing literature (Sherman, 1988; Sherman & Cocozza, 1984; see also Fotheringham, 1970) indicates that institutionalized people with mental retardation tend to come from large families of lower socioeconomic status that are single-parent or in which there is high marital conflict. Poor parental health (physical or mental) or older parental age is also a common factor in placement. Sherman and Cocozza's (1984) review also indicates the significance of community factors, especially professional inclination to recommend placement and a dearth of alternative services.

The specific factors in placement may vary with the nature of the child's disability. Allen (1972) examined applications for admission to the Utah Training School in the mid- and late-1960s, soon after the shift in professional beliefs about the desirability of institutionalization. The largest proportion of applicants (more than one-third) cited threats to family welfare, such as parental or sibling conflict and family instability, as their rationale; most of these applications concerned children with severe or profound mental retardation. Almost 30% of the applicants cited the physical or psychological burden of caring for a child with handicaps, sometimes in regard to parental health. The second largest proportion of applicants consisted predominantly of families reporting difficulties managing their children's severe or moderate retardation. The third largest group of applicants (about one-eighth of the sample) cited social management problems; most of the children involved had mild or borderline retardation.

The age of the children also related to placement decisions. Most (72%) of the children in the first group were age six or older. Even very unstable families may be able to tolerate the demands of young children with mental retardation, but families with multiple problems may not be able to deal with the marked deviance of behavior and appearance of older children with severe or profound mental retardation. On the other hand, most placements sought under the rationale of psychological or physical burden involved young children. The majority (57%) were under age 6, and most (81%) were under age 11. Apparently, when families simply are incapable of dealing with the special needs of children with disabilities, that difficulty is noted early in the child's life.

The complexity of interests that parents must balance is noteworthy. Caring for a child with severe or profound mental retardation is undeniably difficult, especially when the family is subject to multiple serious stressors (see generally Earhart & Sporakowski, 1984; Farber, 1968; Grossman, 1972; Henggeler et al., 1994). Parents often consider the perceived welfare of siblings and neighbors — and their own and their other children's sense of embarrassment in the community — in deciding whether to institutionalize a child (Sherman & Cocozza, 1984).

The nature of these conflicts is suggested in the cases cited by the federal district court in *Bartley v. Kremens* (1975), a famous class-action suit involving institutionalized children in Pennsylvania. One boy with Down syndrome was institutionalized for a couple of weeks so that his parents could take a vacation; if a less restrictive form of respite care were available, it seems likely that it would have been used. Another child with mental retardation was placed because of conflicts with the child's mother and the family's fear that the mother would have a nervous breakdown if placement did not occur. A third child was institutionalized because of "a fear that if the child remained in his home, the mother might break down, the marriage of the child's parents might end in separation, the father's health might fail, and an adolescent daughter might be pushed into a premature marriage to escape an unhappy home" (p. 1044).

Although institutionalization of the child with mental retardation in fact generally has no discernible effect on the well-being of the families who place their children, the concerns involved are quite legitimate, even if at some variance with the child's own interest. Moreover, as in the instance in which the family simply desired to take a vacation, short-term residential placement for the family's benefit actually might be in the child's own interest in the long term, if the parents are then better able (after a break) to care for the child.

Provision of resources and support may help to keep families together. Minnesota's financial subsidy for families of mentally retarded children has had the most effect on helping the most stressed families cope (Zimmerman, 1984). The subsidy was particularly useful in helping to pay for special items for the child, increasing the family's general ability to meet the child's needs, and purchasing specialized child care so that mothers could work outside the home. On the other hand, the availability of a subsidy made no difference in families' *plans* ultimately to place their children with mental retardation outside the home. Mothers who anticipated eventually doing so tended to be younger, work outside the home, have fewer children (note the variance from studies cited earlier on effects of family size), and have a child with mental retardation who was making relatively little progress. As the options for women outside the home continue to increase along with consequent increases in overall family stress, the adverse consequences of having a child requiring extraordinary long-term care may become more significant. This possibility suggested by Zimmerman's (1984) study is another indicator of the complexity of interests involved in placement decisions.

With such conflicts — and resulting guilt and cognitive dissonance — it is perhaps unsurprising that parents of institutionalized persons with mental retardation often have led the opposition to deinstitutionalization (see, e.g., Frohboese & Sales, 1980). Nonetheless, once parents actually experience the markedly better conditions in which their children live when they are moved to community residences (Baker, Seltzer, & Seltzer, 1977), parental opposition to deinstitutionalization tends to evaporate (Conroy & Bradley, 1985; Latib, Conroy, & Hess, 1984).

The growth in the ideology of normalization (see, e.g., Cullen, 1991; Rapley & Baldwin, 1995; Wolfensberger, 1970, 1971, 1975) may have changed the potential familial conflicts engendered by decision making about a child with mental retardation. For families who have not placed their child previously (and, therefore, are not concerned directly with deinstitutionalization), the conflict of interest ultimately may be over *not* placing the child. In current professional thinking, young adults should move into community residences so as to achieve maximal self-sufficiency. For adults with mental retardation, semi-independence in a community residence is *less* restrictive than living at home — and certainly less restrictive than living in an institution. For parents accustomed to thinking of their adult child with mental retardation as infantile and in need of protection, the possibility of some independence for him or her may be threatening. In the context of this book, however, this issue is tangential, in that placement of a *minor* with mental retardation typically occurs for a reason other than encouraging independence. Placement is likely to occur, for example, because of a discrepancy between family resources and the level of demands placed upon the parents for care of the child.

THE EFFICACY OF RESIDENTIAL TREATMENT

Highly restrictive settings might be justified if they provided substantially greater efficacy of treatment for conditions that were sufficiently severe to warrant state attention. However, no evidence thus far supports the notion that efficacy of treatment is correlated positively with its restrictiveness. In fact, where a correlation exists between efficacy and restrictiveness, it generally is negative (e.g., Hoagwood & Cunningham, 1992).

Kiesler (1982a; see also Kiesler & Sibulkin, 1987) examined 10 experiments in which severely disordered adults and, in some studies, late adolescents were assigned randomly to hospitalization or alternative care (see Stein & Test, 1978, for program descriptions). In no case was the outcome of the more restrictive care more positive, and it often was less effective (see Miller & Hester, 1986, for a similar analysis of inpatient substance abuse programs). Clients of alternative care programs were more likely to be employed subsequently or in school, to function adaptively in the community, and so forth. The alternative programs were markedly less expensive, and their clients tended to be much less likely to be hospitalized subsequently. Relying on these studies, Talbott (1985) described the sentiment toward rejuvenating hospital-based public mental health services as "scientifically unsupportable, clinically unconscionable, and economically unfeasible" (p. 48). Similarly, noting the historic isolation of state hospitals, Robert Okin (1985a), former commissioner of mental health in Vermont and Massachusetts, argued that "the most basic problem of the state hospitals is not that they provide an inferior quality of care, but that for the majority of patients, they provide the wrong kind of care in the wrong treatment setting" (p. 743).

Fewer studies have examined residential treatment of children, but they are consistent with the findings about adult inpatient treatment. In one of two experimental studies of hospital treatment for children (Winsberg, Bialer, Kupietz, Botti, & Balka, 1980), Medicaid-eligible children aged 5 to 13 were randomly assigned to an inpatient ward of a municipal teaching hospital or community-based treatment facility. In the former, the traditional combination of pharmacotherapy, psychotherapy, and milieu therapy was provided by psychiatrists on faculty or in residency, and social casework and therapy was administered to families. In the latter, traditional psychotherapy was not provided, but case advocacy (e.g., Melton, 1983a) and social services were provided to the family, and the child received psychoactive medication. The community treatment program was distinguished by "continuous avail-

43

ability of staff, persistent advocacy, and treatment flexibility" (Winsberg et al., 1980, p. 415).

Children in the community treatment group showed significant improvement on all dimensions of the Conners Behavior Rating Scale, the Devereux Elementary School Behavior Rating Scale, and the Devereux Child Behavior Rating Scale, but the children in the hospital treatment group showed improvement only on the behavior rating scale factor of inattentiveness. Both groups made minimal academic gains, with no significant group differences. Parents and families showed no significant change in either group, but the lack of change may have reflected lack of sensitivity of a family functioning measure developed for the study, which contained only a three-point scale (adequate to grossly inadequate) for broad measures of family welfare (e.g., financial conditions, housekeeping).

The second study (Flomenhaft, 1974) involved random assignment of "acutely disturbed hospital admissible patients" to inpatient or outpatient treatment at Colorado Psychiatric Hospital in Denver. Among the 300 patients in the study were 71 adolescents aged 12 to 20, 40 of whom were followed for two to four years after completion of treatment. Their data were analyzed separately. Firm conclusions about treatment outcome cannot be made because of reliance on a Developmental Task Inventory of questionable and unverified validity. About half of each group subsequently was hospitalized at least once. The proportion employed at time of follow-up was similar (about 80%). Although the expected cell values were too small for statistical analysis, there was a clear trend for adolescents in the inpatient group to be placed in long-term institutional or foster care more frequently (29.2%) than those who had been treated on an outpatient basis (6.3%).

Despite the frequency of placement of youth in residential treatment centers, few outcome studies have been conducted in group care facilities and residential schools. The situation that Maluccio and Marlow described in 1972 essentially is unchanged:

> Despite expanded and more sophisticated evaluative research during the past decades, there is no conclusive evidence on the effectiveness of residential treatment. All of the available studies are descriptive, short-term,

44

and follow-up. None has the scope of a comprehensive or definitive work; each is concerned with a small number of children known to a particular center. There has been no longitudinal research, and there has not been any investigation encompassing a wide range of treatment centers or comparing a variety of programs. (p. 241)

Unfortunately, sufficient records often are lacking even to develop a clear clinical impression that services apparently are working. State authorities often fail to monitor residential treatment facilities, especially in the private sector (Kiesler, 1993; Knitzer, 1982). Moreover, even if close scrutiny of programs were maintained, the records may not be very informative to external reviewers. In an audit of group homes in California, the GAO (1985b) found that case plans often were missing or incomplete. In such a circumstance, it is difficult to develop a clear impression of the treatment either in the program as a whole or for individual children.

The data that are available often are not encouraging. For example, in a three-year study of 36 residential treatment centers in a southwestern state, Hoagwood and Cunningham (1992) found that two-thirds of the residents were judged to have made little or no progress or to have been released prematurely. In a comparable proportion of cases, staff believed that placement had occurred only because community-based alternatives were unavailable.

Such findings do not mean that the outlook for treatment of youth with emotional disturbance (typically, conduct disorders) is hopeless — merely that residential treatment is unnecessary or even ill-advised. In a refutation of the "nothing works" hypothesis, Lipsey (1992) conducted a metanalysis of nearly 400 experimental and quasi-experimental studies of delinquency treatment programs reported since 1950. He found that juveniles in treatment groups, on average, had a 10% lower rate of recidivism than juveniles who were not involved in any kind of treatment. The better programs produced 20 to 30% reductions in recidivism rates and improvement on other outcome measures. The most effective treatment programs tended to focus on changing behavior through structured behavior modification or training programs. Specific targeted behavioral foci related to a number of domains: (a) interpersonal relations, (b) self-control, (c) job skills, and (d) school achievement. Lipsey found the most effective programs to be those involving intensive, multimodal treatments, the implementation of which were monitored closely.

Lipsey did not find institutional or residential treatment to be any more effective than community-based programs. Indeed, some recent intensive community-based programs that systematically address the multiple domains in which youth with behavior disorders — even violent youth — and their families need help have shown substantially more positive results than the programs in Lipsey's sample (see, e.g., Henggeler & Borduin, 1995; Henggeler, Melton, & Smith, 1992; Henggeler, Melton, Smith, Schoenwald, & Hanley, 1993; for reviews, see Howell et al., 1995, and Tate et al., 1995).

Lipsey's (1992) findings are consistent with earlier research not only in identifying the particular targets of treatment likely to lead to improvement but also in failing to find support for the notion that more restrictive treatments lead to better outcomes. Those programs that consistently have shown long-term effects have focused on building academic and vocational skills, strong case advocacy, and parallel efforts at community, school, and family change (see Melton 1983a, chap. 4, and Rutter & Giller, 1984, chaps. 9 and 10, for reviews). By their nature, the potent aspects of the treatment program are probably optimally delivered in the community (see, e.g., Massimo & Shore, 1963; Shore & Massimo, 1979; Winsberg et al., 1980; see also Melton, 1977 and 1983a, chap. 5, on clinical advocacy).

Project Re-ED (Hobbs, 1982) is probably the residential program — actually now a network of programs — that best demonstrated the merits of an ecological approach combining psychoeducation of the child with efforts to improve the "fit" between child and social environment. Re-ED relies on specially trained teacher-counselors who try to make the child's environment cognitively and affectively educational. Liaison teacher-counselors help to prepare the community for the child's return. The child's stay is made as brief as possible (under six months). Even during placement, the child returns home on weekends. In short, the hallmarks of Re-ED are an educational rather than a psychodynamic emphasis, brevity of placement, and maintenance and strengthening of community ties. Re-ED challenges many conventional notions about residential treatment. By its emphasis on the child's social system prior to and during placement, it is a "non-residential" residential treatment program that is intended by plan to minimize the restrictiveness and intrusiveness of treatment.

Not only is there little evidence of the effectiveness of residential treatment, especially relative to well-conceptualized nonresidential alternatives, but the primary problem of residential treatment may be *avoiding negative effects*, a point to which we return in Chapters 2 and 5. Institutional litigation since the early 1970s has documented the atrocious, abusive conditions present in many state hospitals and training schools (see generally Melton & Davidson, 1987; Wooden, 1976). The physical facilities themselves often are maintained inadequately, and the facilities are depressing places to live (Gutkind, 1993; Talbott, 1980). Large institutions are known to have particularly debilitating effects on the motivation, social skills and responsiveness, language development, and self-concept of their residents (see, e.g., Goffman, 1961; Lyman et al., 1989; Pilewski & Heal, 1980; Rotegard, Hill, & Bruininks, 1983; Tjosvold & Tjosvold, 1983; Zigler & Balla, 1978; see also Baker et al., 1977, on "mini-institutions"). The stigma of a history of institutional placement also is well known. The effects on youth who are on the verge of applying for jobs, seeking insurance, and so forth may be especially pernicious (see Koocher, 1983).

Of course, not all residential treatment programs have the obvious problems that have been endemic in state institutions. As already noted, some really are *therapeutic* even if their divorce from the community is self-defeating in the long term. Nonetheless, even in those programs, restrictiveness of treatment must be considered. Absent *compelling* evidence of effectiveness — evidence that is clearly lacking — less restrictive settings should be used. This conclusion is the cornerstone of our proposal to restructure various aspects of the child mental health service delivery system.

ALTERNATIVES *ARE* POSSIBLE

Despite the restrictiveness and cost of residential treatment, the disruption of families that it causes, and the dearth of evidence supporting its necessity or even marginal utility, states rarely have attempted to generate a continuum of services for children and youth. Although alternative programs

47

also have been evaluated rarely (in part because they have been instituted rarely), there is sufficient experience with restrictive programs and the alternatives to them to suggest optimal policies for children's services: "(a) develop mainstream, integrated, community-based services, whether children's needs are considered from the perspective of juvenile justice, education, child welfare, or mental health; (b) tailor services in the least restrictive, most normalized environment that is appropriate; and (c) include the family in the rehabilitative process" (Behar, 1985, p. 189).

In discussing day treatment (partial hospitalization) programs for children and adolescents, Lahey and Kupfer (1979) offered a number of reasons to favor such programs over residential treatment. Day programs are less expensive. They provide some relief to families, but they permit families to remain intact. Day programs still provide for some removal from maladaptive family environments, but they also permit families to learn new techniques. In the meantime, day programs often do not disrupt schooling or social life, and they avoid some of the iatrogenic effects of institutions, institutional behaviors. Parents often prefer the less drastic intervention, and day programs avoid the stress of separation for both children and families. Day treatment programs can ease transition to fully normalized living, and they can be used as a base for intensive treatment programs. They also provide opportunity for extended assessments under close supervision without the restrictiveness and intrusiveness of inpatient evaluation.

Lahey and Kupfer (1979) noted, however, that the asserted advantages of day treatment programs are based on logical extensions of research on residential treatment and analyses of partial hospitalization programs but not on direct experimental tests. Some outcome studies (e.g., Kettlewell, Jones, & Jones, 1985; Tolmach, 1985; see also Gudeman, Dickey, Evans, & Shore, 1985) have shown positive treatment effects of day treatment programs with substantially less fiscal cost and intrusiveness than residential programs (see Hoge et al., 1992, for a review). The available research, however, is marred by lack of control groups.

Several model projects have relied on brief, in-home interventions to provide problem-related counseling and support (e.g., Heying, 1985; Hinckley & Ellis, 1985; "Program Update," 1985; Schwartz & AuClaire, 1995), sometimes with impressive results in randomized trials (see, e.g., AuClaire & Schwartz, 1986; Henggeler & Borduin, 1995; Henggeler et al., 1992, 1993; Schwartz, AuClaire, & Harris, 1991). Such in-home interventions may be especially direct ways of keeping families intact when a question arises as to a child's safety or level of control in the home. Even brief out-of-home respite care may be an important way of helping families deal with the stress of caring for a child with special needs and avoid institutionalization (see, e.g., Subramanian, 1985; Upshur, 1983).

Perhaps the most persuasive evidence (beyond the negative evidence on residential treatment) for establishment of alternative programs is that, when such action has been carefully implemented, the use of residential treatment has dropped substantially. In a pioneer effort to establish alternatives, North Carolina developed a variety of programs for the most difficult youth in its state service systems (Behar, 1985). As a result of a class action on behalf of emotionally disturbed, assaultive youth who "are or will be in the future involuntarily institutionalized or otherwise placed in residential programs," North Carolina established an innovative range of services, including in-home crisis services, vocational training, specialized foster care (e.g., Hawkins, Meadowcroft, Trout, & Luster, 1985), respite care, expansive case management, and so forth. These services closely parallel those that we noted previously as having demonstrated efficacy. Despite the fact that the program deals with the most difficult youth in the state (the majority of whom were living away from their families, predominantly in institutional settings), fewer than 10% of members of the class covered by the litigation are judged now to require secure residential treatment. The remainder are being served in the community.

Besides serving as an exemplar of the innovative community services that can accrue from friendly litigation (see also Okin, 1984), the North Carolina experience indicates that states can increase services to the most troubled and troubling youth while minimizing restrictiveness and cost. Analogous findings from an evaluation of the effects of litigation to close Pennhurst State School and Hospital in Pennsylvania show that even children with the most profound mental retardation can be served in the community (Conroy & Bradley, 1985). The North Carolina and Pennsylvania experiences demonstrate that severe need does not imply that services must be delivered in an institution.

This conclusion has been given further weight by the experience in intensive case management programs for youth who have placement histories or are at high risk for placement. In such a program in New York State (Armstrong & Evans, 1992), case managers worked with 10 children and their families. The case managers were on call 24 hours a day, and they had $2,000 per child available as "flex funds" to purchase services not covered by conventional funding streams. This program reduced both admissions and length of hospitalizations (Evans, Banks, Huz, & McNulty, 1994), and it also demonstrated impressive clinical results (Evans, Armstrong, & Kuppinger, 1996).

Similarly, development of a system of care in demonstration counties in California resulted in an extraordinary drop in use of group homes. If the dramatic decline in group home expenditures in the demonstration counties was replicated in a statewide program, the drop in expenditures over a 30-month period would be projected to be almost a quarter of a billion dollars (Rosenblatt & Attkisson, 1992). Because efforts were made for an *interagency* system of care, placements were not simply shifted to other systems (Rosenblatt & Attkisson, 1993). Foster care and residential school placements remained stable or declined in the demonstration counties, and state hospital use declined throughout the demonstration areas.

Similar success in maintaining children with placement histories or high placement risk in the community has also been demonstrated in intensive case management ("wraparound") programs in Alaska (discussed in Melton & Pagliocca, 1992), Florida (Clark, Lee, Prange, & McDonald, 1996), Maryland (Hyde, Burchard, & Woodworth, 1996), and Vermont (Yoe, Santarcangelo, Atkins, & Burchard, 1996). Taken together, however, the experience with wraparound services suggests that they do not automatically improve clinical outcomes. Rather, such programs require careful conceptualization and implementation so that program integrity is maintained and that they do in fact incorporate the flexibility and responsiveness to family needs that community programs — unlike residential programs — have the potential to achieve (Rosenblatt, 1996).

To summarize, the residential treatment system evolved essentially as a "non-system" that traditionally has crossed the lines of mental health, juvenile justice, and special education. It continues to serve predominantly conduct-disordered youth from troubled families. Despite its cost to society in dollars and the intrusions upon the liberty and privacy of individuals and families, its efficacy largely is undemonstrated. Indeed, the evidence tips, in the aggregate, toward *negative* effects of residential treatment programs. Regardless, there has been no demonstration that residential programs are superior to less costly and restrictive alternatives.

Turning again to our task of formulating appropriate child mental health policy, the largely unfettered growth of residential treatment programs should be checked in favor of investment in alternative services on utilitarian grounds alone. The benefits of the residential programs have not been demonstrated to match the costs. The principled ethical and legal rationales for greater care in consideration of the privacy and liberty of troubled youth and families are perhaps even more persuasive and certainly more fundamental. It is those rationales to which we now turn.

•

CHAPTER 2

Restrictiveness and Intrusiveness
of Treatment

Our inquiry into the nature and efficacy of residential treatment in Chapter 1 was oriented toward two broad issues: (a) the breadth of regulation that will be necessary if change is to occur in how treatment is delivered to children and youth, and (b) the utilitarian calculus of the relative costs and benefits of a treatment system based on restrictive modes of service. Our focus in this chapter is more fundamental. Good social policy — our goal, of course — is based in part on what will and will not work. But much more is involved. More or less independent of the marginal utility of residential treatment is the question: Is such treatment consonant with primary ethical and legal values?

The social contract that mutually binds the state and its citizens carries with it reciprocal rights and obligations. Among these is the state's duty to accord respect to and for persons (Rawls, 1971). Within such a framework, state action is constrained by the necessity of provision of primary goods to individuals — those goods that are defined consensually as basic to preservation of human dignity and welfare. Among them are liberty and privacy.

Respect for persons demands respect for their autonomy and maintenance of zones of privacy that protect personal boundaries (Melton, 1983d; National Commission, 1979; Shatz, Donovan, & Hong, 1991). These principles are vindicated in modern constitutional law through the requirement of strict scrutiny when the state seeks to limit the fundamental rights of its citizens (e.g., *San Antonio Independent School District v. Rodriguez*, 1973). Whenever the state infringes rights that are guaranteed expressly or implicitly by the Constitution, it must base its action on a compelling state interest, closely tailor the action to the interest, and use the least drastic means of doing so. In short, infringement of individual rights is ethically and legally legitimate only when countered by unusually strong competing considerations of benefi-cence—the duty to promote social welfare. When such a consideration is present, violation of individual rights should be no greater than necessary. This overriding principle is applicable to children and youth as persons just as it is to adults (Brown, 1982; Melton, 1983d, 1983e; Worsfold, 1974). As one of us (Melton, 1993b) noted elsewhere: "When a society recognizes the personhood of its smallest and most vulnerable members and not only pro-tects them but does so in a manner that protects their dignity, it sets a tone conducive to promotion of democratic ideals. When such conditions are not present, the message is clear that raw power is more important than either reason or caring" (p. 531).

DEFINING THE LEAST RESTRICTIVE ALTERNATIVE

The least drastic means principle has been embedded in both constitutional and statutory disabilities law in the term *least restrictive alternative* (LRA) (see Epstein, Quinn, & Cumblad, 1994, for a review). It is useful to separate *restrictiveness* and *intrusiveness*, because the least drastic means principle is applicable not only to interventions that restrict the exercise of liberty, but also to state-sanctioned intrusions into privacy, among other fundamental rights. Although we will lapse for convenience into use of the LRA term when we are referring to the general application of the concept, it is impor-tant not to overlook the ethical and legal significance of therapeutic pro-cedures that are very intrusive but place few constraints on freedom of asso-ciation and movement (see Melton & Davidson, 1987).

The LRA concept is deceptively simple in other ways. As Hoffman and Foust (1977) showed, the concept is necessarily multidimensional and case-specific, yet it is discussed frequently as if it were unidimensional. Indeed, taken literally, LRA seems to embody merely the least restrictive state intervention. If that were the way the term was intended, the LRA would always be for the state to do nothing!

At a minimum, LRA requirements demand balancing the restrictiveness and intrusiveness of a treatment against its probable efficacy. The LRA is the least drastic means of meeting the state interests that justify involuntary treatment. Perceptions of the marginal restrictiveness of treatment may vary dramatically across professional groups. If the individual's mental disorder is believed to be restrictive, even highly restrictive treatments may infringe the patient's liberty only minimally.

Even if professionals agree, though, about the starting point for balancing libertarian and paternalistic interests, normative disagreements may exist about the appropriate ceiling for compulsory intervention. How fully and with what certainty must the state's interests in an individual's treatment be met? Complicating matters further, the answer may vary across justifications for compulsory treatment. For example, if the justification is the protection of society via police power, the state may require greater certainty that a proposed treatment will be as effective as a more restrictive alternative than if the justification is to the committed person via the parens patriae power. Police power commitments are consonant with society's right to self-defense (e.g., *Jacobson v. Massachusetts*, 1905) and justifiably may require particular certainty that the state's interest is being met. Thus, the interests on either side of the scale vary, weighing more heavily in some contexts and less so in others. Moreover, adjustments on one side of the scale cannot necessarily be compensated for by corollary adjustments on the other. As we indicate in Chapter 5, the relationship between restrictiveness and efficacy may not be linear. More restrictive treatments are not necessarily more effective; indeed, the most restrictive treatments may be least so (see Weisz & Weiss, 1993). Lack of linearity makes identification of an acceptable meeting point between restrictiveness and efficacy difficult.

Even if authorities can agree upon the point at which the LRA occurs in the abstract, other considerations complicate the calculus in the real world. Although a particular treatment may be more likely to be beneficial than an alternative, it also may present greater risk of harm, take longer, or cost more. Although physically less restrictive, it may be subjectively more aversive or intrusive to the client. The importance of the distinction between objective appearance and subjective experience relative to civil commitment was demonstrated strikingly in a recent work by Monahan and colleagues (1996). They noted that

> [s]everal findings cloud the distinction between "voluntary" and "involuntary" patient status (Hoge et al., 1994). First, patients' reports belie the idealized view of the voluntary admission process as involving a patient who recognizes his or her illness, seeks professional help, and initiates hospitalization. We found that 34% of voluntary patients did not believe they had a mental illness. In 49% of cases, someone other than the patient initiated coming to the hospital; indeed, in 14% of the cases, patients were in some form of custody at the time of presentation. (p. 18)

The authors' work did not end with this observation. They found not only that some "voluntary" admissions appeared involuntary, but also that some "involuntary" admissions could have been handled as voluntary ones.

> Our findings also belied the characterization of involuntary commitment as inevitably involving patients who deny they are ill and protest the hospitalization process. We found that 34% believed they were mentally ill. Perhaps more surprising, we found that 22% reported that it was their idea to come to the hospital for help, and 20% stated that they initiated the admission. About half (47%) said that there were no reasonable alternatives to hospitalization. While some (18%) were unaware of their legal status, the great majority of those who knew they had been committed (81%) reported that they were not offered the opportunity to voluntarily enter the hospital, and more than half (56%) of these patients indicated that they would have entered voluntarily if they had been given the opportunity. (pp. 18–19)

Clearly then, a variety of practical considerations, not the least of which is the issue of subjective versus objective restrictiveness, clouds attempts to define the least restrictive alternative.

Where the state has multiple purposes in compelling treatment (or supporting a parent or guardian's "volunteering" a child or ward), these, too, may affect the determination of the LRA. A placement that is more effective than an alternative in incapacitating a youth believed to be dangerous may be less effective in treating the disorder that is perceived to be at the root of the troubling behavior. The treatments also may vary in how much they intrude into family privacy and restrict parental autonomy.

In short, determination of the LRA for a given child may not be a simple matter. Furthermore, even if agreement can be reached about the factors to be used in determining the LRA and how they are to be balanced, other problems may arise. As we will discuss at the end of the chapter, the law may be unclear as to whether the LRA refers to the least restrictive *known* treatment or the least restrictive *available* treatment. The law also may be unclear about the allocation of responsibility for investigating alternatives and, when less restrictive treatments are unavailable, creating them. As we shall see, the resolution of these issues may be critical in determining whether the LRA is more than an empty promise.

RESTRICTIVENESS OF TREATMENT
Does Liberty Matter?

Although we are only beginning to untangle the web of issues surrounding application of the LRA concept, we must look beyond the mechanical operation of this legal doctrine. We must consider the context within which this doctrine operates. Accordingly, we turn to an analysis of restrictiveness and its implications for children and youth. As we already noted, restrictiveness may be defined as the degree of infringement of liberty. Application of the concept to child mental health policy is hindered by two historic, albeit regrettable — indeed, in our view, abominable — assumptions. First, people with mental disabilities have been perceived as incapable of appreciating the loss of liberty or even of recognizing that liberty was being lost (see, e.g., Mill, 1859/1947). Therefore, it has been argued, the loss of liberty is incon-

sequential to them (but see Morse, 1985; Ross, 1996). Second and analo-
gously, minors have been perceived as failing to have any cognizable interest
in liberty. Consider, for example, the Supreme Court's observation just over
a decade ago that "juveniles, unlike adults, are always in some form of custody" (*Schall v. Martin*, 1984, p. 265).

With a double disability of a mental disorder (or at least a perceived need
for treatment) and status as a minor, youth in treatment programs may be
viewed by many people as especially undeserving of liberty or at least as
uncaring about it. This approach to children and persons with mental disorders dates back centuries. Consider the following by Sir William Blackstone (1765–1769/1979): "For the lord chancellor is, by right derived from
the crown, the general and supreme guardian of all infants, as well as idiots
and lunatics; that is, of all such *persons as have not discretion enough to manage
their own concerns* (Vol. 1, p. 451, emphasis added).

The claim that liberty is a trivial matter for mentally disordered adults
should have been put to rest long ago by the Supreme Court's recognition of
the "massive curtailment of liberty" entailed in psychiatric hospitalization
(*Humphrey v. Cady*, 1972, p. 509). The Court has acknowledged expressly
the significance of freedom from restraints even for people with profound
mental retardation (*Youngberg v. Romeo*, 1982). In reviewing when non-
dangerous persons with mental disorders may be confined against their will,
the Court summarized the case as raising an "important question concerning
every man's constitutional right to liberty" (*O'Connor v. Donaldson*, 1975,
p. 573).

On the other hand, the idea that children lack a right to, or interest in,
liberty continues to enjoy some official recognition. In its landmark *Gault*
decision, the Supreme Court noted the long tradition of cavalier treatment
of minors as human beings lacking legal status as persons entitled to respect
for liberty:

> The right of the state, as parens patriae, to deny to the child procedural
> rights available to his elders was elaborated by the assertion that a child,
> unlike an adult, has a right "not to liberty but to custody." He can be made
> to attorn to his parents, to go to school, etc. If his parents default in

effectively performing their custodial functions — that is, if the child is "delinquent" — the state may intervene. In doing so, it does not deprive the child of any rights, because he has none. It merely provides the custody to which the child is entitled. On this basis, proceedings involving juveniles were described as civil not criminal and therefore not subject to the requirements which restrict the state when it seeks to deprive a person of this liberty. (*In re Gault*, 1967, p. 17)

The notion that liberty is inconsequential to minors should have been eliminated finally by the recognition in *Gault* and subsequent Supreme Court cases that "neither the Fourteenth Amendment nor the Bill of Rights is for adults alone" (*In re Gault*, 1967, p. 13); "[s]tudents in school as well as out of school are 'persons' under our Constitution" (*Tinker v. Des Moines Independent Community School District*, 1969, p. 511). However, the Supreme Court more recently resurrected the theory that detention of juveniles in a jail-like facility, even when they have not been convicted of an offense, is an inconsequential infringement of their rights because they "are always in *some* form of custody" (*Schall v. Martin*, 1984, p. 265, emphasis added).

Indeed, the Supreme Court has persisted in treating minors as half-persons for whom liberty is rather trivial, if not totally meaningless. A pattern in the Court's approach to children's litigation has been first to acknowledge briefly that children and youth have a cognizable liberty or privacy interest in a particular context, but then to devote the bulk of the Court opinion to discussion of why the interest is not very important (e.g., *Vernonia School District v. Acton*, 1995). Similarly, the Court frequently has applied a lower level of scrutiny to infringements of minors' rights than to those of adults (e.g., Note, 1984). Whatever the merits of the states' claims that strong bases exist for such policies, the Court has failed to force them to prove that compelling justifications exist in fact. The Court also has ignored the evidence that society historically has imposed substantial burdens of baseless discrimination on minors and people with disabilities generally.

Both common sense and empirical research tell us that freedom and dignity *do* have considerable meaning for children and youth. Consider, for example, the impassioned discussion of the district court in *J. L. v. Parham*

(1976, p. 136) (see chap. 5) about significance of the loss of liberty entailed for institutionalized children:

> [T]his case raises the most important question of every child's constitutional right to liberty, not only the liberty that includes freedom from bodily restraint . . . but also the liberty that includes the freedom of an ordinary, every-day child in the United States of America — the freedom to live with mothers, fathers, brothers and sisters in whatever the family abode may be; the freedom to be loved and to be spanked [a rather dubious right]; the freedom to go in and out the door, to run and play, to laugh and cry, to fight and fuss, to stand up and fall down, to play childish games; the freedom to go to school and to frolic with school mates; the freedom to go to Sunday school and church; the freedom to watch and listen or not to watch and listen to television; the freedom to buy candy at the corner store; the freedom to be a normal child in a normal household cared for by normal parents.

The experience of choice is meaningful and reinforcing even for young children (see, e.g., Brehm, 1977; Brehm & Weinraub, 1977). When applied to treatment and education, it results in greater involvement and achievement (see, e.g., Adelman, Lusk, Alvarez, & Acosta, 1985; Holmes & Urie, 1975; Lewis, 1983; Lewis & Lewis, 1983; Melton, 1983c; Taylor, Adelman, & Kaser-Boyd, 1985a, 1985b). The experience of freedom also increases children and youth's sense of personal efficacy (Rosen, 1977) and socializes democratic values (Melton & Saks, 1985; Tapp & Melton, 1983). Moreover, "a sense that one has little control over one's life . . . is negatively related to mental health, educational achievement, and family planning" (ABCAN, 1993, p. 81). Children generally evince a much better understanding of procedural fairness than adults believe (Gold, Darley, Hilton, & Zanna, 1984).

The provision of liberty clearly has meaningful and positive consequences. Perhaps, though, the key issue is that liberty has ethical significance apart from its effects. Denial of the significance of liberty for children and youth is a denial of their personhood. In our view, children and youth *are* members of the community entitled to respect (Melton, 1983e). Absent compelling reasons to the contrary, that respect must include recognition of their autonomy and preparation for exercise of rights (Brown, 1982; Worsfold, 1974). This view has informed and guided the approach we take herein to reform mental health services for children and adolescents.

Freedom of Movement

Assuming that liberty is meaningful to children and youth, we turn to an analysis of the nature of restrictiveness. Mental health professionals tend to define restrictiveness in terms of the degree of constraint upon freedom of movement, with little attention paid to freedom in decision making (Epstein et al., 1994; Ransohoff, Zachary, Gaynor, & Hargreaves, 1982). Residential treatment programs vary substantially in the degree of constraint they impose on movement, prompting researchers to work toward creation of scales to assess the restrictiveness of physical movement in such settings (e.g., Epstein et al., 1994). Okin (1985b), for example, found that state hospitals in Massachusetts ranged from 0 to 48% in the proportion of patients who had been subjected to seclusion or physical restraints. Earle and Forquer (1995) studied three public hospitals in the New York City area and found that a staggering rate of 33% of child and adolescent patients had been subjected to seclusion. In their three-year study of use of seclusion and restraint in a child psychiatric hospital, Goren, Singh, and Best (1993) found that 28% of the 175 patients during the study period had been secluded or restrained a total of 1,670 times. Of those secluded or restrained, 25% had been secluded five or more times and 32% had been restrained multiple times.

Some residential treatment programs place much greater restraints on their residents' freedom than residents would receive in a home. Indeed, complaints of gross misuse of isolation have been common features of institutional litigation involving children and youth, whether in the mental health or the juvenile justice system (see generally Wooden, 1976). In some cases, youth have been subjected to prolonged isolation with no ability to communicate with therapists or other residents, no opportunity to leave the room except for toileting, no television, radio, or even material for reading, and a prohibition of any clothing other than pajamas or underwear.

The specific facts have been grotesque at times. Consider, for example, a federal court's description of the prolonged solitary confinement for treatment of two girls in a Wisconsin facility (*Mary and Crystal v. Ramsden*, 1980). The girls were subjected to all of the restrictions mentioned above and were confined to a room measuring 7½ ft by 11 ft with no furniture other than a bed and mattress. The door to the room had a small observation window and three large separate locks. Not unsurprisingly, this environment took a psychological toll:

> At trial Mary testified that her stay in isolation [29 days] was made particularly difficult by the fact that her treating psychologist refused to visit her until the day before her release. She experienced frustration at not being able to talk to anyone and complained of physical discomfort which a staff nurse attributed to be a side effect of isolation. In addition, Mary testified that the isolation room was very hot, with an unshaded window, poor ventilation and insect infestation. On one occasion after the room was sprayed with insecticide, Mary was required to remain in the room despite the noxious vapors. Mary's requests to clean her room and to be able to pick out some reading material from the book rack were denied. . . .
>
> Crystal's stay in isolation was more difficult. She was upset and frightened from the beginning. She cried for prolonged periods. She threw her bed around to express her anger and tore her towel to use in a suicide attempt. Her bed and linens were removed as punishment for this conduct and as a preventive measure. . . . Crystal was not visited by a psychiatric therapist until the fourth day in isolation and thereafter once a week. Crystal was required to serve nineteen out of twenty days in isolation despite the effect such confinement was having on her.
>
> Crystal also testified that the condition of her room included insect infestation and that she was required to return to her room immediately after pesticide spraying. (p. 595)

Fortunately, the grossly inhumane conditions to which Mary and Crystal were subjected are probably rare, although, as already mentioned, far from altogether unique. However, serious restrictions on liberty are common in residential treatment programs as part of the "treatment" itself. The structure endemic in institutional regimens deprives residents of many of the choices of everyday life (e.g., Rivlin & Wolfe, 1985). Confusing rights with privileges (see Gutkind, 1993, p. 92; Wexler, 1981, chap. 9), some programs also painfully deprive residents of the most basic freedoms as part of their effort to resocialize youth. Residents in many programs, especially those that purport to treat delinquents or substance abusers, must begin at level zero, complete with restrictions to room or ward, deprivation of visitors and phone calls, and prohibition of street clothes. Any formulation of social policy relative to children's mental health treatment needs must ensure that human dignity is not sacrificed at the altar of treatment efficacy, particularly where, as here, the efficacy is largely mythical anyway.

Freedom of Association and Communication

Several cases have demonstrated vividly the isolation from the outside world that some treatment programs impose as a way of taking control of residents' lives. Even if one does not assume youth themselves to have independent rights to association and communication (as we assume), parents should be able to communicate with their children so that they can guard their interests and make informed decisions about treatment. Under isolation therapy children are held incommunicado in order, presumably, to increase control over them and diminish the possibility that they will be upset by messages from their parents or others outside the hospital or treatment center. Under such approaches, communication is treated as a privilege to be earned. Alternatively, isolation from others on the ward as well as outside the hospital is used as punishment.

Whether therapeutic or punitive in intent, such restrictions are especially pernicious. Besides the loss of liberty, prohibition of communication effectively destroys residents' right to legal counsel and makes informed proxy consent (e.g., Gray, Lyons, & Melton, 1995, p. 60) by their parents impossible. For example, litigation against particularly outrageous psychological and physical brutality at one residential treatment center commenced only after one boy ran away and contacted an attorney and another managed to send a coded letter to his father (for a detailed recitation of the facts, see *Milonas v. Williams*, 1982). Gross restrictions on freedom of association and communication threaten due process generally and permit abusive conditions to go unchecked. Thus, our overall approach to mental health policy for minors embraces methods that not only allow children to retain their fundamental rights but also provide them with at least rudimentary means of vindicating those rights.

INTRUSIVENESS OF TREATMENT
Psychological Intrusiveness

Provo Canyon School in Utah was the private treatment center that was the subject of the litigation spawned by the forbidden phone call and coded letter mentioned above. In the beginning phases of the school program, residents were locked in and required to stand for prolonged periods day after day in order to promote right thinking and social conformity. Mail was censored, visitors were discouraged, and complaints about the school resulted in punishment. To move beyond these totalitarian conditions, students were required to pass a polygraph examination designed to reveal negative attitudes about the school. Students who failed the lie detector test were subject to punishment not only for what they confessed to having done, but also for what they had *thought* about doing. The district court found that the punitive measures included isolation in a bare 4 ft by 8 ft by 9 ft room and a "hair dance" in which staff would grab a resident's arm with one hand and his hair with the other.

The conditions at Provo Canyon were extreme by anyone's standards. Nonetheless, they serve to demonstrate the psychological intrusiveness that can accompany extraordinary restrictions of movement and association. As control increases, so does the likelihood of psychological intrusion. Programs that rely on a strategy of control often have an explicit goal of psychological intrusion; they aim to strip away the existing personality and to resocialize residents.

Although such policies commonly are derived from benevolent — if mis-guided — intentions, the motives of staff may be downright mean spirited. One former director of an adolescent treatment unit was quoted as follows: "At many hospitals, the staff is nurturing and psychologically minded, but at Mayview you don't have that. You just have some not-very-well-educated, not-very-bright people seeing some very disturbed adolescents as bad kids who need to be taught a lesson" (Gutkind, 1993, p. 91). Whatever the legitimacy of motive, such efforts almost necessarily involve an attack on personal integrity, whether through extreme confrontation, highly intrusive monitoring of behavior, or humiliation rituals. Personal privacy is viewed as inconsistent with institutional needs for surveillance of behavior in order to protect children from loss of control (Rivlin & Wolfe, 1985).

Even less extreme measures by good programs to maintain control often are *experienced* as intrusive. For example, Roth and Roth's (1984) study of elementary- and junior-high-age inpatients in a well-known psychiatric teaching hospital showed that "[e]ven under the best circumstances, psychiatric hospitalization is a difficult experience for children" (p. 15). Although children developed more positive feelings about the staff during their stay, they did not change in their negative response to hospitalization per se. The most common complaint was about the forced separation from family. Older children also objected to institutional regimens, medical procedures that they regarded as scary, and fighting among the patients.

Similarly, a survey of 10- to 18-year-old children and adolescents who had been placed at some point in residential treatment as dependent and neglected revealed largely negative feelings about the facilities (Bush, 1980). The survey covered more than 100 different treatment centers. Children in institutional care reported feeling unhappy, unsupported, unwanted, unloved, and uncomfortable. They also regarded institutional life as punitive, demanding (in terms of chores), and lacking in privacy. It is important to note that these responses were not to out-of-home care in general. Children were slightly more positive toward group homes than institutions, but much more positive toward foster homes and other family-like arrangements (e.g., living with relatives other than parents) than either group homes or institutions. A similar work by Piersma (1986–1987) covering a single hospital found adolescent patients to be more critical of their hospitalization than adult patients. Living conditions were the most commonly criticized feature of institutional life.

In interviews of adolescents voluntarily committed by their parents to Western Psychiatric Institute, Lidz, Gross, Meisel, and Roth (1980) found unanimity of belief that hospitalization was inappropriate and a "setback in their lives" (p. 171). They were concerned about both the stigma of status as a mental patient and the possibility that they would be detained for a lengthy period of time.

Perhaps it is not surprising that children and adolescents are dissatisfied with highly intrusive and restrictive placements. Rosen, Heckman, Carro, and Burchard (1994) attempted to delineate the precise factors associated with child and adolescent (dis)satisfaction with their treatment placements. They found that "[i]ncreases in placement restrictiveness were associated with decreased satisfaction" (p. 61). Although overall satisfaction was not related to positive behavioral outcomes, restrictiveness of placement was associated with children's perceptions that they were less involved in treatment planning and implementation ($r = -.62$). On the other hand, participation in treatment planning, combined with a perception of unconditional care, did relate to decreases in problematic behavior on the part of the children.

It is noteworthy that children and their parents differ substantially in their perceptions about the acceptability of various forms of treatment. Child inpatients perceive outpatient psychotherapy as more acceptable than hospitalization (Kazdin, 1986): "[F]or children, the prospect of removal from the home may raise concerns over separation and abandonment, signal removal from friends, and represent a possibly anxiety-provoking situation" (p. 339).

Minors also are sensitive to the intrusion that outpatient psychotherapy represents. Self-disclosure is the treatment risk most often identified by older children and youth, particularly those who have experience in treatment (Kaser-Boyd, Adelman, & Taylor, 1985). About 80% of children and youth in a university-based psychoeducational program objected to the treatment at some point (Taylor et al., 1985a). Lack of choice about participation was the most common complaint. Minors, like adults, are cognizant of the intrusion into private zones that is an inherent element of psychotherapy, and desire to maintain some control over others' access to personal information.

Whether information, physical space, or body is at stake, privacy represents protection of personal integrity (Melton, 1983d). Respect for personal boundaries is a critical element of respect for persons. In keeping with this principle, one of us previously has characterized extraordinary intrusions in the name of treatment as psychologically abusive acts that should be prohibited by state law:

[L]aws and agency regulations governing institutional care should go beyond prevention of physical maltreatment. They also must prevent psychological harm and threats to the dignity of the children and youth directly or indirectly under state care. In that regard, institutions and their staff should be barred from interventions designed to humiliate, depersonalize, deprive of outside communication (other than reasonable restrictions on time, place, and manner), isolate (other than brief periods of seclusion when necessary to ensure safety), or otherwise subject youth to significantly greater intrusion upon privacy than expectable in family life.

Neither a therapeutic justification nor consent by a parent or guardian should be a defense to allegations of psychological maltreatment under such a standard, which subsumes only the most egregious assaults upon the personal dignity of children and youth. (Melton & Davidson, 1987, p. 174)

The concept of intrusiveness focuses more on *what* is done than *where* it happens. Although total institutions, by their nature, are more likely to use highly intrusive procedures, degradation rituals and intense involuntary confrontation are psychologically intrusive whether they occur in a public school, an outpatient clinic, a group home, or a hospital. Child mental health law should regulate such procedures regardless of the nature of the facility involved.

Our argument has been made largely on deontological grounds; we believe that children and youth are *wronged* when privacy is invaded to a degree that it threatens their personhood. However, the insult may be compounded by injury. For example, child and adolescent misbehavior sometimes is more the product of depression than character disorder (Carlson & Cantwell, 1980; Chiles, Miller, & Cox, 1980; Meeks, 1995). When a child already has fragile self-esteem, intense confrontation may extinguish rather than promote any residual sense of self-worth. On the other hand, just as the experience of choice may facilitate treatment (Melton, 1983c; Taylor & Adelman,

1986) and improve mental health generally (e.g., ABCAN, 1993), protection of privacy may enhance self-esteem irrespective of psychopathology (Wolfe, 1978). Golan (1978) found that child psychiatric inpatients who had single bedrooms had significantly more experiences of privacy as chosen aloneness and higher self-esteem than children in multiple-occupancy bedrooms, although the two groups did not differ in the degree of mental disorder ascribed to them by staff.

In eloquent testimony before a West Virginia court, psychologist Robert Hawkins aptly summarized the therapeutic significance of protection of privacy and the link between restrictions on liberty and intrusions on privacy:

> It seems just a natural — the way it is run it seems like a natural outgrowth of the whole institution model. Once they collect that many human beings together who have not been historically very responsible, you inevitably get some cases of . . . physical violence, and such. So the next step to the institution person's point of view is logically to reduce their privacy by making it possible to watch them all the time.
>
> [Q] Would you say that privacy is important for any of the goals that you suggested are important; for example, developing social skills, responsibility, less disruptive behavior and that sort of thing? . . .
>
> [A] Yes, because I think that one of the first things that you have to do in conducting any kind of treatment is remember that whatever you do serves as a model in the youngster. If you show little respect for his dignity, for his value as a human being, as a person, for his integrity, then that is what you are teaching him to show other people whether you intend to or not.
>
> It seems to demonstrate . . . the impersonal way the boys are dealt with there seems to demonstrate that they are not highly valued, that they certainly are not trusted, and I'm afraid that the effect of that on their future behavior and on their willingness to trust you in any way is pretty negative. (*State v. Werner*, 1978, p. 913)

Physical Intrusiveness

Invasions of privacy are not limited to intrusions into zones of personal information. As demonstrated by the line of abortion cases decided by the

Supreme Court, privacy also pertains to control over one's body (e.g., *Roe v. Wade*, 1973). This principle has been applied to mental health law in a series of cases on mental patients' right to refuse antipsychotic medication, also known as neuroleptics or major tranquilizers (e.g., *Rennie v. Klein*, 1981). Although the precise legal basis for such a right has varied[1] as has the level of procedural protection believed necessary to vindicate it,[2] all courts that have decided the issue in reported opinions have found at least a qualified right of mental patients to refuse treatment. In most cases, the decision has its foundation in the federal constitutional rights to privacy and freedom from unjustified threats to personal security or the related principle embedded in the common law of most states that intrusions into bodily privacy require the consent of the subject (see *Cruzan v. Director, Missouri Department of Health*, 1990, for review of state common law provisions).

Litigation thus far has focused almost exclusively on the right to refuse antipsychotic medication, although the principle should apply to other treatments (e.g., Winick, 1989). The focus on antipsychotic medication is based on two aspects of such treatment. First, some courts and commentators have focused on the mind-altering effects of antipsychotic drugs.[3] Because of their effect on thinking processes, such drugs arguably have special potential for intrusion on personal integrity and fundamental freedom. Second, and more generally, the serious and sometimes permanent negative side effects of antipsychotic medication raise particularly grave threats to bodily integrity.

As reviewed by several courts and amicus curiae (friend of the court) American Psychological Association (*Washington v. Harper*, 1990), several side effects on neuromuscular functioning are common results of prolonged use of antipsychotic drugs. Perhaps the most serious of these side effects is tardive dyskinesia, which occurs in roughly one-fifth of chronic users of antipsychotic medication and which often is irreversible (Gardos & Cole, 1980). Tardive dyskinesia (TD) is marked by "pseudoparkinsonian" symptoms (e.g., tremors, facial rigidity and contortions, drooling, lip smacking) that may increase the actual or perceived stigma of mental patients and therefore adversely affect mental as well as physical health.

As Marder and Van Putten (1995) recently observed: "At least 10%–20% of patients treated with neuroleptics for more than 1 year develop TD. In chronically institutionalized patients, the prevalence is 15%–20%. Recent prospective studies indicate that the cumulative incidence of TD is 5% at 1 year, 10% at 2 years, 15% at 3 years, and 19% at 4 years" (pp. 256–257, citations omitted). Some studies suggest that children and adolescents may be particularly susceptible to TD, as evidenced by the fact that some have developed the disorder after treatment periods as brief as only five months (Herskowitz, 1987).

Other adverse neuromotor sequelae, namely, extrapyramidal side effects (EPS), are usually transient but still frightening. Stanilla and Simpson (1995) recently observed, "Gross EPS can have a significant negative effect on treatment outcome by contributing to poor compliance, exacerbation of psychiatric symptoms, violence, and even to suicide" (p. 281). Notably, dystonic effects can occur in which a muscle or group of muscles, such as those in the throat, abruptly contract. "Akathisia is a syndrome of subjective and objective motor restlessness associated with neuroleptic treatment" (Buckley & Meltzer, 1995, p. 628). Although, as noted above, the symptoms may be transitory, they nevertheless are a chief cause of noncompliance with recommended medication (e.g., Buckley & Meltzer, 1995).

Neuroleptic Malignant Syndrome (NMS) is yet another side effect of considerable concern. "NMS is an uncommon (i.e., incidence <0.9%) and potentially fatal complication of neuroleptic treatment" (Buckley & Meltzer, 1995, p. 629). The syndrome is characterized by altered states of consciousness, autonomic instability, rigidity, and fever.

Some other neuroleptic side effects are serious but so rare that they have been given relatively little attention in the psychiatric literature. Consider, for example, Pavor Nocturnus (sleep terror disorder): "The child appears terrified, screams, stares, has dilated pupils, sweats, and has rapid pulse and hyperventilation. He or she is agitated and confused and cannot be comforted. When alert, the child most commonly has no memory of the episode. Return to sleep is rapid when the episode is over, with complete amnesia in the morning" (Dulcan, Bregman, Weller, & Weller, 1995, p. 695).

Relatively recent advancements in psychopharmacotherapies have resulted in the addition of nonneuroleptic medications for the treatment of psychotic symptoms. As Marder and Van Putten (1995) observed, "Until recently, all effective antipsychotic drugs produced significant neurological side effects, and, for this reason, were referred to as neuroleptics. Clozapine and other new drugs are effective antipsychotics, but with fewer motor side effects than conventional antipsychotics. For this reason, the term *antipsychotic* is preferable for describing these drugs" (p. 247).

As implied above, Clozapine is "[t]he prototype atypical antipsychotic agent" (Owens & Risch, 1995, p. 275). Although Clozapine has demonstrated better efficacy in treating psychotic symptoms with a lower incidence of EPS and NMS (see Owens & Risch, 1995, for review), one of its side effects, agranulocytosis, can be fatal. Indeed, the danger of agranulocytosis necessitates weekly monitoring of patients' blood counts. Other side effects of this third generation antipsychotic include high fever, sedation, blurred vision, uncontrolled retention or elimination of urine, hypo- and hypersalivation, orthostatic hypotension, and tachycardia (irregularity in cardiac functioning) and, especially with older patients, anticholinergic delirium (e.g., Owens & Risch, 1995). Clearly, Clozapine and related "third generation" antipsychotics are not without undesirable side effects.

Little attention has been given to the legal policy issues raised by nonconsensual treatment of minors with antipsychotic medication. However, the concerns that the courts have recognized with regard to forcible medication of institutionalized adults have even greater relevance for minors. Several facts are noteworthy in that regard.

Negligent or abusive administration of antipsychotic medication may be especially common in institutions for minors with mental retardation or emotional disturbances.

Antipsychotic medication is a misnomer when prescribed for children and adolescents, except in the case of adolescents with adult schizophrenia. These drugs are most often prescribed for their purported "quasi-sedative" effects in managing the behavior of children with psychosis, mental retardation, or behavioral disturbance (e.g., Attention Deficit Hyperactivity Disorder) (Winsberg and Yepes 1978; see Buckley & Meltzer, 1995, and Dulcan et al., 1995, on sedation as a side effect of neuroleptic use). Even among psychotic children, "antipsychotic" drugs may not have antipsychotic effects. To summarize, "there are few established and carefully researched indications, and little is known of the long-term consequences of such treatment" (Gualtieri, Quade, Hicks, Mayo, & Schroeder, 1984, p. 20). Other psychiatric researchers make similar points. Campbell and Gonzalez (1996) concluded that "[e]ven though neuroleptics are widely used in children, with a few exceptions, systematic large-scale and long-term studies of neuroleptics are lacking in this age group of patients" (p. 1). Prescription of antipsychotic medication for children and youth takes place more on the basis of "medical lore than on a solid and well-developed empirical base" in the service of "diminishing pathological behavior and ultimately encouraging the development of adaptive behavior" (Aman, 1983, p. 456). The gaps in knowledge are stunning: "Still very much needed are studies on the determination of minimum effective doses and on the behavioral toxicity so often manifested in children before any neuroleptic-induced extrapyramidal/parkinsonian side effects appear, as well as systematic research on the effect of neuroleptics on cognition, learning, and academic performance" (Campbell & Gonzalez, 1996, p. 2).

The dearth of studies describing the effects of psychoactive drugs on children and adolescents should result in special care in prescription practice:

> The careful clinician attempts to balance the risks of medication, the risks of the untreated disorder, and the expected benefits of medication relative to other treatments. Clinical experience with the use of a psychotropic drug in adults should generally be substantial before that drug is used to treat children and adolescents. Because pharmaceutical houses rarely undertake the expense and trouble of testing drugs in children and adolescents, the U.S. Food and Drug Administration (FDA) guidelines as published in the *Physicians' Desk Reference* (PDR) cannot be relied upon for appropriate indications, age ranges, or doses. (Dulcan et al., 1995, p. 670)

Nonetheless, thousands of children with widely divergent conditions receive antipsychotic medication each year (Gualtieri et al., 1984). Administration of antipsychotic drugs may be especially common in institutions for persons with mental retardation. Research conducted in the early 1980s showed that one-quarter to one-half of the residents received such medication, typically for very long periods of time and often in dosages exceeding manufacturers' recommendations (Aman, 1983; Lipman, 1982). This practice appeared to continue with deinstitutionalization. Martin and Agran (1985) found that 70% of participants in community programs for persons with mental retardation who have a history of institutionalization received psychotropic medication (usually antipsychotic medication), compared with only 27% of participants without such a history. Very recently, Campbell and Gonzalez (1996) acknowledged the widespread prescription of neuroleptics for children with mental retardation, whether in community or residential settings, and, remarkably, further acknowledged that "only in recent years has there been a concern whether long-term neuroleptic treatment is justified in this population before efficacy and safety issues have been determined through rigorous research methods" (p. 13).

Use of neuroleptics is also widespread in treatment of child and adolescent inpatients, regardless of their diagnosis, especially when they are hospitalized for an extended stay (see, e.g., Parmelee et al., 1995; Zito, Craig, & Wanderling, 1996; see also Cullinan, Epstein, & Quinn, 1996, on use of psychotropic medication among youth in an interagency community-based system of care). In a study of public child inpatient units in New York State, Zito et al. (1996), for example, found that two-thirds of the patients receiving neuroleptic treatment did not have diagnoses of schizophrenia; rather, the modal diagnosis was conduct disorder.

Tardive dyskinesia and other extrapyramidal effects are problems at least as serious among children and youth as adults.
Although research is scant, existing studies show that "tardive dyskinesia does occur among children and adolescents, that the condition embraces a wide range of clinical manifestations, that it is not always reversible and that it may be associated with low doses of neuroleptics over a short period of time" (Gualtieri & Hawk, 1980, p. 59). Withdrawal syndromes, half of them moderate or severe, were observed in 44% of a diagnostically heterogeneous sample of children and adolescents when their physicians decided to withdraw them from such treatment (Gualtieri et al., 1984). Dosage was the factor most consistently related to withdrawal problems, a finding of particular note given the high doses frequently administered to institutionalized minors. The rate of persistent tardive dyskinesia among patients with mental retardation is about 30%, with another third of patients showing withdrawal

dyskinesia (Kalachnik, 1984). Such rates are substantially higher than those reported for adults with schizophrenia. An even higher rate has been observed among children, adolescents, and young adults with mental retardation, with cumulative dosage again being the most important factor (Gualtieri, Schroeder, Hicks, & Quade, 1986). Similar rates have been reported in studies of children with other diagnoses (Campbell & Gonzalez, 1996, and citations therein on p. 12). Atypicality of dyskinesic symptoms appears to be the rule rather than the exception among children and adolescents; the neurochemistry of treatment-emergent dyskinesias thus may be different from that experienced by adults (Richardson & Haugland, 1996). Clinical reports also suggest that dystonic reactions, some of them strikingly severe and potentially fatal, are especially common among younger patients (Gualtieri & Hawk, 1980), especially boys (Dulcan et al., 1995).

Antipsychotic medication often impairs learning.
Perhaps the most disturbing side effect of antipsychotic drugs, in light of their intended purpose, is that they appear actually to inhibit learning and cognitive performance. The FDA's Pediatric Advisory Panel recommended in the mid-1970s that thioridazine (Mellaril), chlorpromazine (Thorazine), and haloperidol (Haldol) contain a package insert warning that such drugs "may reduce learning performance if high doses are used and/or if it is prescribed for long periods of time. Careful consideration of improvement in severe behavior problems should be balanced against possible reduction in learning performance in each individual case" (quoted in Lipman, 1982, p. 268). Dulcan and colleagues (1995) described the problem as follows: "Developmental toxicology refers to the unique or especially severe side effects resulting from interaction between a drug and a patient's physical, cognitive, or emotional development. Interference with learning in school or with the development of social relationships within the family or with peers can have lasting effects. Behavioral toxicity (i.e., negative effects on mood, behavior, or learning) often develops before physical side effects are observed, especially in young children" (p. 671, citations omitted).

Studies conducted since the FDA panel made its report actually have given more substantial basis for concern about the cognitive effects of antipsychotic medication (e.g., Aman & Singh, 1991). For example, children with

Tourette's syndrome treated with haloperidol were rated by their teachers as not working as hard or learning as much as children who were not medicated (Sallee, Rock, & Head, 1996).

There is little evidence for effectiveness of antipsychotic medication in treating behavior disorders in children. Antipsychotic drugs actually may exacerbate inappropriate behavior.

Even scholars of mental health and mental retardation who are generally favorable toward chemotherapy question its use in treating childhood disorders and mental retardation. The comments of Kalachnik (1984) are representative: "Although the author views non-use of psychotropic medication for the individual who may derive true benefit from such medication with as much abhorrence as unnecessarily placing or maintaining an individual upon psychotropic medication for staff convenience or lack of programming, based upon the data [about efficacy] . . . and side effects . . . it may be concluded that the benefit : cost ratio of neuroleptic medication with the mentally retarded is much smaller than desired" (p. 311).

Aman's (1983) comprehensive review of effects of antipsychotic medication on mentally retarded persons showed some positive effects of thioridazine (Mellaril) in altering some maladaptive behaviors but no effect on most social behavior. No clear evidence for effective treatment with chlorpromazine (Thorazine) was found. Dulcan and colleagues (1995), in their discussion of psychopharmacologic treatment of aggression in children and adolescents, noted that "[a]lthough stimulants have been suggested for the treatment of conduct disorder without ADHD, there are as yet no data to support this strategy" (p. 685).

Negative behavioral effects of antipsychotic medication on children are better documented. As already noted, learning appears to be impaired by such drugs. Moreover, behavioral deterioration lasting for several weeks is common in children on withdrawal from antipsychotic drugs (Dulcan et al., 1995; Gualtieri et al., 1984). These behavioral symptoms, which are temporary, ironically may be perceived as evidence for the need for continuing drug treatment and lead to increased use, with accompanying increased risk of permanent and severe tardive dyskinesia (Gaultieri et al., 1984; Kalachnik, 1984).

PROCEDURAL ISSUES

Our review leaves little doubt of the harm engendered by unnecessarily restrictive, psychologically intrusive, or physically intrusive procedures. Not only is there the wrong resulting from threats to autonomy and privacy, but also the most restrictive and intrusive procedures in mental health and mental retardation services have the most dubious efficacy and the most severe negative side effects. More really may be less! More precisely, the relationship between restrictiveness/intrusiveness and efficacy of treatment appears to be curvilinear. Interventions that do not affect multiple aspects of the child's life generally are ineffective (e.g., Epstein, Cullinan, Quinn, & Cumblad, 1995), except for very specific problems (e.g., phobias; see Melton, 1983a, chap. 4). On the other hand, as interventions begin substantially to reduce choices available to a youngster or to increase psychological or physical threats to his or her integrity as a person, efficacy diminishes. Thus, significance of a right to treatment or habilitation in the least restrictive alternative is heightened by the harm resulting from overly restrictive or intrusive services or from failure to provide any services at all.

Vindicating such a right is not easy, though. Besides the confusion engendered by the complexity of the LRA concept, several practical realities may stand in the way of fulfillment of the right to treatment through the least restrictive alternative. Chambers (1978) noted three such obstacles. The first, which is a serious problem when a constitutional foundation for the LRA is posited, is the argument that the restrictiveness of treatment is irrelevant when the placement is voluntary. Because juvenile placements usually are voluntary legally if not factually (i.e., parents appear to have consented voluntarily), the state may bear no constitutional obligation to provide a less restrictive placement when one potentially is available. This obstacle was partially removed by the Supreme Court's decision in *Youngberg v. Romeo* (1982) that patients were entitled to freedom from unreasonable restraint. Regardless, where a statutory entitlement is in place, as often is true (see Epstein et al., 1994, for discussion), barriers to a constitutional claim need not be attacked.

A second and more general problem is when the state's experts argue that the restrictive or intrusive treatment is the only one that will meet the state's interests. Given the deference due professional judgments as matters both of law[4] and fact,[5] such an argument is likely to reduce substantially the likelihood of a court or other legal authority's seeking a less restrictive placement. In that regard, a need exists to challenge myths about hospitalization (Kielser, 1982b) and other forms of restrictive or intrusive treatment — myths that are prevalent among mental health professionals as well as the general public (Kiesler & Sibulkin, 1987).

Finally, perhaps the real crux of the matter is that the lack of a carefully crafted and implemented procedural requirement for exploration of therapeutic alternatives may render an LRA standard moot, even if it is held to apply. An LRA requirement is likely to be meaningless if no one has a clear responsibility (and accompanying time and expertise) to investigate and, when necessary, create alternatives (see *Lake v. Cameron*, 1964).

Creation of such alternatives is, to some extent, a matter of resources. If funds are inadequate, then a continuum of care — and a less restrictive or intrusive placement for a particular child — may not occur, no matter how carefully treatment is planned. On the other hand, restrictive treatments require little ingenuity. Therefore, making the LRA concept meaningful is often a matter of assigning responsibility for real planning: careful consideration of relatively unrestrictive, individualized means of meeting the needs of a child and his or her family and addressing the interests of the state.

Two kinds of response to the need for treatment alternatives are required. First, legal structures with appropriate staffing to ensure adequate exploration of alternatives should be put into place, a matter we discuss in more detail in later chapters. Second, mental health professionals should assume the duty of advocacy for child clients (Melton, 1977). The model of cooperation between attorneys and mental health professionals in the New Jersey Office of Public Advocacy (Perlin, 1981) is an illustration of the ways in which dual advocacy can avoid unnecessarily restrictive treatment for individual children and ultimately stimulate the development of a continuum of services. Chambers's (1978) point in that regard is well taken:

> Mental health professionals bear a heavy burden of responsibility to insure
> [that] searches for alternatives occur. In many parts of the country, judges
> will have been long accustomed to relying on hospitalization as the pre-

ferred mode of care. They cannot be expected to educate themselves about the new era of alternatives to mental hospital treatment. Attorneys, however well informed, will often appear to judges to be starry-eyed idealists spouting high-sounding moral nursery rhymes. Mental health professionals need to get to know judges, gently educate them, cajole them into cooperative projects. Take a judge to lunch. (p. 35)

To be sure, there are problems associated with trying to define the level of care for children that is minimally required but not overly intrusive. Arguably though, we must grapple with these issues because liberty is important to children—notwithstanding Supreme Court proclamations to the contrary. Some forms of treatment infringe liberties so greatly that they threaten the personhood and psychological well being of the very children they are supposed to help. Worse still, some of these treatments (i.e., antipsychotic medication) threaten the physical safety and even the lives of these children. As we focus on the various technical procedures that protect children's interests, it is important to remember just what is at stake.

PART 2

Defining the Commitment Process

•

CHAPTER 3

Problems in Definition

As we have shown, there are effective treatments available to address the needs of children, youth, and their families. Some treatments (i.e., institutional) are to be avoided if at all possible, not only because they may not help but because they may actually harm. We also have argued that appropriate treatment alternatives often may not be offered spontaneously; it may be necessary both to identify an appropriate treatment strategy and to advocate for it. Advocacy can be especially complicated. In a society where resources for the treatment of mental disorders are scarce, it is always tempting to concentrate legislative efforts on securing greater appropriations for treatment. Civil commitment laws and the rights that they protect may sometimes seem either irrelevant or a costly obstacle to treatment. Why should anyone care about commitment laws, especially when they are concerned only with the rights of children?

There are three different answers to this question. First, the scarcity of resources itself demands a reexamination of civil commitment laws. Civil commitment is one of the chief factors in determining the allocation of mental health and mental retardation resources among the children most in need of it. Civil commitment laws force public sector treatment providers to give priority to involuntary patients at the expense of patients who do not meet the commitment criteria but who may, by other standards, be more appropriate for treatment. The laws can discourage the treatment in the private sector of patients who meet neither the legal definition of a voluntary patient nor the criteria for involuntary commitment. As resources grow more scarce, this function of minor commitment law grows in importance so that the judge and the child's defense lawyer often deliberately restrict their concern to assuring access to mental health or mental retardation services.

Second, despite fluctuations in our understanding of the nature of mental disorders, commitment will continue to serve, as it has for the last two centuries, nontherapeutic, political goals, such as public safety and the provision of shelter for the homeless. These traditional goals are independent of, and sometimes in conflict with, therapeutic goals. When it is a child who is being hospitalized, the civil commitment process also is concerned with the education of the child and support for a certain kind of family structure.

Third, as we stressed in the introduction, civil commitment laws have a great and largely untapped potential for tempering the demands for treatment and vindicating parental authority for the normative principle of respect for the personhood of children and youth. For some people involved in the commitment process, the notion of children's rights may seem oxymoronic. Therefore, it is even more important for the commitment laws to be clear in their formulation and protection of those rights.

The legal consequences of a civil commitment of a child are to provide a shield for the minor with severe emotional disturbance and a sword for mental health professionals. As a shield, civil commitment law imposes limits on coercive intervention by mental health professionals into the minor's life. These limits may be substantive, restricting absolutely what is done to the minor, or procedural, restricting how it is done.

As a sword, the law authorizes treatment. Treatment can be coercive in the sense that the minor patient opposes it. Through commitment, the clinician can recruit the assistance of law enforcement officers, social service workers, and others to force treatment. The treatment may be nonconsensual in the sense that the minor, because of actual or presumed immaturity or mental disorder, is unable to make an informed decision to accept or refuse the treatment. Here again, commitment laws encourage others to assist the clinician. Related laws may authorize treatment with the consent of the minor alone because of doubts that mental health professionals may have about the common law incapacity of persons under the legal age of minority to consent. Without these other sources of authority for treatment of a minor, mental health professionals might hesitate to act because of their concern about common law liability for battery or false imprisonment.

These are the practical dimensions of civil commitment law. There is an equally important moral dimension. It is in the civil commitment law affecting minors that society attempts to define and reconcile the competing interests of the minor patient, the parent, and the mental health professional. The problems posed by paternalism in the civil commitment of adults are exacerbated when the patient is not only mentally disordered but also a minor. The problems of parental authority over the health care of the child also are complicated where the child is mentally disordered and the treatment in question has a greater impact on the child's autonomy than does an appendectomy.

Measuring the justice of the civil commitment of children is not accomplished easily. In speaking of the process for adjudicating Social Security disorder claims, Mashaw (1983) defined justice as "those qualities of a decision process that provide arguments for the acceptability of its decisions" (p. 24). He identified three very different kinds of arguments depending on the model of justice that was being followed in that administrative system: "(1) that decisions should be accurate and efficient realizations of the legislative will; (2) that decisions should provide appropriate support or therapy from the perspectives of relevant professional cultures; and (3) that decisions should be fairly arrived at when assessed in the light of traditional processes for determining individual entitlements."

Mashaw (1983) called these three models bureaucratic rationality, professional treatment, and moral judgment models, respectively. The first model is appropriate where legislative standards are clear cut and the accuracy of their application is of primary importance. In the second model (usually called the *medical model* in civil commitment), opaque professional standards and procedures are permitted to determine the best interests of the patient. In the third model, the state and the individual interests are opposed and the standards for balancing those interests are "so open-textured that each decision both defines the nature of the entitlement and awards or denies it to a particular party" (p. 24).

Against which of these models is the justice of a child's commitment to be measured? The question is complicated further by confusion among the actors in commitment. Clinicians sometimes think that the statutory standards are more well-defined than they are and that the standards are unrelated to ordinary treatment standards. Judges and defense lawyers may view themselves as facilitators of treatment standards unrelated to the rule of law, rather than as value definers.

This confusion is increased by the design of most commitment laws because they commonly draw freely from all three models. The criteria of commitment, for example, might require the state first to offer voluntary treatment to the defendant, and to survey the availability of involuntary treatment settings less restrictive than a hospital. This is primarily a bureaucratic function. That is, no interpretation of the law is required to determine whether voluntary placement has been offered and whether a survey of less restrictive alternatives has been conducted. On the other hand, the determination of capacity to consent to voluntary treatment and determination of what treatment modality is the least restrictive also involve elements of professional and moral judgment.

Even where a particular commitment statute *appears* to endorse one of these models primarily, on closer inspection other models may be involved. For example, the commitment criteria might require a diagnosable mental illness and a prognosis that treatment will benefit the patient. These criteria seem to call for an exercise of professional judgment guided by the polestar of the patient's best interests rather than any legal standard. Although this approach appears to afford considerable professional discretion, in fact the law's failure to define precisely the kind of mental disorder required for commitment may reflect a desire to expand the discretion of the judge or

84

other legal decision maker. Moreover, even if a precise definition is provided, that too limits professional discretion. Any definition, even that contained in the current edition of the *Diagnostic and Statistical Manual of Mental Disorders*, restricts the exercise of professional judgment and introduces normative moral elements appropriate for a judge or jury. Ancillary requirements that the diagnosis of mental illness be based on a personal examination conducted within a certain time frame, and documented in a certain way, are appropriate for bureaucratic decision making (i.e., these criteria are clearly met or not).

Finally, the criteria might require a finding that the patient is dangerous. This demands moral judgment. That is, the definition of dangerousness must be applied to a specific individual in a specific community. It does not make sense from the bureaucratic perspective to say that a patient is dangerous except in rare instances where danger is defined thoroughly, as, say, operating a motor vehicle with a blood alcohol level above 0.10. From a professional judgment standard, a finding of dangerousness is meaningless to the extent that it is not synonymous with a threat to the patient's well-being.

The procedures for applying each of these criteria are not always appropriate to the model by which the standard is measured, particularly where the person proposed for commitment is a minor. The statute or the prevailing practice may call for clinicians to decide dangerousness with little real opportunity for the judge or jury to participate in that determination.

Most civil commitment provisions fall somewhere along a continuum with the professional judgment (or medical) model at one end, and the moral judgment (adversarial or judicial) model at the other. Typically, the focus in a commitment process will shift from a bureaucratic standard in which detention is effected by a police officer, to a professional standard in which pretrial evaluation is authorized, to a moral standard on which extended treatment is premised. Child commitment laws differ from those affecting adults in their reliance on the professional judgment model at all three stages.

We have attempted to describe typical structure of laws in the United States providing for the civil commitment of minors without concerning ourselves with the provisions of particular state statutes. In doing so, we make two assumptions: There is a common structure to these commitment statutes. There are ways in which this structure can be improved through the Model Act for the Mental Treatment of Minors, contained in Appendix A.

THE PERSPECTIVE OF DUE PROCESS

The value of looking through the lens of the law at the compulsory treatment of mentally disordered minors is in the power of the lens to bring into clear focus the social values at stake in that treatment. Although fairness and accuracy in determining who receives compulsory treatment are primary objectives of due process, determining what is fair and how accuracy may be assured in commitment proceedings involve considerations of family dynamics, clinical practice, and psychological maturity. Not surprisingly, judges, who typically have little social scientific training, sometimes mis-apprehend these bases of the contemporary constitutional critique of the commitment of minors. Indeed, in a later chapter we argue that the mis-apprehension is so great that it amounts to a deliberate reliance on myths rather than on empirical knowledge. The failure, though, is not a failure of constitutional doctrine; it is a failure of advocacy to bring forth facts about the state of science to which the law can be applied.

The relatively recent "constitutionalization" of civil commitment law is not a symptom of legal chauvinism. Of course, it does require one to concede that parents and clinicians are not above the law altogether with respect to the treatment of mentally disordered minors. In other words, persons who both are under the age of majority and have a mental disorder do still have legally cognizable rights. But, admitting that, it still is possible to contend that those rights will be protected adequately by the parents and clinicians involved in the treatment rather than by judges and attorneys. Indeed, the *Parham* decision essentially held just that (*Parham v. J. R.*, 1979).

Of course, the notion of due process also is useful for discussions of children's rights, as the district court in *Parham* amply demonstrated. *J. L. v. Parham* was a class action, brought before a three-judge federal district court (that happened to include then federal court of appeals judge Griffin Bell, sitting by designation). One of the two children who served as class represen-tatives, J. L., committed suicide before the litigation concluded.

86

Two different kinds of relief were sought by the plaintiffs in *Parham*. To remedy what they thought was an abridgment of procedural due process, the plaintiffs wanted to stop the state of Georgia from admitting children to its mental health facilities on the basis of parental consent or, as often as not, the consent of the state agency into whose custody the children had been placed. While the state called this kind of admission voluntary, the plaintiffs persuaded the court that, because the child had not given consent to the admission, it was every bit as involuntary as a civil commitment except that no hearing of any kind had been offered to the child.

The plaintiffs also argued that there had been a violation of substantive due process. They persuaded the court that the placement of children in state hospitals, regardless of the fairness of the procedure with which it had been achieved, violated the child's right to treatment in the least restrictive setting. The court took the extraordinary step of ordering the state of Georgia to create alternative treatment settings to transfer the children to.

The Supreme Court, without adequate explanation, reversed the district court ruling on the substantive due process issue. On the question of procedural due process, the Supreme Court agreed that admissions on parental consent alone were involuntary, but the Court decided that informal review by independent treatment providers would satisfy the requirement of due process required for an initial admission.

THE IMPACT OF THE COMMON LAW

Practical concerns make the complexity of commitment statutes inevitable. One traditional concern that has developed is the common law liability of the treatment provider for treatment performed without the informed consent of the patient. Without legislation in most states, it is anyone's guess whether the common law (as interpreted by some future court) requires this consent in nonemergency situations where the patient is mentally disordered (Meisel, 1979). Many state statutes of limitations dramatically increase anxiety over future tort actions by allowing the patient to bring suit after the age of majority is reached or the mental disorder is removed, whichever comes later.

One might argue that the common law permits treatment of a mentally disordered patient with the consent of the next-of-kin and that the common law authorization of this treatment is beyond dispute when the mentally disordered patient is a minor and the relative giving consent is a custodial parent. In practical terms, however, this involves predicting what judges and juries will do under a unique set of facts. Ironically, the malpractice defense bars in some states may prefer the ambiguity of the common law. Judges and juries may be biased in favor of treatment providers. Reluctance of treatment providers to testify on behalf of plaintiffs will impede proof of the applicable standard of care. In such states a statutory procedure for assuring authority for treatment, at a minimum, might sensitize patients and their attorneys to the need for authority and, at most, might supply the standard of care in a malpractice action.

PARHAM AND THE NEW RULE OF LAW

How can the authority for treatment be assured statutorily? *Parham*, a decision which was no less an expression of federalism than of medical paternalism, did not permit a state legislature to pass a law conferring wholesale immunity on clinicians for all treatment of mentally disordered minors without their consent (even if the consumerist elements in the legislature would stand for it). *Parham* dictated that some kind of procedure for commitment must be established by statute or regulation, although some judicial and advocate roles at the front end of that procedure might be played by clinicians. The need to provide assurance to clinicians that they have authority to treat, and at the same time provide the minimal protection of the minor patient's rights compelled by the Constitution, results in delicate, often emotionally charged, legislative line drawing.

Whether it is the nature of the social values behind the commitment statute or the mechanics of drafting a commitment proposal, the constitutional perspective is an effective heuristic device for probing the operation of a commitment statute and for comparing, on a practical level, the statutes of different states. The notions of substantive due process and procedural due process assist in sorting, at least provisionally, the elements of a commitment statute in two distinct categories. Chapter 4 examines substantive and, to a lesser extent, procedural due process considerations in the commitment of mentally disordered minors. Here we look at the nature of a commitment process, contrasted with a private admission, and the links between procedure and substance in that process.

In a truly voluntary admission to a psychiatric facility, definition of the process of admission often is neither possible nor particularly important. Of course, many facilities do proceed in a similar, step-wise manner, guided by custom or accreditation standards, to prepare social histories, screen for medical disorders, determine insurance coverage, and have the patient sign a blanket consent to admission and treatment.

Where the admission, denominated as voluntary, of a minor is concerned, this process may include obtaining the consent of the parent as well, although many admissions do not involve the formal consent of either the child or the parent. How numerous these cases are in the public sector is difficult to say because of their low profile, but it is possible that no one involved in the admissions process gives any thought to whether the admission is voluntary or involuntary, and to what the requirements are of each.

Occasionally, controversies surrounding the liability of the local educational agency for treatment or habilitation related to the minor's education, will pressure mental health professionals to graft formal legal procedures onto what otherwise would be a private, informal admission to a facility. The focus of these procedures brought under the Individuals with Disabilities Education Act (1990) or parallel state statutes is the educational necessity of residential psychiatric placement and the consequential liability of the local educational system for the cost of all or part of that placement.

The order in the stages of the commitment process has a bearing on its constitutionality. To use the minimalist, medical model of commitment due process, commitment consists of at least two stages; a review by an independent medical decision maker, and then treatment. Though most commitments proceed in that order, emergency circumstances usually permit a reversal of the order. Because different state and individual interests may be at stake, continued treatment for an extended period of time might require further procedural steps, although the majority of the *Parham* Court did not find it necessary to address that question. A brief review of the Supreme Court's approach to commitment due process demonstrates the Court's tendency to ignore the important links between substance and procedure in the several statutes that it has scrutinized.

FROM PROCEDURE TO SUBSTANCE

The current requirements of procedural due process in the commitment of minors are usually explained by reference to a test developed in *Mathews v. Eldridge* (1976, p. 335; see also, *Parham v. J. R.*, 1979). Important flaws in this test as applied to children's commitment are worth noting here. Although *Mathews* involved a dispute over property (Social Security disorder benefits) rather than liberty, it is cited routinely by the federal courts in questions of procedural due process, whether these questions arise in an administrative law context or a capital murder trial. Still, the *Mathews* test works fairly well as a tool for evaluating the procedures required to protect some liberty interests.

Because standards are inevitably ambiguous in commitment, it is the *fairness* with which those standards are interpreted and applied rather than the accuracy that becomes important. Fairness is more difficult to measure in increments to and balance against cost. In *Addington v. Texas* (1979), the first example of the Supreme Court applying the *Mathews* test to civil commitment, the procedural safeguard in question was the standard of proof in adult commitment cases. The Court's method in *Addington* was to identify (a) the private interest in avoiding commitment, (b) the risk of erroneous deprivation of that interest from the use of the existing, usually lesser procedural safeguard, and (c) the state's interest in avoiding the presumably higher cost of the greater procedural safeguard. These three elements (constituting the *Mathews* test), to the extent that they involve only procedure, must be considered in context. Specifically, they must be considered vis-à-vis the point in the commitment process at which the issue is raised.

Some years later, in *Zinermon v. Burch* (1990), a five-member majority (of whom four since have left the bench) again applied *Mathews* in a commitment case. Burch complained that he had been admitted as a voluntary patient to a Florida state hospital at a time when he was not competent to consent to admission. He argued that due process requirements entitled him to the kind of pre-deprivation procedural protection afforded by a commitment hearing or, alternatively (and minimally), to an evaluation of his competence to consent to admission.

The real issue in *Zinermon* was whether Burch was barred by prior Supreme Court decisions (e.g., *Parratt v. Taylor* (1981)) from bringing a federal civil rights complaint because of the existence of an adequate post-deprivation remedy under state tort law. *Mathews* was employed by the majority to determine whether a pre-deprivation remedy was necessary and, thus, whether Burch had raised a federal claim.

In reaching their decision that Burch had a right to a pre-deprivation remedy of some kind that was available in federal court, the Court ventured through the three steps in *Mathews*. For once, the majority was unequivocal in defining the private liberty interest as one of avoiding a "massive curtailment of liberty" (p. 131). The Court was not asked to determine precisely *what* pre-deprivation procedural safeguards were needed in voluntary mental hospital admissions. The Court's reliance in *Zinermon* on *Parham* and related cases providing only minimal procedural safeguards (e.g., *Goss v. Lopez*, 1975) to demonstrate instances where a hearing was required before liberty deprivation suggests that informal procedures likely would suffice even for adults. In providing Burch with a federal remedy (including statutory attorney's fees), the Court clarified that its laissez-faire policy in commitment hearings did not extend so far as to eliminate federal court jurisdiction altogether.

In *Parham*, the narrow, procedural issue before the Court was whether a hearing in front of a judge was necessary prior to admission of a minor for inpatient psychiatric treatment. One might limit the issue to more than just a consideration of minor patients at this stage of treatment who already had been in community treatment. Unlike *Addington*, the children in the *Parham* case were not assumed to be facing initial admissions of a life-long confinement without the benefit of further procedure. Because the adequacy of procedures in *Parham* was gauged at an earlier point in the commitment process (initial admission) than in *Addington*, procedural due process is satisfied with less rigorous procedural safeguards.

Addington only slightly lessened the safeguards of a traditional criminal trial. It should be noted at this point that children fare differently under Fourth Amendment analysis as well. When asked whether random urinalysis of athletes in public school amounted to an unreasonable search, the Supreme Court upheld the practice through the use of a balancing test strongly reminiscent of *Parham*. Justice Scalia, writing for the majority in *Vernonia School District v. Acton* (1995), weighed the nature of the privacy interest at stake against the legitimate government interests advanced through the search. Scalia began by observing: "Traditionally at common law, and still today, unemancipated minors lack some of the most fundamental rights of self-determination — including even the rights of self-determination in its narrow sense, i.e. the right to come and go at will (p. 2391).

Not surprisingly, when this individual interest is weighed against the governmental interest in "[d]eterring drug use by our Nation's schoolchildren" (p. 2395), the search involved in urinalyses seems to the Court to be reasonable. Thus, even in the Fourth Amendment context where non-utilitarian bases of constitutional rights are established quite well, children's status as minors shifts the Court to a paternalistic and pragmatic approach.

In its landmark decision addressing the right to treatment after admission to a mental retardation facility, *Youngberg v. Romeo* (1982), the Court again approached the question of substantive due process. Although procedural due process demands that the state exercise power over the individual in certain ways (e.g., only after notice and hearing before a neutral decision maker), substantive due process limits the ends to which that power may be used. In *Youngberg*, the Supreme Court required Pennsylvania to provide the mentally retarded residents of Pennhurst with (in addition to food, clothing, shelter, and medical care) reasonable protection from harm, freedom from unreasonable restraint, and sufficient treatment to prevent impairment of these two other rights. On the face of it, no quantity or quality of procedure would permit the infringement of these rights. As *Youngberg* illustrated, however, in providing an operational definition of these substantive rights, the Court's methodology and conclusions sometimes are indistinguishable from those used in procedural due process controversies.

The Court used four approaches to finding in the due process clause substantive rights belonging to the mentally retarded residents of Pennhurst.

First, the Court declared a right to food, clothing, shelter, and medical care on the basis of the defendant's concessions in the pleadings. Second, the Court noted that it had found under the Eighth Amendment a right of prisoners to safety and freedom from restraint. Because the Pennhurst residents had not been placed in state custody for punishment, the Court reasoned the residents at least must be as entitled as prisoners to such rights under the due process clause. Third, the Court deduced from these rights a right to such treatment as was necessary to protect the rights to safety and freedom from restraint. Fourth, the Court said, "In determining whether a substantive right protected by the Due Process Clause has been violated, it is necessary to balance 'the liberty of the individual' and 'the demands of an organized society'" (p. 320). The court implied that this is the same kind of balancing analysis that it used in *Parham* to decide procedural due process challenges to civil commitment.

The standard crafted by the Court in *Youngberg* is the *professional judgment rule*. Under the most conservative interpretation, this rule imposes mostly theoretical limits on the treatment or non-treatment of persons in state mental health or mental retardation facilities. By contrast, some federal circuit courts of appeal (e.g., *Thomas S. v. Morrow*, 1986) have revealed a potential in this rule for forcing precisely the kind of systemic reforms sought by the *Parham* trial court but rejected on appeal as "substantive" rather than "procedural." Despite the characterization of *Youngberg*'s professional judgment rule as substantive, it may have the same effect as the Supreme Court's nominally procedural requirement of independent medical decision making in *Parham*.

The professional judgment rule seems intended to assure a process of deliberate clinical decision making, without attempting to influence the outcome of that process. The most generous readings of that rule, resulting in the creation of new community placements for persons already deinstitutionalized, simply have endorsed the usually unanimous recommendation of the clinicians involved. The professional judgment rule might have been intended by Justice Powell to serve as a shield for treatment providers against liability for violating the patients' rights to treatment. On its face, *Youngberg*, like *Parham*, seems to have endorsed the treatment provider's customary way

93

of doing business. But as applied and extended by the lower courts, the *Youngberg* decision proved to be a formidable sword for the vindication of those patient rights.

This unexpected result seems to have occurred in instances where the unanimous clinical opinion has been that the state's care was a substantial deviation from the care that might be called professional, in the sense that it is too restrictive. Under this set of facts, the deference to professional opinion required by the *Youngberg* decision entitled the plaintiff to a summary judgment.

The professional judgment rule is the fullest development of the trend toward judicial deference to clinical expertise begun in *Addington*. In *Addington*, the perceived difficulty clinicians would have, both in meeting a standard of proof in commitment of beyond a reasonable doubt and in achieving thereby the legitimate ends of commitment, led to the approval of a lesser standard of proof. In *Parham*, the perceived fairness and accuracy of clinical judgment (or perhaps the notorious unfairness and inaccuracy of commitment judges) persuaded the Court to empower clinicians with the authority of a judge. In *Vitek v. Jones* (1980), clinical judgment was endorsed as a substitute for legal advocacy for prisoners facing commitments to mental health facilities. Starting then with a slight easing of procedural requirements of proof, the Court proceeded to replace the judge, and then the defense lawyer, wtih a clinician, although presumably the clinician was obliged to operate under traditional legal standards in both new roles. In *Youngberg*, those standards move closer to becoming whatever the clinician chooses to make them.

In *Parham* (1979, p. 598), Chief Justice Burger could be heard to chide the plaintiff for seeking substantive due process remedies with procedural due process complaints. But in the series of cases we have examined briefly, procedure and substance are related closely , and it does not matter on which aspect of due process the Court focused. Whether a decision was couched in terms of procedural due process or substantive due process, the Court has expressed a clear preference in mental disorder decisions for accuracy, or at least expediency, over fairness. This preference has been based as much on the Court's cynicism about achieving fairness through traditional, judge-mediated proceedings as its naiveté about the accuracy with which mental disorder or dangerousness can be defined and determined.

In part, this preference for accuracy rather than fairness as a measure of due process was expressed by the choice of the *Mathews* test. *Mathews* demanded that costs of procedural safeguards be justified by benefits to the accuracy of decision making. Procedural safeguards, like most individual rights, are impossible to defend on the basis of measurable social utility. Individual rights are what have been called "anti-utilitarian" (Dworkin, 1977, p. 269).

The repeal of the Fourth Amendment's requirement of a search warrant would be one example of a cost-effective way of improving the reliability of law enforcement decisions. Indeed, it is precisely because maximal efficiency would lead law enforcement officers to widespread intrusions on privacy that we need the Fourth Amendment. The rationale for procedural safeguards in children's commitments is related to expediency in treatment, much the way the Fourth Amendment is related to efficient law enforcement. According Fourth Amendment rights to adults accused of criminal conduct may be even more acceptable to some than acknowledging that a child proposed for involuntary hospitalization possesses a right to a fair hearing before an impartial decision maker.

The futility of the individual seeking procedural rights in a commitment proceeding on the basis of *Mathews* can be illustrated by a brief look at another Supreme Court decision. In the context of commitment, the Supreme Court (*Allen v. Illinois*, 1987) has ruled that the defendant has no privilege against self-incrimination. This ruling rested on two conclusions reached by the Court's five-member majority.

First, as it had in the 1974 case upholding the preventive detention of juveniles (*Schall v. Martin*) and earlier yet in *Addington*, the Court found that the commitment in question was not criminal in nature, and thus did not trigger the entire range of criminal procedural protections. Second, the Court, speaking through Chief Justice Rehnquist, answered Allen's alternative argument that even if the self-incrimination privilege did not apply because technically his was not a criminal proceeding, due process independently demanded that he be accorded this procedural protection. The chief justice applied the *Mathews* test of what process is due and found (without any real evidence on the point) that, far from increasing the reliability of decision making, this safeguard actually decreases it.

The significance of this trend for persons interested in legislative reform is twofold. It signaled both practical and conceptual freedom from the traditional forms of judicial decision making imposed by cases such as *Lessard v. Schmidt* (1972). And it added new urgency to legislative reform efforts because of the risks of impact of litigation in this field. Legislators should be more willing to support new initiatives in the civil commitment law affecting minors now that the law is more settled. The single most important teaching of *Parham* is that the state legislature, not the judiciary, is chiefly responsible for deciding how minors' rights at stake in commitment are to be protected.

COMMITMENT LAW AS AN EXPRESSION OF POLICY

One clearly substantive section of commitment laws is devoted to a statement of policy. On the most general level a civil commitment law for minors expresses legislative preferences that thereafter must be implemented by the governor and his or her subordinates, notably the directors of the state mental health and mental retardation programs. There is a bewildering array of policies that commitment law can affect, not always in the intended manner (to the extent that legislative intent ever can be ascertained fully). Policy regarding the priority of populations to be served, the relations among the competing agencies involved in the social control, education, and treatment of minors, the relative prestige of the mental health professions, and, finally, the structure of the family are expressed in most commitment statutes, with differing degrees of explicitness. At most, these expressions of policy will guide the executive and inform the judiciary; at a minimum, they can raise public awareness of certain issues.

The range of permissible purposes or policies of a commitment law is limited very loosely by notions of substantive due process and equal protection. Substantive due process principles affect the choice of policies primarily at the points where those policies are operationalized in criteria for commitment or in prescriptions of post-commitment rights. At those points, due process considerations influence the choice of standards, the precision in expressing the standards, and the relationship among the standards (e.g., the relationship between the criteria of commitment and the conditions of post-commitment treatment). The next chapter considers these dimensions of substantive due process in more detail.

THE ROLE OF STATUTORY DEFINITIONS

The section of a commitment law devoted to definitions is also impossible to classify strictly as either substance or procedure. Both important policy choices and the real meaning of the procedural safeguards often are buried within these definitions. Here it is helpful to look at a few of the Model Act's definitions. There is more discussion of these definitions in Chapter 6.

Of the statutory definitions contained in a civil commitment law, none is more fundamental than that of voluntariness. It is worth remembering that it was the practice, prior to the lower court decision in *Parham*, to conceptualize admission of a minor to a state facility at the request of a parent or a parental surrogate as voluntary.

The Model Act defines voluntary by reference to two other controversial terms, *competent* and *consent*. A voluntary admission is one to which a competent patient gives his or her consent. As more information is required to be communicated for a consent to be valid, and more skill is demanded of the patient in handling that information, fewer patients will be considered voluntary, and more involuntary commitments will occur. Although elsewhere we discuss clinical evidence that many minors in fact have a significant ability to understand the risk and benefits of hospitalization, the ultimate choice of the quantum of information that must be understood, the quality of the understanding, and the degree of freedom of the patient from coercion belong to the legislature.

The Model Act expands the coverage of the commitment law through the use of the term *physically intrusive or restrictive mental health treatment*. Admission to any residential treatment in any setting, psychotropic medication, and certain kinds of aversive therapy are given as examples of treatment that meet this definition. The consequence of falling under this definition is that the provider of nonemergency treatment must obtain consent from the patient or an order from the court. The consequence of treatment, such as psychotherapy, not falling under this term is that neither formal consent nor a court order must be obtained.

This definition takes on greater significance through language in Section 105 of the Model Act that prohibits all physically intrusive or restrictive mental health treatment not provided in accordance with the act. Many existing commitment laws on their face are permissive statutes that say, in effect, that a hospital may admit a patient after the judge's commitment or that a hospital may admit a patient with the consent of the patient, and if the patient is a minor, the consent of the parent of the patient. Hospitals meeting the particular definition of the statutes can avail themselves of this harbor safe from risk of tort liability but, as far as the statute goes, need not do so. Other, newer programs for minors with mental disabilities might not be able to use the safe harbor and are even less likely to believe that they must use it. As a consequence, many commitment laws are failing to protect either the patient or the provider as treatment moves out of the state hospital and into new community settings.

The Model Act attempts to regulate all contemporary treatment modalities according to the degree of risk posed by treatment to the patient's civil rights, and not according to whether the treatment is offered in a state hospital or a local medication clinic. As a consequence, it employs the term *program* rather than *hospital* or *institution* and defines *program* to be all-inclusive. Programs are excluded from regulation to the extent that they do not administer physically intrusive or restrictive treatment.

Within its definition of treatment, the Model Act includes all habilitation services (providing that they are physically intrusive or restrictive) offered to minors with mental retardation. This approach is intended in part to assure that mental retardation services are regulated by the commitment procedures and standards. We have taken the position that a unified approach to the involuntary treatment (or habilitation) of minors with mental disabilities is desirable. This position is consistent with the view that the important question revolves around the degree of threat that the services in question pose to important liberty interests of the minor, and not how those services are characterized and where they are delivered. It is also true that there is often more uncertainty with minors than adults as to whether the primary diagnosis is mental illness or mental retardation.

Because of the scope of mental disabilities and treatment modalities covered by the Model Act, the term *patient* is defined globally to include all of the euphemistic and often misleading labels attached to mentally disordered minors in treatment. Some statutes, at the cost of clarity, avoid the use of any label by referring to the patient constantly as the *person*.

The Model Act's use of the term *provider* is not as critical as it is in many commitment statutes. In the Model Act, a provider is simply an alternative to a program as the source of regulated physically intrusive or restrictive treatment. The term is defined to include only licensed physicians and comparably qualified psychologists because of the assumption that only these individuals will be administering this kind of treatment outside of a program.

The provider is empowered under circumstances described in Section 106 to petition for commitment or to block the petition of a program. This gives the provider an advantage over other mental health and mental retardation professionals who do not meet the definition of provider. It also gives the provider authority that law enforcement authorities lack except in emergency commitments. Although the nature of this authority is somewhat unusual, the strategy of confining discretion in a commitment statute to clinicians with certain qualifications is quite common. Here the justification for selectively conferring authority to petition for commitment is based less on credentials and more on degree of familiarity with the minor.

The Model Act is drafted in sharp contrast to many commitment statutes that, with support from the *Parham* decision, rely on providers to perform quasi-judicial functions. The most common of these functions is to conduct a pretrial clinical evaluation of whether the minor meets criteria related to commitment but not necessarily the same criteria applied by the court. If the provider finds (sometimes in the form of a written *certification*) that the minor meets the criteria in question, several consequences are possible depending on how much weight the statute gives to the provider's opinion.

At one extreme, endorsed by *Parham*, the clinical certification is sufficient to admit the minor on an involuntary basis. At the other extreme, the provider's opinion is considered by the commitment court along with the other evidence. In the latter case, however, judges and juries still tend to follow the provider's advice blindly, especially when he or she is the only expert witness. Because of concern about excessive deference by judges and juries to mental health professionals' opinions, and other concerns discussed later, there is not a requirement of a clinical evaluation or, therefore, a need for a definition establishing the qualification of the evaluator.

It should be clear at this point that definitions function as more than aids to interpretation. They also typically establish the jurisdiction of the statute (i.e., who and what is regulated by the statute). The definitions also express some basic standards, such as the criteria for "voluntary" status.

The Model Act also omits what at first might appear to be the essential definition of *mental illness* and *mental retardation*. Whether or not limited to minors, most current commitment statutes contain some kind of definition of these terms. Often the definitions are tautological — for example, defining mental illness as a mental disorder, without defining mental disorder. Others define mental illness to include considerations of dangerousness. In some cases, courts have saved a statute by reading into its definition of mental illness or need for treatment a requirement of dangerousness. A few statutes and some proposals for reform have attempted precise definitions of mental illness, dangerousness, or both.

Mental retardation is defined less often, although in theory there is at least as much of a need to provide definition. Indeed, in some states, the chief protection mentally retarded persons have against mental health commitment is the effectively undefined requirement of mental illness for those commitments, and even then it is not unheard of for mental illness to be interpreted by a commitment judge as a term embracing any kind of mental disorder.

To the maximum extent possible, the Model Act has attempted to keep the definitions section brief and noncontroversial. Where an extended definition could not be avoided, care has been taken to emphasize that the definitions are meant to be illustrative. The definition of *consent*, for example, states that "consent usually must be preceded by communicating" certain categories of information. Where the Model Act compels or prohibits conduct, it does so through standards or procedures clearly denominated as such, and not through definitions.

Clarifying the commitment process is plagued by a variety of difficulties that the Model Act attempts to overcome. Even our attempt at clarification is limited, though, not only because of ambiguities concerning the sources of law that guide the process but also the relatively unstable status of each source. Each of the major topics within this chapter, such as due process, the common law, and the impact of *Parham*, could fill, indeed has filled, volumes. Yet, clarity remains largely elusive.

As we turn to the specific criteria and requirements of the various civil commitment statutes it is important to remember that these ambiguities remain. To be sure, statutory law helps to clarify matters some. Nevertheless, statutory law is both informed by and constrained by other sources of law — chiefly, those of the ambiguous variety referred to above.

CHAPTER 4

•

The Commitment Process

By what authority may the state confine its mentally disordered citizens? Is that authority different where the persons confined are under the state's age of majority? To answer those two questions, we examine in this chapter the legal and conceptual sources of the state's commitment authority and the statutory provisions — primarily the commitment criteria — through which the commitment authority is realized.

Courts have described the legal authority for civil commitment as emanating either from the state's *police power* or the state's *parens patriae power*. Generally, commitments can be characterized as police power commitments if they are based on a finding of dangerousness, and as parens patriae commitments if they are based on any other criterion, such as inability to care for oneself. It is not always possible to make this kind of distinction, particularly with respect to children's commitment, because of the strong element of paternalism that guides courts in their application of police power commitment criteria.

The police power—the authority to act to maintain or further public safety—is one of the essential functions of the state. The most familiar exercise of the police power is the apprehension and punishment of individuals suspected of a crime. Assuming the fairness of procedures therefor and the fairness of the definition thereof, few people would quarrel with the proposition that the state legitimately may deprive convicted criminals of their liberty. But there is less agreement about the application of the police power to persons who neither have been accused nor convicted of a crime but rather, who may be suspected of having a mental disorder.

Although here we are concerned primarily with the use of the police power to restrain minors who are not charged with delinquency or status offenses, the courts considering the commitment of children are influenced by cases involving all the above categories.

Commitment statutes existed at the time of the writing of the Constitution. Through two hundred years of judicial scrutiny, the most intense of which occurred in the 1970s, the proposition that the state, pursuant to the police power, may limit the liberty of mentally disabled persons never has been questioned seriously. This can be explained by the fact that, although commitment long has been justified by reference to the police power, its principal applications have been assumed to be benevolent. Early on, commitment was a means of placing indigent persons, for whom neither work nor guardianship was a possibility, into poorhouses (Katz, 1986). By contrast, guardianship, a traditional exercise of the parens patriae power, was utilized to secure food and shelter for people with mental disabilities whose estates were large enough to fund the services of a guardian.

Only gradually has commitment come to serve the function of authorizing the confinement of persons with mental disorders, regardless of wealth. At the same time, guardianship has grown in prominence as an alternative to or augmentation of commitment for persons regardless of wealth. This longstanding link between commitment and guardianship suggests that even though the former is an expression of the police power and the latter an expression of the parens patriae power, participants on both sides of the commitment debate have viewed the process as a kind of government paternalism comparable to guardianship. The result of this, particularly in children's commitment, has been failure to examine carefully the nature of the police power underlying commitment.

Some abolitionist critics of commitment are at least as concerned about the impact of commitment on the taxpayer's pocketbook as with its impact on the patient's liberty interests. Many of the judges and defense lawyers in civil commitment proceedings also view the commitment process as conferring a public benefit that the prospective committee is fortunate to be offered. As a result, police power commitment criteria, such as that of dangerousness, receive a nonadversarial, paternalistic reading.

The assaults on commitment statutes that led to watershed cases in the 1970s, despite their libertarian rhetoric, were motivated by a desire to improve the nature of this benefit rather than to abolish commitment. (A short history of civil commitment law fleshing out the contours of this motivation is contained in the initial district court decision of the landmark case *Lessard v. Schmidt*, 1972). The cases looked longingly and perhaps naively to due process as a rationale for improving the quality of services available to civil committees. Some difficulty in accomplishing this goal was to be expected because in this country a constitutional basis for an affirmative right to government services is far more difficult to derive than the negative rights to substantive and procedural protection from government incursions on personal autonomy.

Subject to these concerns about the appropriate reach and quality of government paternalism, the contemporary inquiry into the police power to commit has concentrated on the necessity and definition of dangerousness as a criterion for the commitment of adults. The inquiry has been largely unproductive because of errors in thinking (see previous chapter). Dangerousness is believed wrongly to be a condition, such as tuberculosis, that someone either does or does not have, and that can be detected (or "predicted," if we are speaking of violence) with a certain degree of accuracy. We have argued that dangerousness is a moral attribution that can be made with varying degrees of fairness but not accuracy. The case law on dangerousness does not refine the inherently open-textured definition of that commitment criterion, but it does tell us something about the value of the dangerousness criterion in assuring fairness and is worth further exploration for that reason.

Broad exercises of the police power that result in the confinement of children are often justified, in part, by reference to the second source of commitment authority, the parens patriae power. For example, the *Schall v. Martin* (1984) case leaves no doubt that our Supreme Court is willing to allow the commitment of children on grounds that rely on extremely vague notions of dangerousness. No doubt in considering pretrial delinquency detentions in *Schall*, the Court was as concerned with circumscribing the liberty interests of the child for paternalistic reasons, as it was with law and order — the usual targets of the police power. The presence of an alternative, paternalist rationale for commitment has the effect of diminishing any normative effect that the dangerousness criterion otherwise might have had on the court's discretion.

Although it is not difficult to understand the paternalistic motives of civil commitment, it is difficult to identify the source of authority allowing the state to act on those motives. Recall that the paternalistic rationale for civil commitment had its origins in revenue collection rather than a concern for disabled persons. The earliest example of a state's exercise of the parens patriae power is found in the 14th-century precursors to our adult guardianship laws. The state-invoked guardianship procedures were used to maximize feudal revenues from the lands of a people with mental disabilities. Incidental to that purpose, the state assured the provision of food, clothing, and shelter to someone who, by reason of mental disability, could not secure them otherwise.

Although today guardianship has lost its purpose of feudal land management, its principal application is still the management of fiscal affairs of wealthy persons with mental disorders. A mechanism is required to assure people who do business with children or with adults who have mental disabilities that the transactions will not be voided later. Such a mechanism also protects the child or the adult with a mental disability from exploitation.

To the extent that the provision of mental health and mental retardation services involves a contract, it is not surprising that parens patriae power also should be relied upon to authorize treatment of a person who cannot give informed consent to (i.e., freely contract for) that treatment. Of course, the consumerist emphasis on the contractual nature of these services, as evident in the requirement of informed consent, is a relatively recent development in the treatment of persons with mental disorders. There is still a widespread assumption among lawyers and treatment providers that there is not the same need for formality in surrogate treatment decision making on behalf of persons with mental disorders as there is in management of their wealth, perhaps because the potential for conflicts of interest is more obvious in financial transactions.

Concern about liability for treatment of persons without informed consent, even after they have been committed, has intensified interest in guardianship as a mechanism for authorizing treatment. In some jurisdictions, even the combination of a commitment and guardianship have been ruled to be insufficient to authorize treatments such as antipsychotic medication without specific court approval (e.g., *Rogers v. Okin*, 1980). In the case of adult commitments, these decisions are important as illustrations of different limits of paternalism inherent in commitment, guardianship, or a combination of both. Presumably, in the case of a child's commitment, neither the commitment nor the parent's treatment decision can confer more authority to treat than the combination of commitment and guardianship of an adult.

The uncertain boundaries of paternalism in commitment are expressed in the *inability to care for self* criterion of commitment. This criterion, which might be thought of as one of passive dangerousness, can be distinguished from the active dangerousness criterion premised on the police power. The parens patriae criterion is used to restrict behavior that is not, and does not threaten to become, subject to criminal sanction.

Here again this debate over the precise formulation of the criterion has limited significance in the commitment of children. No matter how narrowly drawn the parens patriae criterion is in the commitment of adults, it usually will be too broad for the fair commitment of children. Many children with mental disorders, whether they ought to be hospitalized, will be "unable to care for themselves," because of immaturity, lack of resources, or the legal disability imposed by virtue of their status as minors. Some states have attempted to narrow the impact of the inability to care for oneself criterion by additionally requiring proof that another criterion, such as decision-making incapacity, also is met. However, many children who do not require commitment nevertheless lack the capacity to make treatment decisions, if only because state law denies them that capacity. Consequently, this commitment criterion does not narrow the application of the law. All of the difficulties inherent in drafting appropriate parens patriae commitment criteria for adults thus are intensified in the context of commitment of children.

SUBSTANTIVE DUE PROCESS CONSIDERATIONS
The practical importance of the constitutional limitation of the police power and the parens patriae power is to shape the criteria for commitment. To satisfy principles of substantive due process (i.e., the constitutional requirement of fairness in standards of decision making) the commitment criteria must be related reasonably to the police and paternalistic powers of government. Another requirement is that the criteria are drawn narrowly to confine the discretion of the decision maker. This gives the prospective committee notice of the standards that are applied in commitment so that a defense can be prepared. It also gives the appellate court a standard by which to measure the justice of the result reached in the commitment. A commitment order based on no legislative criteria or on vague criteria might be complained of as "arbitrary and capricious," however well reasoned the decision otherwise may be.

Commitment criteria can be delineated with sufficient precision to restrict the decision maker's discretion, but they still may run afoul of another substantive due process principle. If the criteria do not limit commitment to populations legitimately subject to police or paternalistic powers, they should be condemned as overbroad. In determining whether criteria are overbroad, courts have had to look both at questions of vagueness and at the scope of the police and paternalistic powers. These questions are not independent. The more vague a standard is, the more susceptible it is to overly broad application. The greater the scope of the commitment power as interpreted by the courts, the less vulnerable the commitment criteria will be to a challenge of overbreadth.

THE DANGEROUSNESS CRITERION
The dangerousness criterion guides the exercise of the police power in many contexts. The Supreme Court has reviewed five contexts wherein dangerous-

ness is at issue: (a) civil commitment, (b) commitment of persons found not guilty by reason of insanity, (c) the preventive detention of minors accused of delinquency, (d) the denial of bail, and (e) the imposition of the death sentence. In each of these contexts except the last, a finding of dangerousness is used to justify a preventive detention. In death sentencing, a finding of future dangerousness is an aggravating factor that, under some state statutes, permits the imposition of the death sentence.

At first blush, this discussion seems to bring us far afield of the original purposes furthered by commitment, as we outlined earlier. Is it fair to call commitment an example of preventive detention? Although it could be contended that civil commitment, particularly of children, is or ought to be primarily a means of authorizing treatment for persons unable or unwilling to give consent, and not preventive detention, "[t]his argument depends . . . on limiting involuntary commitment to those patients who are treatable in the setting to which they are being sent, actually providing the indicated treatment, and detaining them only long enough to accomplish the needed intervention. If any of these conditions are absent, the mental health system is in fact being used for preventive detention purposes" (Appelbaum, 1988, p. 780).

The case in which the dangerousness criterion of commitment was explored first by the United States Supreme Court was that of *O'Connor v. Donaldson* (1975). Certain features of the case bear on its general applicability.

First, this heavily qualified ruling was more significant for what it did not decide about pre-reform era commitment laws than what it did decide. Second, as a consequence of that ruling and widespread legislative reform of the 1970s, most contemporary commitment laws are so different from the law by which Kenneth Donaldson was committed that the decision in his case tells us very little about what changes in contemporary commitment laws might be permissible. Finally, subsequent decisions by the Supreme Court on dangerousness and on the procedural aspects of commitment have shown that, particularly in the case of children, a commitment criterion of dangerousness is, by itself, no assurance against an unfair commitment.

O'Connor is a case that might have been about the right to treatment. Kenneth Donaldson was confined for nearly 15 years in the Florida State

Hospital. During that time he received no treatment. During that time he was dangerous neither to himself nor to others. During that time he had an opportunity to be released to the care of a halfway house, Helping Hands, Inc., and to the care of a college classmate. The Court held: "A State cannot constitutionally confine without more a non dangerous individual who is capable of surviving safely in freedom by himself or with the help of willing and responsible family members or friends" (1975, p. 576).

The opinion deliberately evaded the thornier question of Donaldson's right to treatment. The Court might have reasoned that because O'Connor did not have the right to treat Donaldson, it did not make sense to consider whether he had a duty to treat him. The Court also declined to consider whether the provision of treatment might have justified the commitment of a nondangerous person, because Donaldson had not received any treatment.

The qualification ("without more") appearing in the holding and the fact that Donaldson received no treatment (in part because the hospital respected his religious objections to treatment) left open the possibility that the provision of needed treatment would render lawful the commitment of a non-dangerous person. The opinion, and Chief Justice Burger's concurrence, is replete with dicta rejecting the Fifth Circuit's position that treatment would justify commitment. The Supreme Court denounced commitments of persons who are "physically unattractive or socially eccentric," and declared that mental illness alone does not "disqualify a person from preferring his home to the comforts of an institution." It is possible, however, to conceive of non-dangerous persons whose disorder nonetheless is more than mere social eccentricity, and for whom hospitalization represents more than simply an enhanced standard of living — like the only means of survival. There is nothing in *O'Connor* that squarely proscribes commitment under such circumstances.

O'Connor thus allowed state legislatures to craft a criterion of commitment that deliberately disregarded dangerousness and looked instead at the more traditional issue of the patient's need for treatment, as long as the latter criterion also avoided problems of vagueness and overbreadth.

Suppose the Court had insisted on dangerousness (or inability to survive with the help of family or friends) as the sine qua non of civil commitment. Could the state legislature define dangerousness to include behavior that did not threaten violence to the patient or others? Two cases that followed *O'Connor* demonstrated that there are no discernible constitutional limits to what the state might call dangerous, especially with respect to minors.

In *Jones v. United States* (1983) the Court was asked to strike down the commitment of a man found not guilty by reason of insanity in the attempted shoplifting of a jacket. This commitment had lasted 10 years by the time it came under the scrutiny of the Supreme Court.

In addition to turning aside the argument that the commitment should not exceed the maximum sentence that might be served upon conviction, the Court rejected the plaintiff's arguments that dangerousness to the plaintiff himself is unpredictable. If the science of prediction is so primitive, Justice Powell observed, that is all the more reason for the Court to avoid meddling with state legislative attempts to come to terms with the matter. To the assertion that Jones's offense was not really dangerous, Justice Powell replied that the state is free to define dangerousness at least as broadly as the criminal code defines it.

In *Schall v. Martin* (1984), a six-member majority of the Court led by Justice Rehnquist approved the preventive detention of juveniles detained on delinquency charges. Such detention, which could last as long as 17 days prior to a trial under the challenged New York law, was premised on a finding of "serious risk" that the minor "may before the return date commit an act which if committed by an adult would constitute a crime." All states and the District of Columbia had such laws on their books in 1984 when the decision was rendered by the Court.

Both substantive and procedural questions were before the Court in *Schall*. The inability to predict dangerousness was approached at different points in the litigation as a substantive issue and as a procedural issue. The primary substantive issues concerned whether the preventive detention, however accomplished, was fundamentally fair. The Court saw this as requiring a two-pronged inquiry. First, the loss of liberty must be justified by the social purposes served. Second, the detention of a person not convicted of a crime must not amount to punishment.

In striking down the preventive detention statute, the lower courts also looked at whether substantive due process was violated, because the dangerousness criterion was unrelated to the purpose of protecting society even if that purpose was legitimate. Because no one could predict which minors would commit criminal acts while awaiting trial, the district court and the court of appeals concluded that dangerousness could not actually be established. Thus, the decision to detain a minor would not promote the goal of protecting society from dangerous persons and, for that reason, violated the due process clause.

Both the majority and the dissenters in the Supreme Court treated the problem of predicting dangerousness as both substantive and procedural in nature. As to its substantive nature, the majority decided that the protection of society from the dangerous conduct of minors who had not been adjudicated delinquent was a purpose of sufficient importance to outweigh the minor's interest in liberty, because that interest is diminished by minority status already. The majority particularly annoyed Justice Marshall, the author of the dissent, by casually likening the loss of liberty incurred through preventive detention to the loss incurred through parental custody and reasoning that, in light of the latter, the former is less significant for minors. Just how much of the Court's decision in *Schall* turned on the issue of the minority status of the persons whose liberty interests were under examination was suggested by its subsequent decision in *United States v. Salerno* (1987). That case upheld the denial of bail to adult defendants on the basis of predictions of dangerousness.

If *O'Connor* demands a finding of dangerousness for the commitment of minors, *Jones* and *Schall* remind us that the dangerousness criterion, especially in the commitment of minors, is more an expression of the legislature's ultimate goal than a real limitation on the discretion of the decision maker. Both the critics of commitment who point to the invalidity of predictions of violence and the proponents of a more medically dominated commitment procedure who claim that attributions of dangerousness ought to be a clinical diagnostic procedure have ignored the real issue in the use of the dangerousness criterion. It is the open-textured nature of that criterion that deserves more attention. This aspect of commitment has not changed much over the centuries. The decision maker, as he or she always has been, is charged with a nearly legislative responsibility for determining at a given time and in a given community what behavior merits commitment. The commitment criterion of dangerousness guides the decision maker, not only in applying the law to a set of specific facts, but also in making a law that implements a very basic and unarticulated policy of protecting society against the patient.

Fairness in finding and applying this policy might be achieved short of interposing procedural safeguards between the proposed patient and the threatened loss of his or her liberty by one of two different strategies. The first involves an articulation of the definition of dangerousness. The second requires the conjunctive consideration of other, unrelated criteria of commitment to assure that whatever definition the court gives to the concept of dangerousness it is kept in its proper context. Most commitment statutes employ both such strategies.

Commitment statutes specify only a few of a wide range of elements of dangerousness. Where an element is unspecified, the decision maker is given greater discretion to define the concept. Depending on the nature of the element that is specified, the role of the judge, jury, or expert witness may be expanded. For example, if a recent overt act of dangerousness must be proved, the role of the fact finder is expanded at the expense of the role of the expert witness. If, on the other hand, the commitment statute is drafted so that it may be interpreted to require only proof of the recent expression of the symptomatology of mental illness, the expert witness's role is expanded. Even in their use of the term *prediction*, researchers on dangerousness assume that a legislature could define all the elements, and the values they reflect, in such a way that the accuracy of a prediction of dangerousness could be measured. A brief survey of some of the basic elements of dangerousness that could be specified legislatively, but often are not, suggests that it always will make more sense to speak in terms of fair attributions of dangerousness than in terms of accurate predictions of dangerousness. The relevant provisions of the Model Act are contained in Section 110(B)(1)(b).

- *The kind of harm that commitment is supposed to prevent*
  This harm might be injury to persons or property. It might be bodily harm or psychological harm to persons.
- *The potential victim of the harm*
  The statute might require that other persons or the patient or both

be threatened with harm. A few statutes require that where the harm is psychological the prospective victims reside with the defendant. The Model Act uses respite care (under Section 112) rather than commitment to prevent harm directed to family members.

- *The magnitude of the harm*

    Must the harm be serious? Not all statutes explicitly require the decision maker to find that the anticipated harm is serious, substantial, or significant or that it rises to the level of a criminal offense.

- *The likelihood of harm*

    In the absence of incapacitation by commitment, is there a greater than 50% probability that the harm would occur? If the relevant dangerous act is defined as an act that would constitute a felony and there is less than a 1% probability that the average person will commit a felony (within the foreseeable future), should a person who is 40 times more likely than the average person to commit a felony be regarded as dangerous, despite the probability that he or she actually will not commit the felony? (Of course, there is a relationship between the *magnitude* and *likelihood* of harm criteria — in most cases, the lower the threshold of harm, the greater the likelihood it will materialize.) The most libertarian statutes require the decision maker to find that the harm is "likely." If that means that a prediction of probable harm is required to commit, no one could be committed under that standard. For that reason, even under the most libertarian formulation of this element, decision makers will be tempted to inquire instead whether the defendant's dangerousness is "significantly more likely than other persons'."

- *The temporal proximity of the harm*

    One fairly common substantive due process safeguard is the requirement that the harm be imminent, or anticipated to occur in the near future, or within a certain number of days (e.g., 30) of the commitment. If there need not be a probability of this harm actually occurring within that time, this provision is less significant. Many decision makers informally will consider relatively unlikely and distant harms both sufficiently likely and imminent where the harm is great. This kind of balancing is done in tort cases under the rubric of foreseeability. The Model Act calls for a comparable finding that the anticipated harm will occur in the foreseeable future to stress that the task here is one of defining values rather than of predicting events.

- *The etiology of the harm*

    At a minimum, commitment statutes commonly, at least implicitly, require the anticipated harm to flow from a mental disorder. The disorder can be defined to include or exclude mental retardation or substance abuse. Additionally, the more libertarian statutes have demanded that the prospective committee be shown to have manifested his or her dangerousness in an overt act or threat occurring "recently" or within a specified period, such as 20 days, prior to the hearing. The overt act requirement is analogous to requirement of an act in the criminal law in giving persons subject to commitment clearer notice of what conduct, as opposed to diagnoses, will result in the loss of liberty. The Model Act omits the overt act requirement because of the reduced likelihood that children would benefit from the notice it provides. Whether the requirement of an overt act results in more accurate attributions of dangerousness is not as significant a question, given the undefined values inherent in those attributions, as whether it adds to the fairness of commitments. The overt act requirement also alters the character of the commitment proceedings by introducing issues in all cases of facts and credibility of witnesses.

    Sometimes these issues would arise in the absence of an overt act requirement simply because the petitioner must adduce sufficient evidence to meet the burden of proof. The Model Act depends primarily on the higher standard of proof—that of clear and convincing evidence—to elicit evidence of prior conduct when it is relevant.

- *Justifiability of the harm*

    Rarely, a commitment statute will demand proof that the anticipated harmful conduct would be unjustified. Although this may be easier than proving that the hypothetical conduct would be criminal, it is still an exercise in speculation, in narrowly identifying both the nature of that conduct and the morally relevant circumstance that would occur in the absence of commitment. The Model Act does not require proof that the harm would be unjustified.

Whether the statute takes a position on each of these seven issues, the decision maker will consider each issue in applying the dangerousness standard. Where the statute is silent, the discretion of the decision maker increases.

The operational meaning of the dangerousness standard is complicated further by the necessity of applying it conjunctively or disjunctively with other standards. The parens patriae criterion for commitment, which sometimes is formulated in terms of passive dangerousness, is an alternative or disjunctive criterion for commitment. This criterion calls for proof that the intended patient is passively dangerous to himself or herself in the sense that he or she is unable to provide necessary self-care because of a mental disorder. In a few jurisdictions, there is a third alternative or disjunctive criterion that authorizes commitment on proof of a serious deterioration in functioning.

Whether the petitioner alleges that the prospective committee is dangerous, unable to care for him- or herself, or has deteriorated seriously, civil commitment statutes typically require that other criteria also be met conjunctively, that is, simultaneously. These other conjunctive criteria require proof of a specified mental disorder and, in some states, proof of an inability or unwillingness to give informed consent, treatment need, or treatment amenability.

Additionally, there are other slightly less substantive criteria which often must be met either in addition to dangerousness or as alternatives to it. They are less substantive because they do not impose absolute limits as much on *who* can be committed as on *how* they may be committed. The requirement contained in the Model Act that an individualized plan of treatment be prepared as a condition of commitment is a good example of a nominally substantive criterion that really calls for a certain process to be completed and nothing more.

The criterion that the proposed commitment is the least restrictive alternative is also often in practice a procedural rather than a substantive safeguard. That is, it requires only that the court go through the process of surveying alternatives to institutional confinement before ordering commitments but otherwise does not define or restrict the populations subject to commitment.

ALTERNATIVES TO THE DANGEROUSNESS CRITERION

As our reading of the Supreme Court's 1975 *O'Connor* decision concludes, there may be constitutionally acceptable alternatives to the dangerousness criterion for commitment. These alternatives are of particular importance in commitment statutes applicable to children because of a pervasive reluctance on the parts of courts, clinicians, and parents to make the attributions of dangerousness customary in the commitment of adults. These alternatives typically are justified by reference to the state's parens patriae authority.

The two most important alternatives to the dangerousness criterion of commitment are a parens patriae criterion permitting commitment of someone who is unable to care for himself or herself because of mental illness and a parens patriae criterion that authorizes commitment of someone who has suffered a serious deterioration in mental health. Each of these alternative criteria raises different problems of fairness and accuracy in commitment.

The inability to care for self criterion, standing alone, suffers from nearly insurmountable problems of vagueness and overbreadth. The cause of the inability may be choice, lack of resources, mental disorder, or, more often, a combination of all these factors. The statute may be unconstitutionally overbroad if it authorizes a deprivation of liberty solely on evidence of a poor choice or indigence. The presence of a mental disorder that is not the primary cause of the patient's inability to care for himself or herself does not make the deprivation any more fair.

The Model Act takes the position that, at least in the commitment of children, the focus of a parens patriae commitment should be on incompetency. Only after incompetency is demonstrated should the inquiry turn to questions of the benefits of treatment and the risks of nontreatment, one of which is inability to care for self.

The Model Act attempts to guide the decision makers' discretion by requiring (in bracketed language) that the mental disorder or mental retardation preclude performance of "basic" tasks of personal hygiene and so forth. The decision maker then must decide what is sufficiently "basic" to qualify as grounds for coercive intervention. Presumably, most children without serious disabilities will be able to perform "basic" tasks. Of course, even at law the question of a particular child's self-efficacy at a certain point in his or her life should be informed by reference to norms provided by developmental psychology (e.g., Melton, 1984a). These provisions, representing the Model Act's formulation of the inability to care for self criterion, are in brackets to indicate the authors' view that, once incompetency is proven fairly and the other criteria are met, it is permissible to commit the child. Because of the inclination of decision makers to be influenced in the determination of incompetency by the fact that the patient is not performing certain basic tasks, it may not be fairer to the patient to link the performance of those tasks in any way to the determination of incompetency.

THE LEAST RESTRICTIVE ALTERNATIVE CRITERION

Joining the inability to care for self criterion with the least restrictive alternative criterion also may help with the slightly different problem of vagueness. At what point does a patient's self-neglect become an inability to care for himself or herself? The answer required by the least restrictive alternative criterion is, in effect, when no intervention less restrictive than commitment will negate the harm of the self-neglect.

This strategy for curing the parens patriae criterion of vagueness and overbreadth avoids the more fundamental issue of how much harm is sufficient to justify commitment. As the least restrictive alternative criterion usually is formulated, it raises other questions about what other interventions must be considered and how restrictiveness is measured.

The least restrictive alternative criterion had its origins in First Amendment jurisprudence. The decision in *Shelton v. Tucker* (1960) struck down, because of the existence of a less drastic alternative, a requirement that public employees report membership in all organizations. *Shelton v. Tucker* was cited by Justice Stewart in *O'Connor v. Donaldson* for the proposition that "while the State may arguably confine a person to save him from harm, incarceration is rarely if ever a necessary condition for raising the living standards of those capable of surviving safely in freedom, on their own or with the help of family or friends" (1975, p. 575).

O'Connor's implicit endorsement of the principle that the state may infringe individual liberty only when and to the extent that there is no less restrictive alternative resulted in the widespread adoption of least restrictive alternative criteria in state commitment codes, some of which simply required for commitment a showing that the prospective committee was not "capable of surviving safely in freedom, on [his or her] own, or with the help of family or friends" (1975, p. 575; see also *Thomas S. v. Flaherty*, 1988).

As we argued in Chapter 3, it is not always useful in looking at the elements of the commitment process to make a distinction between an element of the process that is procedural and an element that is substantive. The least restrictive alternative criterion is the best example of such an element in a commitment process, and it deserved more consideration by Chief Justice Burger on its merits in *Parham*.

The least restrictive alternative criterion is difficult for many clinicians to understand, because they view treatment as an augmentation, and not a diminution, of the freedom of a person with a mental disorder. Chief Justice Burger's dictum that a person who goes without treatment of his or her mental disorders is not more free than one who is committed demonstrates that this perspective is not unique to clinicians. Even legal professionals who accept the legislative decision that there is an inverse relationship between treatment and freedom sometimes think that the "amount" or quality of freedom at stake is minimal. Dicta in the *Schall* (1984) decision suggesting that children have an attenuated interest in liberty makes it all the more difficult to craft a least restrictive alternative criterion that anyone will take seriously.

The Model Act takes an intermediate position on the criterion itself by conditioning treatment on proof that "[t]here is no comparably effective treatment currently available that is less physically intrusive or restrictive." Formulations of the least restrictive alternative criterion which, like that in Section 110 of the Model Act, require the court only to compare commitment to "currently available" alternatives, in themselves, do not assure a reduction in the overuse of institutional treatment. Courts accustomed to ordering institutional placements by doing so reduce the demand for alternatives and, consequently, the number of alternatives that are "currently available." Fluctuations in the availability of funding or third-party reimbursement for less restrictive treatment have the potential for making this criterion a dead letter. Accordingly, the Model Act seeks to promote the creation of less restrictive alternatives by means other than the commitment criterion of the least restrictive alternative.

Those who stress the need for an individualized education plan that is consistent with commitment pursue a new strategy for assuring the child is in the least restrictive placement. The federal Education for All Handicapped Children Act of 1975 (now known as the Individuals with Disabilities Education Act), and state special education laws implementing it, require education placements in the "least restrictive environment." Because the local educational agency is potentially liable for all of the nonmedical costs of commitment regardless of the magnitude of these costs, involvement of the educational agency in the commitment process ought to reduce the overuse of residential treatment.

Since the emergence of federally funded community mental health centers in 1963, commitment codes have tended to place responsibility on local mental health and mental retardation agencies to assemble evidence relevant to the least restrictive alternative criterion. This shift in responsibility has proven to be unfortunate in areas where local government had pressured these agencies to advocate institutional treatment because the treatment was paid by the state or by insurance rather than by local funds, and because it supposedly benefited public safety in some cases. Local educational agencies, of course, sometimes have tried to "mainstream" children with mental disorders who needed residential treatment simply because it is vastly less expensive. Although it does not address this mainstreaming problem explicitly, the Model Act would not allow a penurious school system to impede treatment needed to prevent harm to the child.

To achieve the substantive effect of placing the child in a nonrestrictive setting regardless of the current availability of that setting now, Section 115 of the Model Act requires extensive reporting of any treatment that is more restrictive than necessary as a result of fiscal restraints. Section 116 imposes on a single agency responsibility for assuring a continuum of service to children and youth proposed for commitment. These two provisions in themselves, taken together, would not prevent an unnecessary commitment. However, they would form a sound statutory basis for the kind of relief provided in the *Thomas S. v. Flaherty* (1988) decision and thereby increase the likelihood that more "comparably effective" and less restrictive modalities of treatment are "currently available."

The process of civil commitment is confusing, in part, because it is guided by considerations on many levels. At a macro level of analysis, the process often involves a merger of two ostensibly incompatible legal rationales for detaining citizens, namely, the police power and the parens patriae power. More mediately, the process involves issues of both substantive and procedural fairness. Finally, at a micro level, the process relies upon poorly defined, and sometimes arguably inappropriate criteria for commitment. All of these complexities comprise the backdrop against which we begin our exploration of specific problems with the civil commitment of children and proposed solutions thereto.

Assumptions Underlying
Child Mental Health Policy

CHAPTER 5

•

Parham and Paternalism:
Mythology in Public Policy

As we have shown, the formulations of truly informed policy to address the mental health needs of children and youth must incorporate important considerations from widely disparate substantive fields of inquiry. Part 1 of this volume addressed the practical realities of treatment efficacy and policies that erode the personhood of minors. Part 2 examined the existing legal framework that provides for the mental health treatment of minors, as well as the broader impact of that framework on child and adolescent mental health delivery systems. In Part 3 we describe a new approach to such policy. We begin by exposing some of the myths that heretofore have plagued child social policy in hopes of avoiding repetition of those mistakes.

The 1979 Supreme Court decision in *Parham v. J. R.* that parents may commit their children voluntarily to mental hospitals without a formal due process hearing can be characterized fairly as indicative of a legal paradigm shift. The Court was remarkably out of step in its unanimous holding that the only constitutional requirement for procedural due process prior to admission was an informal review of the child's need for treatment by a physician acting as "neutral factfinder." Although the Court did find that some form of post-admission review was required constitutionally, it found formal, adversary hearings to be unnecessary. Indeed, Chief Justice Burger's disparagement of such procedures as "time-consuming procedural minuets" (p. 605) demonstrates the extent to which the Court was *un*willing to protect the legal interests of children and youth.

Parham represented a remarkable shift away from a judicial trend to recognize independent civil rights of children and to provide both substantive and procedural due process protections for persons threatened with the "massive curtailment of liberty" (*Humphrey v. Cady*, 1972, p. 509) that psychiatric hospitalization brings. Although not without qualification (see generally Melton, 1983b), the Supreme Court within the previous 12 years had held that minors have constitutionally protected rights to due process in delinquency proceedings (*In re Gault*, 1967), freedom of political expression in public schools (*Tinker v. Des Moines Independent Community School District*, 1969) and privacy in decisions involving abortion (*Planned Parenthood of Central Missouri v. Danforth*, 1976) and contraception (*Carey v. Population Services International*, 1977). The abortion cases appeared to provide considerable impetus toward recognition of due process rights for minors independent of their parents, because they rested explicitly on an assumption of inherent conflict between parents and child in abortion decisions.[1] Surely there was no less potential for conflict in parents' difficult decisions regarding psychiatric treatment of their minor child. The child's alleged need for hospitalization itself signaled a fractionation of the family and some breakdown in the unity of interests between parents and child. To hold otherwise would require a conceptualization of the balance of power among parents, child, and state decidedly different from the Supreme Court's analysis in the preceding abortion cases (Annas, 1979).

Parham, therefore, marked a pronounced turnabout in the assumptions believed to underlie juvenile mental health law. In engineering this reversal, Chief Justice Burger relied on a panoply of psychological assumptions (see Table 1) without supporting evidence. Indeed, it is the contention here (see also Melton, 1984a, 1984b, 1987a), that the majority opinion in *Parham*

124

Table 1. Psychological Assumptions in *Parham*

---

(1) There is no evidence of the use of mental hospitals as a "dumping ground." (pp. 597–598)

(2) "The state through its voluntary commitment procedures does not 'label' the child." Rather, stigma results primarily from the "symptomatology of a mental or emotional illness." (pp. 601–601)

(3) "The law's concept of the family rests on a presumption that parents possess what a child lacks in maturity, experience, and capacity for judgment required for making life's difficult decisions. Most important, historically it has recognized that natural bonds of affection lead parents to act in the best interests of their children." (p. 602)

(4) "Most children, even in adolescence, simply are not able to make sound judgments concerning many decisions, including their need for medical care or treatment." (p. 603)

(5) The state restricts use of "its costly mental health facilities" to persons in "genuine need." (pp. 604–605)

(6) Adversary proceedings will deter parents from seeking needed treatment for their children. (p. 605)

(7) "Time-consuming minuets" (i.e., due process hearings) take mental health professionals away from patient care. (pp. 606–606)

(8) Provision of a "neutral factfinder" adequately protects against erroneous admissions. (pp. 606–607)

(9) "Here the questions are essentially medical in character." The opinions of mental health professionals are necessary to determine "the meaning of the facts" in a determination of whether an individual meets legal requirements for admissions. (p. 609)

(10) Judicial review does not heighten the reliability and validity of psychiatric diagnosis. "Common human experience and scholarly opinions suggest that the supposed protections of an adversary proceeding to determine the appropriateness of medical decisions for the commitment and treatment of mental and emotional illness may well be more illusory than real." (p. 609)

(11) Adversary proceedings will exacerbate preexisting familial conflicts. (p. 610)

(12) "It is unrealistic to believe that trained psychiatrists, skilled in eliciting responses, sorting medically relevant facts and sensitive to motivational nuances will often be deceived about the family situation surrounding a child's emotional disturbance." (pp. 611–612)

(13) The state's mental health professionals are competent, conscientious, and dedicated. (pp. 611–616)

(14) There is no evidence that the state acts differently from parents in committing its wards. (p. 618)

---

represents a construction of the supposed reality of how hospitalization occurs, derived from idyllic notions of how the family and the mental health professions should be. As such, this opinion reflects both a representation of myths (of wishes for a world that isn't and perhaps never was) as facts and an antiempiricist bias among the Court's conservative members.

THE CASE FACTS

Before proceeding to a more detailed analysis of the majority's assumptions in *Parham*, it is useful to examine the facts presented at trial, case facts that stood in sharp contrast to the social facts asserted by the chief justice. The suit in *Parham* was brought by two boys (J. R., age 12, and J. L., age 13) — both of whom had been patients at Georgia state hospitals for more than five years — on behalf of themselves and the class of approximately 200 minors in Georgia's mental hospitals. They contended that they had been deprived of liberty without procedural due process or attention to whether the hospital was the least drastic environment for their treatment.

J. R. had been removed from his natural parents at age three months because of severe neglect. He lived in a succession of seven foster homes before being placed by welfare authorities at age 8 in Milledgeville State Hospital after the authorities had failed to find an adoptive home. Initial diagnoses were borderline mental retardation and unsocialized aggressive reaction of childhood. After hospitalization for about two and one-half years, hospital personnel began requesting long-term foster care or an adoptive home for J. R. because they feared he would regress if he was not placed in a suitable home very quickly. Three years later, he was still in the hospital.

J. L.'s young life was equally tragic:

J. L. at birth on October 1, 1963, was adopted. His parents divorced when he was three, and he went to live with his mother. She remarried and soon gave birth to a child. On May 15, 1970, his mother and step-father . . . applied for his admission to what is now Central State Hospital; he was admitted. Hospital personnel found that J. L. was mentally ill and diagnosed his illness as "Hyperkinetic Reaction of Childhood 308.00." On September 8, 1972, he was discharged to his mother, but she brought him back to the hospital and readmitted him ten days later. He then remained in confinement and at the time this lawsuit commenced had been in confinement for five years and five months of his twelve years, one month of life. In 1973 hospital personnel indicated to the Department of Family and Children's Service that J. L. needed to be removed from hospital confinement and placed in specialized foster care. His records show that the Department of Family and Children's Services indicated that the department could not pay for institutionalized (private) foster care unless J. L. was eligible for such care to be paid for by A.F.D.C. or Social Security funds. He was not an A.F.D.C. eligible child. (p. 117)

J. L. and J. R. were not unusual cases. The state had stipulated that at least one-fourth of the hospitalized children in Georgia could be cared for in less restrictive settings. The majority of the institutionalized children were said to be wards of the state and not psychotic. In short, the picture emerging from a review of the *Parham* facts was that many, perhaps most, of the hospitalized children in Georgia, a state with a relatively well-developed community mental health system, were in the institution because their families were unable or unwilling to care for them and the state had not developed alternative residential services. As we saw in Chapter 1, Georgia is hardly unique in this respect.

THE *PARHAM* ASSUMPTIONS

The scenario developed by the chief justice seems almost totally divorced from the record developed at trial. Drawing from the "pages of human experience" (1979, p. 602) — that is, his own intuition — Burger established a series of social "facts" by judicial notice (see Table 1). Specifically, the Court generated particular concepts of the family, the mental health system, and the effects of various procedural forms on both of these institutions.

The Family
The Court's view of the family may be summarized as follows:

Parents, including the state acting in loco parentis, almost never dump children into mental hospitals. Rather, children are placed there because their parents (unlike the children themselves) have the wisdom to judge the children's need for treatment accurately. Parents' and children's interests are coextensive, because parents can be assumed validly to act in their children's best interests.

Several of the assumptions underlying this idyllic view of the family — specifically, of parental authority — are questionable. Most fundamentally, the deference to parental authority in *Parham* was based at least ostensibly on minors' incompetence and the potential harm of badly reasoned decisions. However, there is ample evidence that adolescents, including those in clinical samples, comprehend salient aspects of treatment and its risks and benefits. Indeed, research generally has failed to distinguish adolescents from adults in their reasoning about treatment decisions in health and mental health. (For representative studies and reviews, see, e.g., Adelman et al., 1985; Ambuel & Rappaport, 1992; Bastien & Adelman, 1984; Belter & Grisso, 1984; Bersoff & Glass, 1995; Garland & Besinger, 1996; Ginsburg et al., 1995; Grisso & Vierling, 1978; Kaser-Boyd et al., 1986; Koocher, 1983; Loff, Trigg, & Cassels, 1987; Melton, 1981; Weithorn, 1982; Weithorn & Campbell, 1982. But see Gardner, Scherer, & Tester, 1989, arguing that the research base remains too thin for confident conclusions; see also Scott, 1992; Scott, Reppucci, & Woolard, 1995; and Steinberg & Cauffman, 1996, arguing for a focus more on "maturity of judgment" than on cognitive capacity.)

There is a need for research on the generalizability of the existing studies of children's competence to consent to mental health treatment to samples at risk for hospitalization. Ideally, such research would tap seriously disturbed adolescents' *capacities* for reasonable decision making about mental health treatment (e.g., through responses to hypothetical situations presented in laboratory interviews) as well as their *in vivo performance* when given options during admission and interviews, when level of stress is probably high and pressures for voluntary admissions may be great (Gilboy & Schmidt, 1971; Lidz et al., 1984). Obviously, in such circumstances decisional competence (i.e., the *intelligence* of the decision) may be compromised by stress, or the adolescent may perceive no real choice, even if the decision is theoretically the prospective patient's to make.

Recent work by Appelbaum and Grisso (1995; Grisso, Appelbaum, Mulvey, & Fletcher, 1995; Grisso & Appelbaum, 1995) provides an ideal conceptual and empirical framework through which to assess children's decisional competence relative to psychiatric treatment. After describing the types of specific competencies at issue in such decisions and prior research on the matter (Appelbaum & Grisso, 1995), the researchers report on their efforts at validating measures to assess the abilities involved (Grisso et al., 1995) and describe their findings when the measures were administered to clinical samples (Grisso & Appelbaum, 1995). This program of research appears to be quite sound methodologically and theoretically and begs for extension to child and adolescent populations.

A first step in this direction was taken recently by Mulvey and Peeples (1996), who compared the hypothetical decision making of mental health outpatients and social service clients between the ages of 14 and 18 with a comparison sample matched on relevant demographic variables. The adolescents in the clinical sample did not differ from those in the community sample in their ability to comprehend and retain information about treatment, but the clinical sample did show less ability to reason about the alternatives. Interestingly, however, gender accounted for much more of the variance in reasoning (girls did better than boys in applying verbal skills to the social situation) than did clinical status.

Even assuming for the purpose of argument (contrary to most of the available evidence) that minors do often lack competence to make reasonable decisions concerning admissions to psychiatric facilities and that they need someone's help in making them, the chief justice probably overestimated the ability of parents to maneuver the system on behalf of their mentally disordered children. The Court's faith in caseworkers to act as concerned parents was particularly circuitous: Georgia expects social workers to act in their wards' best interests; therefore, they obviously do so. The empirical invalidity of such an assumption is demonstrated well by a study of children in foster care in Illinois (Bush & Gordon, 1978) which found that only 60% even knew who their caseworker was. Of these, about 25% had not seen the caseworker for at least six months. Fifty percent of the sample had lived in at least four homes since entering foster care. The general lack of continuity for children who are wards of the state is documented well (Mnookin, 1973). No basis exists for the belief that caseworkers can be expected to act as real parents for all of their children or that children will come to perceive their casework-ers as surrogate parents (see, e.g., ABCAN, 1993, p. 34; Lidz et al., 1980).

When one abandons a de jure conception of *parents* as inclusive of *guardians* of state wards, the picture is not as bleak. Nonetheless, the Court's view of typical parent-child relationships certainly was filtered through rose-colored glasses. First, it must be acknowledged that, although most parents probably do strive to guard their children's best interests, the family as an institution has been under considerable stress. The average number of adults in families has been on the decline, and the economic and social supports available to them have also been declining, at the same time that the demands on the family and the threats to the safety of its youthful members have been increasing (see, e.g., ABCAN, 1993; Garbarino, 1995; Melton, 1993a, 1995; National Research Council, 1993). Meanwhile, the health care environ-ment — and, therefore, the knowledge and time needed to navigate it skill-fully — has become ever more complex. In such circumstances, parents may lack the energy, knowledge, and resources needed to advocate vigorously for alternatives to hospitalization.

Second, it is fallacious to assume that general expectations of parental concern can be applied uncritically to parents of children being considered for admission to psychiatric hospitals. As we noted in Chapter 1, many minors who are admitted to hospitals have already been separated from their families. Even when such a history is not present, the mere fact that there has been an attempt at hospitalization suggests a fractionation of parental and child interests, as the *Parham* dissenters argued. Simply imagining such a separation and the short-term relief from the child's behavior that it may bring to the parents and siblings may be enough to build an emotional wall (Blacher & Baker, 1994).

Family integrity is thus directly diminished by the attempt to institutional-ize a child, particularly for the relatively lengthy periods characteristic of placements for juveniles. Unity of interests becomes particularly difficult to maintain when the bases of institutionalization are chronic misbehavior (e.g., conduct disorders) and lack of another place to go (rather than "mental illness"), and there is significant conflict or emotional distance among family members (as is common in families of youth with conduct disorders; see, e.g., Farrington, 1995; Loeber & Stouthamer-Loeber, 1986).

In making this point, we continue to adhere to our fundamental thesis that the allocation of decision-making authority is not the key issue. As Blacher (1994) noted in regard to placement of youth with mental retardation, placement typically is not a discrete event. Rather, it is often the product of years of thinking about the possibility; "once parents actually begin to look at placement options (behaviorally defined as visiting a facility), placement is almost inevitable" (Blacher, 1994, p. 220). Although psychiatric hospitalization sometimes may more closely approximate a crisis response, it too often is the end of the road of attempts by the family to find a solution to its problems—often including other placements of the child. As Blacher (1994) lamented, "Formal services often arrive too late to families—if they arrive at all—long after these families have endured an overload of stress, adjustment difficulties, and even financial hardship" (p. 227). Moreover, parents often find themselves between the proverbial rock and hard place as legal, health, welfare, or educational authorities urge placement lest even more intrusive actions are taken in their own and their child's lives. The clear need, as we argue throughout this book, is to develop legal structures that will result in meaningful alternatives for families so that children will not find themselves in the position of having no place to go.

In short, although we are sympathetic to parents facing the hospitalization of their child, the simple picture of parents seeking inpatient psychiatric treatment for their child as they would for a child in need of a tonsillectomy or an appendectomy is clearly naive. The range of unnecessarily restrictive treatment alternatives may leave parents, through no fault of their own, with an accurate perception of little choice. Moreover, where the "parent" is the state, such a perception is plainly erroneous, given the problems in the foster care system in most states. Thus, our approach to a new child mental health policy acknowledges that sometimes parents are unable to act in the best interests of their children, however well-intentioned parents may be.

Mental Hospitals

The Supreme Court's view of state mental hospitals was almost as positive as its concept of the family. The picture the majority painted of state institutions was almost free of blemish. It can be summarized as follows:

State mental hospitals work well without external judicial review. Staff are competent, and physicians almost always evaluate families and children validly. Civil commitment is, after all, a "medical" issue, and physicians, of course, will not allow a child to be admitted to or remain in the hospital unless medically necessary.

Quality of care. Compare the Court's assumptions with the summary of the literature about state hospitals by Morse (1982), an articulate critic of involuntary hospitalization:

The inadequate conditions of public mental hospitals have been a feature of state mental health care for over a century. Many of the psychiatrists are poorly qualified, if qualified at all; physical condition and staffing are inadequate; and satisfactory treatment is a myth. Periodic exposés and calls for reform have not yet led to acceptable improvement. Although courts have shown a willingness to supervise public mental hospitals when the level of care provided drops beneath a minimally humane level of decency, there is still no evidence that legislatures are willing to allocate the money necessary to ensure optimum care and treatment. Indeed, states faced with right to treatment decrees that force them to expend far greater resources on their patients have responded by dumping the patients into the community instead of treating them with the degree of care and expertise dictated by decency and medical ethics. This is not to say that there have not been improvements in state hospital care; it is simply to underscore the reality of inadequate care and treatment nearly everywhere. Arguments that what is available is better than nothing are unacceptable. People who are locked up because they are allegedly disordered must be treated properly. If they are not, we should admit that the major goals of involuntary hospitalization are preventive detention and warehousing and proceed to analyze the system on that basis. (pp. 81–83; footnotes omitted)

Public mental health systems have gone far in their development of services for adults with serious mental illness (Huxley, 1990–1991; Mowbray, 1992). Indeed, the innovations that have occurred for that population have arisen primarily in the public sector — as is the case for new service models for treatment of children and adolescents. Nonetheless, dismal conditions remain in many state hospitals, as even the psychiatric establishment itself (e.g., Stone, 1982; Talbott, 1980, 1985) has recognized (see Gutkind, 1993, for a description of contemporary state hospital conditions).

The problems may not be merely ones of inadequate financing and difficulty recruiting high-quality professionals to work with patients who are chronically and severely disordered or simply hard to manage. Rather, the hospital model of treatment may be inherently ineffective for many patients (e.g., Eamon, 1994). The debilitating effect of total institutions long has been documented in the sociology of deviance (Goffman, 1961; McEwen, 1980). Some adult patients become institutionalized to the point where they find it so much easier to cope in the institution than in the community that they actively avoid discharge through presentation of themselves as sick (Braginsky, Braginsky, & Ring, 1969). Such a problem may be particularly acute for minors in view of the relatively long hospital stays common for that age group (see Kiesler, 1994; Lundy & Pumariega, 1993) and the nature of total environments. Reviewing data on the frequency of seclusion and physical restraint of children in psychiatric hospitals, Goren et al. (1993) concluded: "The culture of psychiatric hospitals encourages coercive staff behavior. . . . Clearly, institutions organized around coercion and control will have difficulty teaching non-coercive behavior to children and their families" (p. 71).

Most basically, empirical evidence simply does not exist to support the assumption of efficacy of hospital treatment (see chap. 1). As Okin (1985a) and Talbott (1985) argued, the problem is not just one of underfunding, archaic physical plant, and so forth. Hospitals are *inherently* expensive, restrictive, and maladapted to the goal of facilitating independent living. Moreover, even the most ardent advocates of retrenchment in deinstitutionalization are unlikely to argue that mental hospitals are suited well to meeting the needs of the conduct-disordered adolescents who populate the children's wards. As Lundy and Pumariega (1993) have lamented, the lack of less restrictive alternatives "has led to the utilization of child psychiatric hospitalization in ways for which it is poorly suited, such as long-term placement or as a crude form of family and environmental manipulation" (p. 2). Therefore, as we approach the task of fashioning a mental health policy for children and adolescents, we do so with the view that psychiatric hospitalization is rarely helpful and may often be harmful.

Reliability and validity of diagnosis. Even if one assumes that psychiatric hospitalization is beneficial for some children and adolescents, there still remains a substantial liberty interest in avoiding erroneous commitment — an interest that the Supreme Court recognized but underemphasized. The underemphasis seemed to stem primarily from two factors: a characterization of the commitment decision as a medical decision and a denial of risks of error in the admitting clinician's assessment of the situation. Secondarily, the Court assumed that whatever minimal risk of error existed would not be reduced by the provision of judicial review.

The Court's concept of the commitment decision is fallacious at its root. The decision to deprive an individual of liberty is an ethical and legal determination, not a medical one (Morse, 1978). Line drawing as to the limits of "mental illness" for legal purposes is a legal determination about which mental health professionals have no expertise. Other elements of decision making about involuntary admission also expressly involve legal and social value judgments (e.g., determination of the least restrictive alternative; see chap. 2), even though they may appear deceptively simple and empirical.

Moreover, the Court ignored the fact that decisions to institutionalize a child often are based on considerations other than the child's so-called objective illness. For example, as discussed in Chapter 1, Warren (1981) found that delinquents and status offenders frequently have been transinstitutionalized into the mental health system as the gates have closed to the juvenile justice system. A survey of administrators of residential treatment programs (Quay, 1984) starkly documented these extraneous pressures. About half of the respondents expressed agreement with a statement that "agencies often accept and discharge clients based on agency need or convenience rather than the needs of the child" (p. 13). About two-fifths of the respondents admitted that "treatment decisions are more often influenced by agency policy than by a child's needs," and a majority acknowledged that professionals often increase the severity of a child's "label" to ensure that the child will receive services. A survey of social-welfare caseworkers (Billingsley, 1964) indicated similar supremacy of bureaucratic pressures over client needs in many cases. Although, as we noted in Chapter 1, many of these features are by-products of the professional, therapeutic, social-service bureaucracy, transfer of responsibilities to the private sector may accomplish little. Indeed, with privatization, these pressures may be assuming still greater importance. When hospitals actively advertise among the general public for new minor patients (e.g., Dawley, 1985; Division of Child, Youth, & Family Services, app. B), it is hard to believe that admitting professionals are apt to turn away many potential admissions, especially where third-party reimbursement is easily available.

Assuming for argument, though, that legal concepts of mental illness are interchangeable with clinical concepts and that diagnosis is free of political and social distortions, there is no reason to believe that problems of diagnostic reliability and validity endemic to psychological or psychiatric assessment of adults (von Talge, 1995) are any less profound for assessment of children and adolescents. Indeed, the child and adolescent diagnoses are more problematic, with the most acceptable reliability occurring with major *adult* diagnoses among adolescents (Strober et al., 1981). Existing clinical diagnostic systems for children are conceptualized poorly, largely unrelated to the empirical literature on symptom clusters, and subject to mediocre reliability across raters and settings (Achenbach & Edelbrock, 1978).

The most commonly used diagnostic system — the Diagnostic and Statistical Manual of Mental Disorders (American Psychiatric Association, 1994) — is fraught with problems that undermine its diagnostic utility. As one eminent scholar on child diagnosis (Quay, 1986, p. 156) noted, "with the exception of the Attention Deficit Disorder category, there are a considerable number of DSM-III categories for which there is no empirical counterpart." Quay's opinion about the inadequacy of DSM-III's child and adolescent diagnoses is shared by other authorities (e.g., Achenbach, 1980) and, for the most part, is as applicable today as it was when he first articulated it. The manual has undergone numerous revisions, but even the most recent revision (American Psychiatric Association, 1994) appears to provide little in the way of improvement in diagnostic reliability. A number of significant weaknesses reflected in the manual have been identified. These include (a) inherent problems with classification systems in general, (b) classificatory problems specific to the DSM taxonomy, (c) inadequate definition of mental disorders, (d) the absence of discrete homogeneous diagnostic categories, (e) the lack of empirical foundation, (f) poor reliability and validity, (g) inadequate consideration of cultural and religious issues, and (h) atheoretical and noncausal diagnosis (von Talge, 1995).

Going beyond DSM and other "official" diagnostic systems, some syndromes that are empirically derived via factor analyses of behavior ratings do seem to generate acceptable agreement between raters and across time but only mediocre reliability across situations (Achenbach & Edelbrock, 1978; Quay, 1979). These research-based taxonomies have seldom found their way into clinical practice, however. Moreover, this body of research is not translatable in any clear way into prescription of services for children matching a particular classification or syndrome (Achenbach & Edelbrock, 1978).

There is even less reason to believe that family assessments will be largely error-free, notwithstanding the Court's assurances that mental health professionals are unlikely to be fooled by the picture the parents initially present. Psychologists have expended little effort to validate techniques for assessing family interaction (Achenbach, 1974). Most commonly, in fact, clinicians rely on parental reports as the principal bases for judging the child's behavior (McCoy, 1976). Although some reason exists for doing so (i.e., parents are likely to have the most cross-situational knowledge of the child), the clinician has little basis in an admission interview for determining points of distortion or scapegoating in the parent's report (e.g., Klein, 1991; Loeber, Green, Lahey, & Stouthamer-Loeber, 1990; Simmonds, 1976). As Meeks (1995, p. 306) observed, "Frequently, the nature of the illness has eroded parental self-confidence, produced destructive countermeasures, and resulted in extreme emotional distancing from the youngster." In that regard, it is interesting that children may be more likely than parents to identify child mental health problems as family issues rather than as problems of an "identified patient" (Small & Teagno, 1979).

As Ellis (1974) put it:

The law distorts the choice between family integrity and personal autonomy, for it bases its choice on the perception of the family situation held

136

by one part of the family—the parents. . . . In the case of juveniles, the law's method of discovery is, in effect, a conclusive presumption that the parents' perception is correct. The greatest drawback accompanying this presumption is that parents often cannot address their own role in family problems. If the child in a family is disturbed, the parents may be the disturbing agent. (pp. 861–882)

Although Ellis's one-way causal theory may be too pat, the point is well taken that admitting mental health professionals are apt, with legal sanction, to hear a one-sided view of the family dynamics and the juvenile's problems. That the parents' version may represent only one side was evidenced by a recent study reporting considerable disparity between children's self-reports and the reports of their parents (Duchnowski, Johnson, Hall, Kutash, & Friedman, 1993). Although it is difficult to determine which side was more correct, it is worth noting that parents reported their families as significantly more cohesive than did their children patients—most of whom already had been placed outside the home! The reality probably cannot be sorted out in an admission interview, even if the clinician is motivated to hear all sides and consider alternatives to hospitalization. The evidence is anecdotal, but mental health professionals apparently share Ellis's skepticism that trained mental health professionals are seldom, if ever, "deceived about the family situation surrounding a child's emotional disturbance" (*Parham v. J. R.*, 1979, pp. 611–612). When we have discussed *Parham* before audiences of mental health professionals, the point that the assumption of unfailing clinical insight was applied by the Supreme Court to the initial interview invariably has stimulated laughter.

The fact that may be hard to accept—the Supreme Court did not—is that assessment of children and adolescents is inherently difficult. Not only must child clinicians assess situations that are developmentally in flux (see, e.g., Levitt, 1971, on "developmental symptom substitution"), but also they are apt to encounter unwilling clients who are reluctant to share critical information. Although older children and adolescents can be reliable informants about their history (McKinney, Chin, Reinhart, & Trierweiler, 1985), they may not wish to contribute to an assessment based on assumptions that they do not share (Adelman & Taylor, 1986; Taylor et al., 1985a):

137

Children's contacts with the mental health system are fundamentally different from those of adults. With few exceptions, adults accept the role of patient (or client) and actively contribute to the diagnostic process and the negotiation of treatment. In short, children do not share the disease model of treatment for psychopathology. As a consequence, diagnosis of children is based much more on observation by parents, teachers, and clinicians than the self-reports so central to the diagnosis of adults. (Achenbach, 1980, pp. 396–397)

In the end, though, the emphasis on diagnostic unreliability may be misplaced. The claim that a hospitalized child or adolescent has a major mental disorder is rare. More fundamentally, diagnosis is meaningful only in the context of research on treatment efficacy (who should get what). That literature gives little basis for matching diagnostic groups with need for residential treatment. Indeed, it calls into question the assumption that residential treatment, or at least its more intrusive and restrictive varieties, is ever the least restrictive alternative (see chaps. 1 and 2). If assessment for placement is not a crap shoot, neither can it be described as a scientifically based procedure. These conclusions compel us in our approach to mental health policy to be somewhat skeptical of the clinical assessment procedures at the time of admission. This skepticism is reflected in the model statute as well as in our broader recommendations.

ADVERSARY PROCEDURES

Besides underestimating the risk of error in commitment of children, the Court asssumed that whatever error does occur would not be reduced by judicial review, and indeed that formal hearings would create substantial harm:

> Adversary proceedings disrupt both the family (including presumably the family of the state welfare worker; see American Psychiatric Association, 1982b) and the hospital, without benefit to the child.

The notion of the lack of effectiveness of adversary procedures was based on two assumptions. First, it was argued that the decision to commit is a medical decision; therefore, lawyers will add little to the process. As already noted, this construction of the commitment decision seems plainly wrong.

138

Second, the Court referred to several articles suggesting that the legalization of commitment had caused only minimal changes in what actually happens in commitment hearings. Interestingly, the authorities cited used such evidence to argue that more, rather than fewer, stringent procedures were needed. In fairness, there is an argument to be made from such data that civil commitment proceedings carry an inherent high risk of error and that moderate reforms will not work (Morse, 1982). It does not follow, however, that risks of error should be accepted passively when deprivation of liberty is at stake. Moreover, evidence from some jurisdictions (e.g., Zander, 1976) indicates that adversary procedures and clear standards do have an impact on commitment proceedings when judges take the due process provisions seriously.

Pressures to hospitalize people with serious mental illnesses may reduce the probability of courts' adopting such a stance (Morse, 1982), even when the bar receives special training in the examination of mental health professionals (Poythress, 1978). Nonetheless, the Court's suggestion of deference to mental health professionals in commitment proceedings is ironic when, at the same time, it bemoans the ineffectiveness of formal civil commitment procedures. When courts routinely defer to clinical judgment, commitment proceedings, of course, will be nothing more than hollow rituals.

Data regarding the actual psychosocial effects of juvenile commitment hearings are sparse. One is left to speculate largely on the basis of anecdotal reports and of laboratory experiments testing the effects of various procedural reforms on adults' perceptions of justice (see Thibaut & Walker, 1975, 1978).

The most systematic collection of outcome data from juvenile commitment hearings was conducted by the New Jersey Division of Mental Health Advocacy, which examined the cases of the 213 minors it had represented over the period 1975–1977 (Perlin, 1981). There were a variety of individual dispositions. Sixty-five of the juveniles were released at or prior to a hearing. Hospitalization in psychiatric facilities occurred in 90 cases (38 cases, voluntary admission; 22 cases, commitment; 30 cases, confinement continued). In the remainder of cases, an alternative placement (e.g., residential school) was arranged. Thus, the role of counsel was not limited to "a finite commit/release paradigm" (Perlin, 1981, p. 157); formal advocacy by counsel also extended to investigation and negotiation concerning other possibilities (e.g., Wexler, 1981, pp. 98–101). Without independent representation for the child, such exploration of alternatives with less devastating effects on liberty might not have occurred.

Moreover, the dire consequences the Court posited for families did not occur. Although the data presented in Perlin's article were gathered unsystematically by trial counsel themselves (and perhaps, therefore, subject to bias), the interview material presented suggests that parents generally welcomed the pushing for the child that adversary counsel undertook. Even well-intentioned parents are likely to have limited knowledge of resources potentially available to their child and the child's counsel actually may be helpful to parents in attempts to obtain less restrictive treatment. Counsel also may be able to use patterns of unnecessarily restrictive treatment across cases as the basis for lobbying or class litigation to increase the availability of alternative services.

Finally, existing social psychological research and theory suggest that adversarial proceedings may produce positive psychological benefits for the child. Having had some control over the process (a form of control inherent in a truly adversarial system) is likely to enhance a child's sense of perceived justice (e.g., Gold et al., 1984; *In re Gault*, 1967) and perhaps decrease resistance to treatment if it ultimately is ordered (e.g., Melton, 1983c; Melton & Lind, 1982).

Such a view was expressed by staff at a Pennsylvania teaching hospital after adolescents were given the right to a hearing if they objected to hospitalization (Meisel & Roth, 1976). Staff believed that the procedure was "helpful to children" for the following reasons:

1. The procedure gives the child the opportunity to tell you how he feels. He has had an opportunity to express his objection.
2. The procedure crystallizes the issue of the need for treatment. It makes the child (and the family) confront the issue of whether or not the child really wants or needs to be hospitalized.
3. It makes the kids feel they have been treated fairly; if they do object they will have an impartial hearing.

4. The procedure affords the child some measure of control over his own destiny.

5. This procedure is a step in the patient's involvement in planning for his own care.

6. The judge will only release the child if he or she does not need to be hospitalized. (Meisel & Roth, 1976, pp. 384–385)

Similar, more systematic data have been reported by researchers at the therapeutic school at UCLA (Taylor et al., 1983, 1985b). When given the opportunity to participate in special education hearings, students have expressed a desire to do so, perceived themselves as competent to do so, and perceived the experience as satisfying. Teachers and parents generally have recognized the children's participation as valuable and effective. Perhaps the critical aspect of the UCLA program has been that staff apparently have perceived children as partners in their treatment and have made genuine efforts to prepare them for participation in decision making (Taylor & Adelman, 1986). Such behavior by clinicians is in the true spirit of requirements for informed consent — respect for the humanity and dignity of clients, who are *participants*, not *objects* in treatment (Katz, 1984; Weisbard, 1986; Weithorn, 1983).

OUTDOING *PARHAM*:
THE AMERICAN PSYCHIATRIC ASSOCIATION'S POSITION
The American Psychiatric Association Guidelines
Despite the lack of support for the *Parham* assumptions, the American Psychiatric Association (1982b) adopted a model statute for civil commitment of minors that out-*Parhams Parham* in its deference to physicians and its underlying faith in institutional care. Minors under age 16 would be voluntarily admissible by their parent (inclusive of "a person or agency judicially appointed as legal guardian of the child," p. 971) with the concurrence of the admitting or treating physician. Sixteen- and 17-year-olds would be able to admit themselves voluntarily. Any parent or custodian could petition a court for certification of a 16- or 17-year-old for 45 days initially, with the next commitment for 90 days, and subsequent commitments of six months.

For involuntary commitment, the petitioner would be required to show

(i) that the child has a mental disorder, (ii) that the child is in need of treatment or care available at the institution for which certification is sought, [and] (iii) that no less structured means will be as effective in providing such treatment or care" (p. 972). *Structured* is not defined further. Presumably, the term was chosen euphemistically to avoid the negative connotations of *restrictive* and *intrusive*. In any event, the term is not used in the manner that least restrictive alternative typically is (see chap. 2). The standard proposed by the American Psychiatric Association demands the choice of the most effective alternative; only if two treatments were equally effective would the level of restrictiveness and intrusiveness be relevant. No balancing is envisioned between state interests in effective treatment and individual interests in liberty and privacy.

For both voluntary and involuntary admissions, only minimal post-admission review is required. The statute provides only for "internal medical review" of treatment plans and an opportunity for "independent medical review of the appropriateness of decisions made either to discharge or to continue hospitalization of the child" (p. 973). This provision for supremacy of medical judgment is consistent with the model statute's purpose "to enable medical decisions to be made in response to clinical needs and in accordance with sound psychiatric judgment" (p. 971). (Reflecting the narrowness of the review contemplated by the statute, the American Psychiatric Association (1982a) later adopted a statement drafted by Alan Stone and Richard Bonnie acknowledging that some mental health professionals advocate more extensive review when lengthy hospitalization is proposed and when children are wards of the state.)

The theme of unfettered medical judgment is especially pronounced in the unpublished commentary by the drafters of the model statute. As revised and approved by the American Psychiatric Association's (1981) Assembly, the commentary notes a frankly defensive basis for the drafting task force's work in "the *strident cries of lawyers* for due process and civil rights and the *anguished concerns of embattled psychiatrists* seeking to retain their freedom to prescribe and treat" (p. 2, emphasis added). An underlying assumption was that protection of procedural due process would feed adolescents' resistance to treatment (American Psychiatric Association, 1982a, p. 975).

The commentary also is euphoric in its assessment of institutions and prejudiced in its description of urban group homes "located in a neighborhood where criminal elements may be close at hand" (American Psychiatric Association, 1981, p. 21). The task force concluded, without references, that less restrictive settings commonly raise youths' anxiety. Without supporting data (which indeed are not available), the task force also asserted that "well-run hospitals and other 'institutions' generally fare much better than smaller units such as group homes in providing . . . services, cost being one of the factors" (pp. 21–22).

The lack of scientific foundation for the assumptions underlying the American Psychiatric Association's model statute is illustrated most glaringly by the threshold age (16) for a requirement of judicial review of admission of minors by their parents. The task force originally had chosen 14, an age that research shows approximates the age of achievement of adult-like competence in decision making (e.g., Bersoff & Glass, 1995; Grisso & Vierling, 1978; Melton, 1981). However, a substantial proportion of psychiatrists in the APA Assembly favored deference to parental authority and medical judgment for all minors. Sixteen, the age actually adopted as the threshold age in the model statute, thus was a political compromise between 14 and 18. The commentary was changed simply by whiting out 14 everywhere it appeared and replacing it with 16. In so doing, statements ostensibly of scientific fact about developmental changes were magically transformed, sometimes absurdly. For example, the commentary now reads that 16 "is the age of entry into high school, an event which has a significant impact on maturation" (American Psychiatric Association, 1981, p. 14).

Related Commentary

A position similar to that of the American Psychiatric Association was also espoused in a group of articles by mental health professionals in North Carolina (e.g., Burlingame & Amaya, 1985; Silverstein, 1980). The tenor of this commentary is illustrated by Burlingame and Amaya's (1985) ascerbic attack on "untrained judges" and "attorneys of varying quality" whose "manipulations" provided "unsavory models" for the delinquent youth who constituted the majority of their inpatient population:

[D]elinquently-oriented adolescents who, as a group tend to deny, rationalize, and project responsibility for their acting out, find the adversarial hearing made to order for legalistic maneuvering and manipulation—thus continuing their refusal to assume personal responsibility for their dilemma while essentially prolonging treatment as a function of enhanced resistance. The very nature of the proceeding suggests to the delinquent what he craves to hear: The crux of this issue is that others may infringe on his rights and that he is entitled to resist in order to continue in his narcissistic, omnipotent, and antisocial activities. (pp. 238–239)

In other words, forcing treatment providers to comply with the law will interfere with their attempts to get their clients to comply with the law.

In the same vein, Silverstein (1980) concluded that "the adolescent must realize that it is a great deal easier to attempt to manipulate a lawyer or judge than to work toward internal change" (p. 1154). Silverstein also suggested that, when youth use legal procedures to protest admission, "the teenager is pursuing legitimate means and may only be mirroring the distrust for the hospital that the legal procedures imply. As such, these procedures may serve to foster in the teenager the negative feelings about the treatment process, thus making trust that much more difficult to achieve" (p. 1155).

The North Carolina group displayed a crabbed and mistaken view of the law. They ignored the possibility (confirmed by the available empirical evidence) that being treated fairly increases perceived justice and treatment efficacy (e.g., Lind & Tyler, 1988). Rather than teaching "manipulation," experience in the legal process can be a means of teaching legitimate ways to express ideas and resolve disputes (Melton & Saks, 1985; Myers, 1990; Tapp & Levine, 1974; Tapp & Melton, 1983). Legal procedures, when taken seriously, are fully consonant with the values that underlie the ethics and theory of the mental health professions. For example, the most recent promulgation of the Ethical Principles of Psychologists "has as its primary goal the welfare and protection of the individuals and groups with whom psychologists work" (APA, 1992, Preamble). More specifically, the code requires that "[p]sychologists accord appropriate respect to the fundamental rights, dignity, and worth of all people" (APA, 1992, Prin. D).

Perhaps the most telling critique of Burlingame and colleagues' views is the fact that, if valid, their arguments would apply as much to the juvenile and criminal justice systems as juvenile commitment proceedings. Apparently they would prefer to deny defendants vigorous legal advocacy lest the defendants learn to exercise their rights! During a decade of work as a law enforcement officer, one of us observed (not *too* unhappily) that the courts are not terribly receptive to law enforcement officers who whine that the Constitution and laws of criminal procedures hamstring efforts at promoting public safety. A defensive response by mental health professionals to the application of due process is no more compelling than similar reactions by the police. Intrusions on liberty and privacy are serious matters, and the care taken to ensure both the appearance and the reality of fairness should be commensurate. Consequently, our policy recommendations include procedures to provide minors with legal remedies for protection of their rights.

TREATING CHILDREN WITH RESPECT

Parham and related commentary are replete with the assertion of myths as facts (see Melton, 1984a, 1986). The assumptions seem to start from a concept of the proper ordering of child, family, and state, and then to rest on an illogical inference that empirical reality matches these ideals — that parents are motivated always exclusively by "natural bonds of affection" for their children, who are incompetent and, therefore, properly dependent; that practice in the public mental health system is efficient, competent, expert, and respectful of clients and, therefore, deserving of deference.

When the presentation of myths as facts is used to obscure the real values of underlying policy, it reflects a breach by policy makers of their duty of fidelity to the electorate. As a practical matter, assertion of myths as facts also results in inaccurate policy analysis and diversion of attention from the central policy issues. For example, the symbolic clash over the nature of childhood that *Parham* emphasizes and provokes may wrest attention from the critical policy dilemmas related to ensuring that troubled youth and families under stress have a place to go for services that are no more restrictive and intrusive than necessary. By the same token, debate about the efficiency of commitment proceedings and the nature of lawyers' behavior avoids the central problem of ensuring fairness and respect for persons in decisions about admission to mental health facilities.

In the end, perhaps it is not myth per se, but a confusion of the nature of myths, that marks child mental health policy. As Melton (1987a) noted elsewhere, Bellah (1975) posed the important distinction: "Myth does not attempt to describe reality; that is the job of science. Myth seeks rather to transfigure reality so that it provides moral and spiritual meaning to individuals or societies. Myths, like scientific theories, may be true or false, but the test of truth or falsehood is different" (p. 3).

Just as psychologists can lift the cover of myths when used to obscure empirical reality, they can confirm and "preserve those myths that express respect for human dignity and, in so doing, embody the highest principles of Western thought. The social contract that creates a duty of respect for autonomous persons in a state of equality (Rawls, 1971) is mythical, but its meaning is true. . . . When we respect the autonomy and privacy of child clients, . . . we reify the symbols of personhood and the myths of equality in the moral community" (Melton, 1987a, p. 352).

The ethical imperative of respect for persons is sufficient to require rigorous due process in any infringement of liberty and privacy. Even if that were not the case, however, it should come as no surprise that fair procedure has therapeutic meaning and effect. Respect for personal privacy is in itself significant in individuation and a sense of self-efficacy and control (see chap. 2; Melton, 1983d, 1987b; Wolfe, 1978). Similarly, ensuring that children are heard increases the probability that attention will be given to their concerns (which are not necessarily those that clinicians commonly hypothesize; see, e.g., Melton, 1987b; Mulvey & Pieffer, 1993; Yamamoto, 1979) and that children will be invested psychologically in the treatment plan (see, e.g., Adelman et al., 1985; Adelman & Taylor, 1986; Holmes & Urie, 1975; Lewis, 1983; Taylor et al., 1985a). As already noted, the right to have a say, which is embedded in an adversary system, is related to perceptions of justice (Lind & Tyler, 1988; Thibaut & Walker, 1978). As a more general matter, actual control (in this instance, overproduction of evidence) is related, not surprisingly, to perceived control, which, in turn, is related to positive psychological and physiological states (see generally Lind & Tyler, 1988; Perlmuter & Monty, 1979).

Due process itself may be mythical. It is an amorphous, flexible concept, but the myth affirms fundamental values of respect for persons. Due process also is clearly a normative concept; it describes what *should* be done, not how proceedings typically *are* conducted. When myths (e.g., the ideal family) are presented as facts, truth is distorted, and normative principles are heeded sub rosa even while other principles are followed overtly. Attention needs to be redirected toward both the critical myths of moral philosophy and the social facts that must be considered in fashioning policies that reflect our underlying values. Procedural rules must provide the process that is due persons entitled to fair treatment and respect.

•

Toward Respect for Children, Youth, and Families: Framework for a "New" Mental Health Policy

Like adult mental health policy (Kiesler, 1982b), child and adolescent policy has departed significantly from the principles that purported to guide it. Although some steps have been taken recently toward development of a continuum of services, child mental health systems generally have neither facilitated preservation of family integrity nor ensured that treatment, when provided, was delivered in the least restrictive and intrusive manner.

This discrepancy between stated and de facto mental health policy has resulted from a variety of factors. First, as we discussed at length in Chapter 5, the empirical assumptions that have guided child mental health law have frequently been erroneous. Policymakers often have underestimated adolescents' ability to make decisions about treatment and overestimated the responsiveness of state youth service systems, and they often have shown little awareness of the model characteristics of institutionalized youth and their families.

Second, because of erroneous assumptions and the complexity of problems of child mental health policy, policy makers often have failed to analyze policy alternatives fully. The policy debate has focused abstractly on the question of the unity of interests among child, family, and state, with substantially less attention to the realities of the lives of troubled and troubling children and youth. Policy makers, clinicians, and the public frequently have assumed that "mental illness" in children (and adults) necessitates residential treatment. Even when such assumptions have not been operative, policy makers have not attended sufficiently to the elimination of fiscal and regulatory incentives for overly restrictive and intrusive services.

Third, beyond empirical errors and insensitivity, policy makers have been led astray by a lack of respect for the personhood of childhood and youth. In fact (see chap. 5; also Melton, 1987a), the empirical errors themselves may have resulted from an attempt to promote myths that justify treating children as nonpersons or half-persons. In that regard, authorities often have underestimated the harm to minors from restrictions on their liberty and intrusions on their privacy. Besides the ethical wrongs engendered by such misconceptions, the efficacy of treatment has been reduced by children's lack of participation in decision making and planning (see chap. 5).

Although the policy that we propose in this volume departs significantly from policies prevailing in most states and supported by the Supreme Court in *Parham* (*Parham v. J. R.*, 1979), our recommendations actually are more consonant with commonly stated policy goals. Because *Parham*-style policies result in unnecessarily restrictive treatment, they neither will preserve families nor facilitate treatment (see chap. 1). Although our analysis starts with a premise of respect for children's personhood and, therefore, their privacy and autonomy, the policy we propose is more likely than prevailing policies to meet paternalistic goals.

As a practical matter, *respect for the privacy and autonomy of minors is consistent in most cases with support for family welfare and the healthy socialization of children and youth.* Relatively unrestrictive services not only protect the interests of the minor but also promote family integrity. Well-designed home-based services provide the opportunity for families to become stronger and remain intact while also serving the treatment needs of the child. Services that are intensive but respectful of clients' privacy and autonomy usually are more effective than highly restrictive or intrusive services (see review in chap. 1). Therefore, services in the least restrictive alternative are apt also to promote the state's interest in the welfare of future workers and voters.

This chapter and the following appendix provide the legal foundation for a "new" child mental health policy based on historic values and the state of the art in mental health and mental retardation services. Specifically, this chapter outlines the assumptions underlying the model commitment statute that we drafted (app. A; hereafter, Model Act) and that the American Psychological Association's Division of Child, Youth, and Family Services (Division 37) endorsed. Some of these assumptions are empirical conclusions to the research reviewed in the preceding chapters. Others are normative: our assumptions about how the mental health system *ought* to serve children, youth, and families. These normative assumptions are consistent with the Ethical Principles of Psychologists (American Psychological Association, 1992). They are derived from the metaprinciples (e.g., respect for persons; beneficence) that appear to underlie the Ethical Principles and other contemporary professional and legal standards for ethical practice in the mental health professions (see Beauchamp & Childress, 1983, for review).[1] Our normative assumptions also are consistent with constitutional deference to due process and the protection of liberty and privacy.

ASSUMPTIONS TO GUIDE POLICY

I. *As persons, minors are owed respect for privacy and autonomy in treatment decisions.*

A. *Minors are persons.*

Even if some jurists have been reluctant to recognize the implications of the answer, the questions of minors' personhood is settled as a matter of constitutional law (e.g., *In re Gault*, 1967; *Planned Parenthood of Central Missouri v. Danforth*, 1976; *Tinker v. Des Moines Independent Community School District*, 1969). More fundamentally, as a matter of ethics, we believe that the basic humanity of children and their moral personhood should be recognized.

Whether potential or full members of the moral community, children should be treated in a manner that connotes respect. Entailed in such respect is fulfillment of the right to primary goods, including facilitation of future access to such goods (Brown, 1982; Rawls, 1971; Worsfold, 1974).[2] Therefore, justice demands that minors' autonomy and privacy are honored, except when fulfillment of such rights would result in a wrong greater than failing to respect personal freedom and integrity.[3] By the same token, children are owed special entitlements (e.g., education, treatment) necessary to permit them ultimately to enjoy full participation in the moral community (Brown, 1982; Melton, 1983a, 1989). Thus, rights to privacy and treatment are both consistent with respect for the personhood of children and youth.

B. *Protection of autonomy in private decisions is basic to respect for human dignity.*

As we discussed in Chapter 2, future self-determination is not the only way in which autonomy and privacy are significant in child and youth policy. Such concepts are important to school-aged children and youth in everyday life. Failure to recognize such significance increases emotional reactance (e.g., Brehm, 1977; Brehm & Weinraub, 1977; Melton, 1983d; Wolfe, 1978).

Therefore, when children are in residential treatment and by that fact suffer greater threats to privacy than "those ordinarily encountered in daily life," the Model Act (§ 102.C) would ensure that care be taken to avoid violation of personal dignity. Freedom of association and communication would be preserved, and privacy of space would be taken into account (e.g., Melton, 1983d; Rivlin & Wolfe, 1985).

C. *Mental health treatment, particularly in forms that are unusually intrusive, invades zones of privacy.*

Mental health treatment is concerned with the most private aspects of human experience and behavior (e.g., *Lora v. Board of Education,* 1977; *Merriken v. Cressman,* 1973). For example, psychotherapy commonly touches on matters of family life, other intimate relationships, sexuality, and thoughts and feelings that the client would not disclose in most other contexts. When individuals, including children and youth, lose control over personal information, they often experience a sense of degradation, and they may suffer stigma or embarrassment from such disclosures.

The Model Act recognizes the significance of privacy in psychotherapy by preserving competent minors' access to confidential treatment (§§ 101.F, 103.B.3, 113.A, and 113.C). The Model Act also reflects an awareness of the need to protect minor clients from intrusions on privacy that may take place in therapeutic programs outside of hospitals (§ 101.E). Special protections are invoked whenever treatment is physically intrusive (e.g., involves use of antipsychotic medication; see chap. 2) or is so psychologically intrusive that it "presents substantially greater risks of harm, embarrassment, or loss of autonomy . . . than those ordinarily encountered in daily life" (§ 102.C).

D. *Most older minors are competent to make informed treatment decisions.*
Adolescent patients are typically capable of understanding and weighing the risks and benefits of treatment (see chap. 5). Even elementary-aged children often are able to understand the nature of treatment and the reasons for it and to participate in making decisions about their mental health care (see, e.g., Lewis, 1983; Lewis & Lewis, 1983; Taylor & Adelman, 1986; Taylor et al., 1983; Weithorn, 1983).

E. *Minors' participation in decisions should be facilitated to a degree consistent with their level of competence.*
When minors are capable of making competent treatment decisions, those decisions should be honored in most circumstances. When not capable, they should be permitted to participate insofar as possible. Consistent with the purposes of the doctrine of informed consent, we heartily endorse a model of shared decision making — of making parents and children partners in treatment.[4]

F. *Treatment should be in the least restrictive and intrusive alternative.*
The concept of the least restrictive alternative (LRA) has both

substantive and procedural components (as noted in chap. 2). Substantively, it involves a commitment to invade constitutionally protected interests no more than necessary to meet the state's compelling interest in the health and welfare of the child. Accordingly, determination of the LRA should be a threshold question in treatment planning.[5] Procedurally, for the right to be vindicated, responsibility must be established for reviewing the restrictiveness of treatment alternatives and creating less restrictive alternatives, where possible but unavailable. The Model Act would vest the responsibility for establishment of alternatives in the providers of services, and it would provide an advocate to act as a gadfly and assist in the location of less restrictive alternatives (§ 114.B). The Model Act also would create a duty of the state to develop a continuum of alternatives necessary for the treatment of minors (§ 116.A).

The recognition of the LRA concept is based on more than simply preservation of autonomy. Given the evidence that restrictive and intrusive treatment often is iatrogenic, it also is derived from the duty of nonmaleficence. At a minimum, the state owes dependent persons the right of protection from harm, corollary to the right of personal security (e.g., *Halderman v. Pennhurst State Sch. & Hosp.*, 1985; *New York State Ass'n for Retarded Children, Inc. v. Rockefeller*, 1973; *Youngberg v. Romeo*, 1983).[6]

II. *Minors with mental disorders and minors with mental retardation have an interest in the integrity of the family.*

   A. *In general, families are better able than the state to care for children, even those with significant disabilities. The dismal record of the state in providing stable foster homes (Bush & Gordon, 1978) or institutional settings (Bush, 1980; see chap. 5) has been established well.*
   The unfortunate reality is that, even in family situations that are harmful to children, the question before placement must be whether invocation of state jurisdiction would not be worse (Melton & Davidson, 1987). Thus, the first response of state authorities to family distress should be to try, whenever possible, to provide

supports to the family to permit it to remain intact. Such a strategy is consistent with both the constitutional right to family privacy (e.g., *Roe v. Wade*, 1973, pp. 152–153; and *Santosky v. Kramer*, 1982, and citations therein) and the state's interest in preservation of the family as an institution for the socialization of children.[7]

B. *Care for minors with mental disorders and minors with mental retardation is often stressful.*

The strain, often both psychological and economic, on families of children with special needs is obvious (see generally Earhart & Sporakowski, 1984; Farber, 1968; Grossman, 1972). Dealing with behavior problems and providing basic care are tiring and frustrating. Stress is likely to be especially great in those instances in which a child's behavior is so problematic that parents cannot even go out for an evening because a babysitter would be unable or unwilling to care for the child. Families also often incur special financial burdens in the care of mentally disabled children, such as costs of specialized medical or psychological evaluation, therapy, and respite care. For families already experiencing significant social or financial problems, the stress of caring for a child with special needs indeed can lead to the "last straw" of institutionalization or surrender of custody to the state (see review in chap. 1).

C. *The state should support family-based alternative care, including respite care, as a means of preserving families and ensuring that alternatives to placement are possible.*

Intensive home-based services have had success in supporting families through crises (see, e.g., Henggeler et al., 1992; Scherer, Brondino, Henggeler, Melton, & Hanley, 1994; Subramanian, 1985). Day treatment (see, e.g., Hoge et al., 1992; Tolmach, 1985), and financial supports (see, e.g., Zimmerman, 1984) also may be helpful. The Model Act would require the state to develop such a continuum of care (§ 116.A).

Section 112 of the Model Act provides special authority for out-of-home respite care. The section was necessitated by the fact that, for reasons described in Section V below, the definition of program was made broad so that it would include restrictive treatment generally, regardless of whether the program called itself a hospital. At the same time, we did not want to foreclose establishment of out-of-home respite care programs that might provide parents and siblings with breaks necessary for them to be able to care for the child with mental disabilities at home. A de facto prohibition of such programs would be outside the clear intent of the Model Act to preserve family integrity and prevent unnecessarily restrictive treatment.

On the other hand, it was important to limit the criteria for unreviewed respite care in order to avoid a "loophole" for judges looking for a way to justify involuntary commitment of an otherwise uncommitable child. Therefore, the Model Act specifies the circumstances in which out-of-home respite care might be appropriate (§ 112.A), provides a presumption in favor of in-home respite care (§ 112.B), and prohibits respite care in lieu of treatment (§ 115.A).

The Model Act also shows deference to family integrity in other ways. For example, it would provide parents with a veto of commitment of their child (§ 106.C). Such a right would apply in all cases except an emergency, unless parental custodial rights have been relinquished for the protection of the child. The act also requires "maximum involvement of the patient's family" in treatment planning, as long as such involvement is consistent with the child's interests (§ 103.B.3).

D. *Provision of advocacy services and formal review of treatment plans typically will facilitate both family integrity and child autonomy by ensuring less restrictive and intrusive services.*
The provision of advocates to ensure that less restrictive alternatives have been considered is likely to be welcomed by parents interested in ensuring effective services and protecting the integrity of the family (see chap. 5; Perlin, 1981).

III. *The state should ensure access to mental health treatment and mental retardation habilitation.*

   A. *Children should have a right to treatment or habilitation.*

     A humane society with great wealth should provide adequate mental health care for those in need of it. Such a duty of beneficence is a corollary to the principle of distributive justice (see Beauchamp & Childress, 1983). Beneficence assumes special significance in the case of children. Not only is the future acquisition of the benefits of full participation in the community jeopardized by failure to provide needed treatment, contrary to the principle of respect for persons, but also the state has a special duty because it enforces the dependency of children and thus renders them less able to seek help for themselves when they are competent to do so in fact. In such a circumstance, an implicit social contract to provide needed care arises, as would be codified in the Model Act (§ 115.A).[8]

   B. *Access to treatment or habilitation should be facilitated for children desiring and in need of it.*

     Access to treatment entails two concepts: (a) the treatment should be available, and (b) it should be obtainable. The Model Act would provide both a substantive right to treatment, effected through requirements to search for and develop a continuum of services (including aftercare for children in restrictive placements), and a right of services (including aftercare for children in restrictive placements), and a right of competent minors to consent to treatment independently and confidentially (e.g., Koocher, 1983).

   C. *Treatment or habilitation should be individualized.*

     For a right to treatment in the least restrictive alternative to be meaningful, it must be tailored to the needs of the child. Therefore, the Model Act would require the development and periodic review of individualized treatment plans (§ 115.F.1).

   D. *The state has a duty to create minimally restrictive and intrusive alternatives when such alternatives are effective in meeting the state's interests.*

This principle is a corollary to the state's duties to provide needed treatment (§ IIA, above) and to do so through the least restrictive alternative (§ IF, above). Given such a combination of duties, if the principle of least drastic intervention is to be effective (cf. *Shelton v. Tucker*, 1960), then the state must provide treatment not simply in the least restrictive alternative *available*, but in a setting no more restrictive than is necessary for effective treatment, given current mental health technology.

E. *Procedural mechanisms are necessary to ensure fulfillment of the right to treatment or habilitation in the least restrictive and intrusive alternative.*

As already noted, a right to treatment in the least restrictive alternative is hollow without allocation of responsibility for ongoing exploration, review, and development of therapeutic alternatives (Chambers, 1978).

IV. *Because many children subjected to restrictive and intrusive treatment or habilitation lack parental care, the state has a special duty to facilitate their access to treatment or habilitation in settings respectful of their dignity.*

As the dissenters in *Parham* noted (1979, p. 638, Brennan, Marshall, and Stevens, JJ., concurring in part and dissenting in part), the notion of identical interests between foster child and guardian is simply nonsensical. With the turnover in state social workers, large case loads, and, most importantly, lack of family ties, the contention that guardians can and will protect the interests of their wards in the same manner as watchful parents defies common sense. To be clear, we do not suggest a lack of concern on the part of most caseworkers. Nonetheless, the fact remains that social workers must find a place to put children in their care, many of whom have significant mental health problems. They may be satisfied, as a result, with placements that are less than optimal.

Also, because state social workers are a part of the very bureaucracy that is responsible for the administration or regulation of residential treatment facilities, they may have little discretion in monitoring the welfare of their wards placed within them (e.g., Billingsley, 1964).

Criticism or mere monitoring may be perceived by agency administrators as insubordination. At a minimum, state social workers are apt to have the appearance of a conflict of interest. Therefore, rejection of the myth of "voluntary" placement of children is especially important when the admitting "parent" is a state guardian.

V. *To be effective in meeting its goals, child mental health policy must take into account the interlocking systems of services for children.* (The foundation for the following conclusions is provided in chap. 1.)

    A. *"Treatment" for children is provided in diverse systems: mental health, child welfare, juvenile justice, and special education.*

    B. *There is a trend toward increasing use of restrictive and intrusive services — frequently private and "hidden" — in each of these systems.*

    C. *Each of these systems has focused its restrictive and intrusive services on "troubling" minors, especially conduct disordered adolescent males, many of whom are wards of the state.*

    D. *A prevailing, seldom-articulated, but probably unalterable assumption is that minors, including adolescents, must be in custody.*
   Therefore, the key questions in child mental health policy may be not *whether* children will be in care, but *where* and with what level of restrictiveness and intrusiveness and with what quality of care.

    E. *If regulatory attention is focused on just one of the restrictive and intrusive systems of treatment for minors, it is likely to push them into other systems.*
   Therefore, to be effective, the scope of regulation must cross systems and forms of care and include private services. The Model Act would decrease the probability of transinstitutionalization (Costello & Worthington, 1981; Warren, 1981) through its jurisdiction over *all* facilities with therapeutic purposes, not just those that define themselves as hospitals or other mental health facilities or that are in the public sector (§ 102.F).

F. *Integration of children's services is critical if they are to be effective.*
Given the diffuse boundaries among the various systems that serve children and youth, a common theme in discussion of children's services is the need for *coordination* of services. However, this term is unfortunate. Often the argument for coordination of services is premature, because a range of services has yet to be *developed*.

Furthermore, the critical concept is not coordination but *integration* of services. Regardless of the system that is the primary conduit of funding and accountability, therapeutic services for children and youth with significant mental health problems will not work, or at least will be less than optimally effective, if affective (mental health), cognitive (educational), and social (welfare) concerns are not addressed (see Melton, 1983a, chap. 4, for review). Thus, the most successful programs for treatment of children and youth with serious emotional disturbances have been those that included interventions planned to address the needs of the developing child in an integrated way. To use Hobbs's (1982) felicitous term, treatment for children with serious emotional disturbance is *reeducation.* The program and its staff should reflect the intertwined goals of teaching, counseling, and community and family change.

Although the Model Act would not require such an approach, which perhaps is insusceptible to legislative mandate, it does make clear a strong policy preference for integrated services. Several elements of the statute are based partially on this policy. The statute would diminish incentives for abdication of responsibility to other agencies by its scope over therapeutic programs across agencies. It also would provide for careful and ongoing treatment planning, and it would require that treatment planning not be divorced from special educational planning (§§ 103.B.3, 110.B.3., 116.F.2).[9]

G. *The public schools may be best able to assume the lead in the integration of children's services.*
The ease of administration of children's services in particular agencies is dependent on the overall structure of state and local agen-

cies and therefore varies across jurisdictions. However, the schools may be the agency of choice for integrating treatment for children. Such a focus is consistent both with the psychoeducational, skills-oriented philosophy that is common in alternative services and the public schools' legal and historic responsibility for universal services for children (Hobbs, 1975). The requirement under the Model Act of integrating education and treatment whenever possible reflects this emphasis. However, it also leaves the possibility of other agencies' assuming the lead role.

H. *Standards for commitment should reflect children's interest (and that of the state) in treatment or habilitation.*

Because of the special interests of the state in the health of its developing citizens and the needs of minors who are so immature that they are unable to make independent decisions competently, adult standards for commitment may be too narrow. Therefore, the Model Act would permit the involuntary treatment of a minor incompetent to consent to a treatment (§ 110.B.1.a) that he or she needs and would find beneficial (§ 110.B.2).

VI. *Procedural protections should be designed to prevent unnecessarily restrictive and intrusive treatment or habilitation.*

A. *More process is due when treatment or habilitation is involuntary.*

When a client does not enter treatment voluntarily, the infringement of autonomy invokes a special burden to prove the justifiability of the corollary intrusion on privacy. In keeping with this principle, voluntary admission under the Model Act would be contingent only on the clinical judgment of the provider that consent is competent and that treatment is needed and likely to be beneficial, except when treatment is physically intrusive or restrictive (§ 103.A). Lengthy restrictive treatment would require the post-admission approval of a court or an administrative board (§ 104.A). On the other hand, nonemergency involuntary treatment would be possible only after a pre-admission judicial hearing, in which adversary procedures would apply, including the rights to notice of the allegations in the petition, cross-examination of witnesses, representation by counsel, and presentation of testimony under the ordinary rules of evidence (§ 109).

B. *Consent by a third party, including a parent or guardian, cannot be reasonably construed as voluntary.*

By definition (§ 102.G), voluntary consent to infringement of personal boundaries can take place only for oneself. Thus, for example, the federal regulations for research involving minors vests authority to *give permission* in parents, who are presumed unable to consent on behalf of their children, and authority to *assent* in their children, who are presumed incompetent to consent.[10]

C. *More process is due when treatment or habilitation is restrictive or intrusive.*

Serious threats to personal autonomy, privacy, or security merit greater scrutiny in order to protect the interest of minors. Because of their circumstances, even competent minors may be more susceptible to coercion to accept treatment not in their best interests. Greater care is appropriate to ensure that potentially harmful treatment is not inflicted. Therefore, as described above, the Model Act would require more scrutiny of planned treatment when it is restrictive or intrusive.

D. *Adversary procedures are most likely to be just in situations that merit substantial procedural care.*

Because adversary procedures reserve to the parties the right to control the presentation of their cases — to have a say — they are likely to be perceived as fair (Thibaut & Walker, 1978). Therefore, as noted above, respondents in commitment proceedings, with the assistance of counsel, would be able to present evidence and cross-examine witnesses.

E. *Such proceedings need not, and usually will not, pit parent against child.*

As we discussed in Chapter 1, parents of children with mental disorders or mental retardation often themselves are reluctant volunteers who would welcome measures to make less restrictive treatment and support for the family available.

VII. *To ensure protection of family integrity and child autonomy and privacy and to enhance the efficacy of treatment or habilitation, a "continuous" system of alternative care should be developed, and disincentives for its maintenance should be eliminated.*

Finally, we wish to emphasize that our intent is positive. To be sure, we have been appalled by the lack of respect that often has been shown for children, youth, and families in the mental health, juvenile justice, and social service systems. On the one hand, we wish to protect minors' freedom *from* unjustifiable or unnecessary infringements of liberty and privacy. On the other hand, this emphasis is consistent with our intent to provide minors with a right *to* those resources that will permit them ultimately to enjoy the primary goods due all persons. Like Stroul and Friedman (1986), we advocate a continuum of services for mentally disordered children and their families. Development of such a continuum cannot depend purely on procedural due process.

At the same time, we recognize that without such protections children and youth with no place to go are apt to be transinstitutionalized into restrictive forms of treatment that often are easily accessible and reimbursible. We are mindful that a functional continuum of services demands innovation in the design and implementation of treatment alternatives. But it also requires elimination of laxity of procedure and diffusion of responsibility. Only then will troubled and troubling children and youth have some place to go that isn't no place to go.

APPENDIX A

•

A Model Act for the
Mental Health Treatment of Minors

DIVISION OF CHILD, YOUTH, AND FAMILY SERVICES
OF THE AMERICAN PSYCHOLOGICAL ASSOCIATION
COMMITTEE ON THE CIVIL COMMITMENT OF MINORS

116. Responsibility of the state.
117. Prevention.

Sec. 101. *Policy statement; short title.*

    A. The (legislature) finds that mentally disordered minors and mentally retarded minors have an interest in the integrity of the family. It is rarely appropriate to treat or habilitate mentally disordered minors or mentally retarded minors outside of the home and school. To prevent unnecessary hospitalization of such minors, it shall be the policy of the state to offer respite care and intensive home-based services for families who care for mentally disordered minors or mentally retarded minors within their homes.

    B. The (legislature) further finds that persons under the age of majority have the fundamental right to make decisions regarding mental health treatment or mental retardation habilitation, absent compelling and carefully defined state interests. The traditional authority of parents to make health care decisions on behalf of their minor children is diminished where the child is competent to make the decision and the decision has critical and irreversible consequences for the child's autonomy, as decisions involving mental health treatment or mental retardation habilitation do.

    C. The (legislature) further finds that the state has an interest in the healthy socialization of its citizens. It shall be the policy of the state to provide minors with access, when needed, to mental health treatment or mental retardation habilitation.

    D. The (legislature) further finds that most older minors are sufficiently competent to make informed decisions to seek or refuse mental health treatment or mental retardation habilitation. For many minors the assurance that treatment or habilitation will be rendered confidentially is essential to their willingness to accept or benefit from treatment or habilitation. The efficacy of treatment or habilitation is enhanced by the patient's active participation in decision making about treatment or habilitation.

E. The (legislature) further finds that physically intrusive or restrictive mental health treatment or mental retardation habilitation often is provided outside a hospital. Residential treatment or habilitation provided outside the hospital also may resemble treatment or habilitation provided in hospitals in the purpose of treatment or habilitation and the restriction of the residents entailed by this treatment or habilitation.

F. In order that the health, privacy, and liberty of citizens of this state are protected regardless of their age, the (legislature) hereby declares that the laws of (the state) henceforth shall recognize the rights of minors to seek or refuse mental health treatment or mental retardation habilitation.

G. The provisions of this act shall be known and may be cited as "The Mental Health Treatment of Minors Act of 1998."

Sec. 102. *Definitions.*

As used in this act:

A. "Competent" means having an understanding of information about the nature, extent, and probable consequences of the proposed course of treatment and alternatives to that treatment, and an expression of a preference as to the course of treatment to be taken, consistent with the patient's values and goals. For the purposes of this act, the fact that a patient is a minor, or mentally disordered, or mentally retarded, shall not give rise to a presumption that the patient is not competent.

B. "Consent" means the voluntary, express, and informed agreement by a competent patient to an action by a program or provider. The fact that a patient currently is receiving physically intrusive or restrictive treatment, such as residential treatment, does not, by itself, render that patient incapable of giving consent, but it does call for added diligence by the program or provider to assure that content is voluntary. To be voluntary, the consent must be given by a patient so situated as to be able to exercise free power of choice without undue inducement or any element of force, fraud, duress, or any form of constraint or coercion. To be express, the consent usually must be in writing. To be informed, consent usually must be preceded by communicating to the patient the following kinds of information:

1. a fair and reasonable explanation of the action proposed to be taken by the program or provider and its purpose, including the identification of any research involved and if so, how the results of the research will be disseminated, and how the identity of the patient will be protected;
2. a description of any adverse consequence or risk to be expected and, particularly where research is involved, an indication as to whether there may be other significant risks not yet identified;
3. a description of any benefit reasonably to be expected;
4. a disclosure of any alternative action that might be equally advantageous for the patient;
5. an offer to answer any inquiries by the patient;
6. notification that the patient is free to refuse or withdraw his consent and to withdraw from participation in any treatment to which consent is required without fear of reprisal against the patient or prejudice to the patient.

C. "Physically Intrusive or Restrictive Mental Health Treatment" means any planned intervention intended to improve a patient's functioning in those areas which show impairment as a result of a mental disorder or mental retardation, and which presents substantially greater risks of harm, embarrassment, or loss of autonomy, considering magnitude and probability, than those ordinarily encountered in daily life. Residential treatment, intrusive somatic treatment including antipsychotic medication, and aversive therapy or habilitation that employs painful or noxious stimuli shall be considered physically intrusive or restrictive mental health treatment within the meaning of this act. Outpatient evaluation or psychotherapy, day treatment, and intensive home-based services are not physically intrusive or restrictive mental health treatment within the meaning of this act. "Treatment" includes habilitation and training.

D. "Patient" means a person under the age of eighteen (or whatever the age of majority is) who is receiving or is proposed to receive treatment whether that person is referred to as a client, resident, student, consumer, recipient, inmate, or some other term.

E. "Provider" means a licensed physician or (licensed) (certified) (clinical) (doctoral-level) psychologist."

F. "Program" means any hospital, intermediate care facility, group home, mental health clinic, or other facility that provides or offers to provide treatment for mental disorders or mental retardation.

G. "Voluntary" means with the consent of a patient.

[COMMENT: This section contains several key definitions. The definition of "competency" is part of the standard for determining which minors may consent to services and which may refuse services. Because a single standard for both acts is used, a less demanding standard would permit more minors to acquiesce to treatment and more minors to refuse treatment. The definition of "program" and the definition of "physically intrusive or restrictive treatment" describe the breadth of regulation proposed. Most existing statutes only address the admission of minors to state hospitals.]

Sec. 103. *Voluntary admission and treatment.*

A. A program or provider may admit a patient for the purposes of treatment and treat until discharge or transfer, until the patient requests discharge, or is no longer competent, whichever occurs first, provided that, if the patient receives physically intrusive or restrictive mental health treatment, the period of treatment consented to pursuant to this section shall not exceed ninety days, where it appears to a provider, after personal examination of the patient, that admission criteria in paragraph B of this section are met.

B. Voluntary admission criteria:

1. The patient has given consent to any physically intrusive or restrictive treatment; and

2. The patient is in need of the proposed treatment for a mental disorder or mental retardation, and likely to benefit from the treatment; and

3. An individualized plan of treatment shall be written by the staff and consented to by the patient. The plan shall include specific provisions for the placement and aftercare upon completion of treatment, and specific behavioral goals against which the success of treatment may be measured. The plan shall be developed with maximum involvement of the patient's family, consistent with the patient's desire for confidentiality and with his or her treatment needs; and

4. The proposed treatment has been adopted as part of the patient's individualized education plan, or if there is none, it has been determined by the examining provider that there is no likelihood that the educational system will make treatment part of the individualized education plan or otherwise provide minimally adequate treatment soon enough to prevent harm to the patient. (and

5. A person described in Sec. 106 consents to any physically intrusive or restrictive treatment, provided that notification of this person of the patient's desire for treatment, or that person's refusal to consent to treatment does not result in harm to the patient.)

[COMMENT: This section authorizes a period of voluntary treatment on the consent of a competent minor. Treatment not involving physically intrusive or restrictive treatment does not require consent, and thus does not require a determination of competency. (Where involvement of a parental figure in treatment does not present a risk of harm to the minor patient, parental consent also is required for physically intrusive or restrictive treatment.)]

Sec. 104. *Judicial review of voluntary admission and treatment.*

A. Upon the petition of either the patient or the program or provider, any judge of the juvenile (or domestic relations) court may authorize the voluntary admission of a patient for any period up to one-hundred eighty days where, after hearing and by clear and convincing evidence, it finds:

1. The admission criteria of Sec. 103 (B) are met; and
2. There is no comparably effective treatment currently available that is less physically intrusive or restrictive.

B. Notwithstanding the foregoing, the approval of voluntary admission and treatment may be made by a committee of not fewer than three providers not involved in the treatment of the patient, pursuant to regulations promulgated by the (department of mental health, health, etc.). Such regulations shall assure the appointment, prior to the committee's hearing, of an advocate to articulate the patient's values or preferences and to investigate the nature of the treatment proposed, and shall assure that no patient is admitted without the patient's informed consent.

[COMMENT: This section may be used where an admission under Sec. 103 extends beyond ninety days. It also may be used (rather than an involuntary commitment proceeding) where the competency of a nonprotesting minor patient is in doubt. An alternative administrative review of voluntary admissions is available subject to promulgation of agency regulations. Because the length of admission is greater, an additional criterion of admission is imposed: admission under this section must be the least restrictive alternative.]

Sec. 105. *Involuntary commitment and treatment; general applicability.*

Notwithstanding any other laws to the contrary, no patient not admitted pursuant to Sec. 103, Sec. 104, or Sec. 111, shall be admitted to a program involving physically intrusive or restrictive mental health treatment except in accordance with an order of involuntary commitment or respite admission entered pursuant to the following procedures and standards.

[COMMENT: While many commitment laws authorize certain kinds of treatment, few prohibit all other kinds of treatment. This section is intended to make compliance with this act essential to

169

lawful mental health treatment of minors, regardless of the setting, if the treatment is physically intrusive or restrictive.]

Sec. 106. *Involuntary commitment; who may petition.*

A petition for the involuntary commitment of a patient to a program for mental health treatment may be brought only by one of the following persons in the priority listed, and provided that no persons in a higher priority object to the petition:

A. A legal guardian;

B. An adoptive parent having custody of the patient;

C. A natural parent having custody of the patient;

D. The director, or his or her designated representative, of a public agency having custody of the patient;

E. An adult sibling;

F. A noncustodial parent, who has not been deprived of custody because of abuse or neglect of the patient;

G. A foster parent;

H. A provider currently treating the patient;

I. The director, or his or her designated representative, of a program proposing to provide treatment.

[COMMENT: This section limits the authority to petition to persons in a parental role, and establish a priority among those persons. This priority is used elsewhere in the act. The alternative approach would be to limit the authority to petition to a "parent" and to list these persons and their priority in the definition of "parent." This section in effect assures a parental veto to the commitment of the child, which may be overridden in emergencies or through extinguishing the parent's custodial rights for abuse or neglect.]

Sec. 107. *Involuntary commitment; contents of petition.*

The petition for involuntary commitment shall indicate the name and address of the petitioner, the patient, and the program to which the patient is proposed to be committed, and shall set forth in general terms why the petitioner believes the patient meets the criteria in Sec. 110(B) for involuntary commitment. The petition shall be under oath. The petition shall list the names and addresses of any witnesses the petitioner intends to call at the involuntary commitment hearing.

[COMMENT: This section identifies the minimal contents of notice to a minor facing involuntary commitment. Little formality is required, although the petition must be under oath. Where these requirements cannot be met, the only recourse is to seek treatment on an emergency basis under Sec. 111.]

Sec. 108. *Involuntary commitment; notice and appointment of counsel.*

After any petition is filed with the (juvenile or domestic relations) court, a hearing shall be conducted no sooner than 24 hours and no later than 72 hours after the petition is filed. Copies of the petition, together with a notice of the hearing, shall be served immediately upon the patient, and all persons, if they exist and are reasonably available, described in Sec. 106. No less than 12 hours before the hearing the court shall appoint counsel to represent any patient, unless it has determined that the patient has retained counsel. Upon the request of the patient's counsel and after notice to the petitioner and all other persons receiving notice of the hearing, the court may continue the hearing once for a period not to exceed 96 hours.

[COMMENT: This section requires notice. A reasonably prompt hearing is required, but no sooner than twelve hours after counsel is appointed. The hearing may be delayed only on request of the defense counsel. The purpose of this continuance is to prepare for trial.]

Sec. 109. *Involuntary commitment; hearing.*

The court shall summon to the hearing all witnesses requested by either the patient or the petitioner. All testimony shall be under oath. The ordinary rules of evidence shall apply. Both the petitioner, patient, and, with leave of court for good cause shown, any other person, shall be given the opportunity to present evidence and cross-examine witnesses. The hearing shall be closed to the public unless the patient and petitioner request that it be open.

The patient or petitioner shall have the right to appeal (*de novo*) the outcome of the hearing to the (court) within thirty days of any final order committing the patient or dismissing the petition.

[COMMENT: The question of whether the appeal is *de novo* or on record must be answered by reference to the judicial system of the state enacting this law. Specifically, if the hearing is to be held initially in a court not of record, then the appeal should be *de novo* to the trial court of record. If the initial hearing is to be held in a court of record, then the appeal should be on that record. Additional rights of the defendant to a written transcript of proceedings then should be specified.]

Sec. 110. *Involuntary commitment; criteria.*

    A. The court shall order the involuntary commitment of the patient to a program for treatment for a period not to exceed ninety days, if after a hearing conducted pursuant to this act, it finds by clear and convincing evidence that the involuntary commitment criteria presently are met.

    B. Involuntary commitment criteria:

        1. The patient is either

            a. not competent to make the decision voluntarily to admit himself or herself for treatment [and as a consequence of a mental disorder or mental retardation is or in the near future, if not provided treatment in the manner proposed, will be unable to perform independently the basic tasks of personal hygiene, hydration, nutrition, self-protection, or education], or,

            b. [significantly more] likely [than other minors] as a consequence of mental disorder or mental retardation to inflict or attempt to inflict seriously bodily harm upon himself/herself or others in foreseeable future, if not provided treatment in the manner proposed; and

        2. The patient is in need of the proposed treatment for a mental disorder or mental retardation, and is likely to benefit from the treatment; and

3. An individualized plan of treatment that includes specific provisions for placement and aftercare upon completion of treatment, specific behavioral goals against which the success of treatment may be measured, and maximum involvement of the patient's desire for confidentiality and with his or her treatment needs, has been written and presented to the court by the program to which commitment is proposed; and

4. The proposed treatment has been adopted as part of patient's individualized education plan, or if there is none, it has been determined by the court that there is no likelihood that the educational system will make treatment part of the individualized education plan or otherwise provide minimally adequate treatment soon enough to prevent harm to the patient; and

5. There is no comparably effective treatment currently available that is less physically intrusive or restrictive.

[COMMENT: Paragraph 1 contains the two traditional alternative criteria of commitment. The bracketed (optional) language in subparagraph 1(a), the parens patriae criterion, adds behavioral standards to the criterion, which may focus the judicial inquiry more narrowly. The bracketed language in 1(b), the police power criterion, makes it clear that the likelihood of harm need not rise to the level of a 50%+ probability. Instead, commitment would be required where the probability of harm was significantly greater than the probability (which is less than 1%) in the general population of minors. Threats of psychological harm to family members are addressed through respite care in Sec. 112.]

Sec. 111. *Emergency treatment.*

A person described in Sec. 106, provided no person in a higher priority objects, or a law enforcement officer may detain a patient, and transport and admit him or her to a program or provider for all treatment reasonably necessary, prior to an involuntary commitment hearing, when it is reasonable to believe:

A. The patient is in need of treatment for mental disorder or mental retardation;

B. A twenty-four hour delay in treatment more likely than not would result in serious harm to the patient or others;

C. A petition for the involuntary commitment of the patient is pending, or, if not pending, is filed within four hours of detention.

[COMMENT: This section provides the authority for pre-hearing detention. Sec. 108 requires the hearing to be held within three days of the initial filing of the petition. This section requires the petition to be filed within four hours of detention. Note that after counsel is appointed for the patient, the hearing may be continued for up to eight additional days, on the request of that counsel. Thus the maximum pre-hearing detention and treatment is eleven days and four hours. While this is a substantial period of pre-hearing hospitalization, the alternatives are reducing the time in which a defense may be prepared or complicating the process with a preliminary hearing in which a lower standard of detention (such as "probable cause") is applied.]

Sec. 112. *Respite admission.*

A. If after a hearing pursuant to Sec. 109, the court finds that, although the patient is mentally disordered or mentally retarded, the criteria and Sec. 110 are not met, the court nonetheless may authorize the involuntary commitment of the patient for a period, or for nonconsecutive periods, not to exceed a cumulative total of forty-five days, if it finds by clear and convincing evidence that:

1. The patient resides with his natural, adoptive, or foster parents;

2. The admission of the patient to the program is necessary to give his or her custodial parents and other members of the household respite from the care of the patient;

3. The patient's needs for care are substantially greater than those of minors of the same age, such that specialized care is

174

required in the absence of the custodial parents; provided that a finding that the patient is mentally disordered or mentally retarded shall not in itself be sufficient to establish that such specialized care is required;

4. The ability of the custodial parents to continue to care for the patient in the household would be reduced without respite from the care of the patient;

5. The patient has been accepted by the program to which respite admission is proposed;

6. The custodial parents themselves have sought mental health treatment and assistance in caring for the patient.

B. Whenever possible, respite care shall be provided by childcare workers in the patient's home or in a program located outside a hospital, which has as its primary purpose the provision of respite care. Respite care within the patient's home that does not involve physically intrusive or restrictive treatment does not require the patient's consent or judicial approval pursuant to this section.

C. Respite care shall not be used as a substitute for treatment.

D. If respite care for which approval is sought is to exceed fourteen days, an individualized plan of treatment or habilitation shall be provided to the court for its approval. The plan shall be to the maximum extent possible consistent with and responsive to the patient's individualized educational plan, if one exists.

[COMMENT: This section is intended in part to prevent distortion by sympathetic courts of the involuntary commitment standards to permit respite care. This section seeks to preserve what is usually the least restrictive placement, the patient's home, and to prevent psychological harm to family members. It is as well an example of the ways in which the act acknowledges the needs and prerogatives of parents.]

Sec. 113. *Treatment records.*

A. A program or provider may disclose any record of a patient or former patient only under one of the circumstances described in subsection B.

B. A program or provider shall disclose any record of a patient or former patients in any of the following circumstances:

1. To other programs or providers in an emergency to the extent necessary to prevent serious bodily harm to the patient or others;

2. To the patient or former patient, his or her current program or provider, or his or her attorney, with the consent of the patient or former patient.

3. To a person described in Sec. 106, if the patient or former patient is not competent to give consent to the disclosure of the record, and no person in a higher priority objects.

4. To any person who presents written documentation of consent of the patient or former patient, if believed by the provider or program to be competent to give that consent; and if not believed by the provider to be competent to give that consent, with written documentation of the consent of a person described in Section 106, provided a person in a higher priority does not object. The program or provider may impose a reasonable charge for the reproduction of records pursuant to this paragraph.

5. To child protective services to the extent required by law.

C. The recipient of any record disclosed pursuant to this section may not redisclose that record, unless otherwise required by law, without the consent of the patient or former patient, if competent to give consent, or, if the patient or former patient is not competent to give consent, without consent of a person described in Sec. 106, provided a person in a higher priority does not object.

Sec. 114. *Discharge; periodic review of status.*

A. At any time that a patient no longer meets the criteria of voluntary admission, involuntary commitment, emergency admission, or respite admission on which he or she was admitted, he or she shall be discharged, unless readmitted under the provisions of this act.

B. The program or provider shall review the status and current conditions of each patient no less frequently than every thirty days to ensure that the criteria on which the patient was admitted currently are met, and that their individualized treatment plan is responsive to the patient's current treatment needs and preferences and is not more physically intrusive or restrictive than is necessary to meet those treatment needs.

C. The patient shall have a right to a judicial hearing, seventy-two hours after request is made to the court or to the program or provider, no more frequently than every thirty days, to determine whether he or she meets the criteria on which the patient was admitted. If the fact-finder determines that the admissions criteria are not presently met, the patient shall be discharged.

Sec. 115. *Rights of patients.*

In addition to the foregoing rights, each patient shall have a right to treatment.

A. This right includes the right to be furnished by the program with food, shelter, clothing, and medical care, as well as a range of treatment modalities that is suited to the individual needs of the patient and that is calculated reasonably to enhance measurably the patient's enjoyment of basic liberty interests.

B. For the purposes of this section, treatment includes the provision of transitional care and care after discharge to the extent that it is reasonably necessary to recover social skills as a consequence of admission or to prevent injury to the patient.

C. A private program may fulfill its obligations to a patient who is not capable of paying its customary charges by making diligent efforts to transfer the patient to a program operated by state or local government, or which provides treatment to indigent patients, and by seeking reimbursement from the parents, appropriate local educational agency, and third-party payers.

D. A program operated by state or local government, or which receives governmental support through direct support, contract payments, Medicare, Medicaid, or tax-exempt status, shall fulfill its obligations to the patient without regard to cost or administrative convenience.

E. In fulfilling its obligations under this section the program may seek reimbursement from the patient according to the patient's ability to pay. The program may seek reimbursement from the patient's parents according to their ability to pay, provided that, if the patient is competent, no treatment information shall be provided to the parents or their insurers without the consent of the patient.

F. In the event that fiscal constraints prevent a patient from receiving treatment that is less physically intrusive or restrictive than that which it is providing currently or proposing to provide to that patient, and the current treatment is permitted otherwise under the provisions of the law, the current treatment may be provided, subject to the following conditions:

  1. A periodic report, prepared by the program no less frequently than every thirty days, of the nature of the current treatment, the alternative treatment less restrictive than current treatment, and the additional financial costs and therapeutic benefits, if any, of that less restrictive treatment shall be prepared and sent to the patient, the court, if any, committing the patient, the Department of Mental Health [Youth Services, Social Services, Mental Retardation Services] and to a person providing advocacy services as described in this section.

  2. The filing of a request with the appropriate local educational agency that the agency designate the patient as a handicapped child, and provide at its expense any less restrictive treatment that the program is unable to provide because of fiscal constraints.

Sec. 116. *Responsibility of the State.*

A. Department of Mental Health [Youth Services, Social Services, Mental Retardation Services] (hereafter in this section, "the Department") shall ensure the availability of a continuum of therapeutic service for minors, including, at minimum, individual, group, and family outpatient treatment, parent education, day treatment, intensive home-based services, respite care, therapeutic foster care, and residential treatment. Such services shall be available to minors of all ages in or near their home communities, in such proportion as to provide for treatment in the least restrictive alternative.

B. At least annually, the Department shall report to the legislative committee responsible for appropriations for mental health and retardation services in regard to its compliance with subsection A of this section. Such report shall contain, at a minimum,

  1. statistics regarding the nature and frequency of reports by programs pursuant to Sec. 115.F.1 and

  2. a plan for remediating any gaps or imbalances in services noted therein.

C. The Department shall monitor

  1. The short-term and long-term effectiveness of mental health services to minors and

  2. The programs' compliance with the rights enumerated in this act. This provision shall not abrogate the responsibility of any other agency authorized to license or regulate programs.

D. At least annually, the Department shall report to the legislative committee responsible for appropriations for mental health and retardation services in regard to

  1. the finding of the studies conducted pursuant to subsection C of this section and

  2. its plans for future studies.

Sec. 117. *Prevention.*

A. The legislature finds that

  1. Mental health prevention reduces the short-term and long-term social and economic costs of mental health problems of children and youth, and that

179

    2. mental health prevention is consistent with the state's interest in the healthy socialization of its citizens.

B. The Department shall develop a plan for primary and secondary prevention of mental health problems of children and youth. This plan shall be developed in consultation with the departments of education and health and shall include provisions for mental health preventative services in the public schools and pediatric health services.

C. At least annually, the Department shall report to the legislative committee responsible for appropriations for mental health and retardation services in regard to the Department's progress in prevention of mental health problems of children and youth.

•

Division 37 Position Statement: Revised Resolution on Advertising by Inpatient Programs

The Division of Child, Youth, and Family Services of the American Psychological Association is seriously concerned about deceptive advertising in the marketing of child and adolescent inpatient programs to the general public. We urge psychologists, consistent with the revised Ethical Principles, to make reasonable efforts to prevent facilities with which they are affiliated from engaging in advertising that is false, deceptive, or fraudulent concerning the provision of psychological services, either because of what it states, conveys or suggests, or because of what it omits.

Advertising about teenage suicide and parent-child conflicts can present a powerful image, but in some instances may be materially inaccurate or use exaggeration in a potentially deceptive manner in depicting mental disorders of childhood and adolescence. It may in such instances foster unwarranted fear in parents and youth or exacerbate the stigma sometimes associated with mental disorders of childhood and adolescence. Also, marketing an inpatient program's attributes may in some cases be deceptive by omitting mention of the availability of alternative forms of service, an omission that can lead parents and youth into unnecessarily restrictive and intrusive care.

As the range of health services that are commercially marketed expands, the importance of professional self-regulation is heightened. Individual psychologists and the profession as a whole have a weighty obligation to guard the interests of clients and prospective clients.

Notes

INTRODUCTION

1. The term *continuum of care* was defined by Knitzer (1982) as "a range of services that can meet both the diverse needs of a varied group of children and the needs of an individual child as they change with time" (p. 29). She added that "[i]t is not enough to develop a range of nonresidential, residential, and case advocacy services for children. These services must be organized so individual children can move easily from one to another depending on their age and needs, and so multiple services can be delivered to children, adolescents, and families in a way that is helpful, rather than confusing or overwhelming" (p. 48).

2. Public Health Service Act §, 42 U.S.C. § 290cc-13 (1988 & Supp. II, 1990), amended by ADAMHA Reorganization Act, Pub. L. No. 102–321 §§ 115, 116, 106 Stat. 323, 346–348 (1992) (to be codified at 42 U.S.C. §§ 290bb-32, 290bb-32).

3. "That inquiry must carefully probe the child's background using all avail-

able sources, including, but not limited to, parents, schools, and other social agencies. Of course, the review must also include an interview with the child." (pp. 606–607).

4. The Court likely did not intend to limit the term "neutral factfinder" to psychiatrists. In discussing its concern over the use of formal proceedings, for example, the Court noted, "One factor that must be considered is the utilization of the time of *psychiatrists, psychologists, and other behavioral specialists* in preparing for and participating in hearings rather than performing the task for which their special training has fitted them." (pp. 605–606, emphasis added).

5. "[T]he District Court did not decide and we therefore have no reason to consider at this time what procedures for review are independently necessary to justify continuing a child's confinement. We merely hold that a subsequent, independent review of the patient's condition provides a necessary check against possible arbitrariness in the *initial* admission decision." (p. 607, n. 15).

1. RESIDENTIAL TREATMENT

1. The fact that children with "serious emotional disturbance" are within the scope of IDEA, whereas children who experience "social maladjustment" are without its protections has engendered considerable controversy as to whom the act covers (see, e.g., Skiba & Grizzle's 1992 rejoinder to Slenkovich (1992)). IDEA's reference to the use of "medical services" "for diagnostic and evaluation purposes" implies that one way of resolving the question on a case-by-case basis is to consult a physician to determine whether the child suffers from a diagnosable mental disorder that might qualify as a "serious emotional disturbance." Indeed, some have argued that IDEA promotes heavy reliance on consultation with physicians (e.g., Bateman, 1995).

2. Such was the case in *Parham v. J. R.* (1979), a case we revisit throughout this volume. In *Parham*, as in many such cases, the child already was a ward of the state. The Court noted that "the determination of what process is due varies somewhat when the state, rather than a natural parent makes the request for commitment" (p. 617), but "conclude[d] that the

differences in the two situations do not justify requiring different procedures" (pp. 617–618).

3. The Court in *Parham* invoked the analogy as follows: "Simply because the decision of a parent is not agreeable to a child or because it involves risks does not automatically transfer the power to make that decision from the parents to some agency or officer of the state. The same characterizations can be made for a tonsillectomy, appendectomy, or other medical procedures" (1979, p. 603). Of course, the Court is right—if the issue is "simply" one of "[dis]agreeab[ility]" or "risk." We argue, though, that it is not. The conflict of interests, for example, that exists when parents are confronted with a decision whether to institutionalize a child generally is not present for similar decisions relative to physical health concerns.

2. RESTRICTIVENESS AND INTRUSIVENESS OF TREATMENT

1. In *Washington v. Harper*, (1990, pp. 221–222) the Court found that the petitioner "possesse[d] a significant liberty interest in avoiding the unwanted administration of antipsychotic drugs under the Due Process clause of the Fourteenth Amendment. In *Aden v. Younger* (1976, p. 679) the court observed that the state, in forcible administration of psychotropic medications, was "attempting to regulate the use of procedures which touch upon thought processes in significant ways," and found the practice to violate the freedom of thought protected by the First Amendment.

2. Lower courts have tended to use the strict scrutiny test (i.e., the state must prove that it has a compelling interest in the goal to be achieved and that its means for achieving the goal are narrowly tailored so as not to infringe protected rights unnecessarily) in evaluating the state's attempt to force administration of psychotropic medications (e.g., *Aden v. Younger*, 1976; *Rennie v. Klein*, 1976). The Supreme Court, however, in *Youngberg v. Romeo*, expressed concern that the strict scrutiny standard was too high and "would place an undue burden on the administration of institutions . . . and also would restrict unnecessarily the exercise of professional judgment as to the needs of residents" (pp. 321–322).

3. This view was articulated (although not very clearly) in *Rogers v. Okin* (1980) as follows:

> We begin our analysis with what seems to us to be an intuitively obvious proposition: a person has a constitutionally protected interest in being left free by the state to decide for himself whether to submit to the serious and potentially harmful medical treatment that is represented by the administration of antipsychotic drugs. The precise textual source in the Constitution of the protection of this interest is unclear, and the authorities directly supportive of the proposition itself are surprisingly few. Nevertheless, we are convinced that the proposition is correct and that a source in the Due Process Clause of the Fourteenth Amendment for the protection of this interest exists, most likely as part of the penumbral right to privacy, bodily integrity, or personal security. (p. 653)

4. For example, "Instead of second-guessing defendants, the court should have taken as true their asserted difficulties . . . and fashioned a ruling. . . ." (*Rogers v. Okin*, 1980, p. 656.)

5. E.g., "[N]either judges nor administrative hearing officers are better qualified than psychiatrists to render psychiatric judgments." (*Parham v. J. R.*, 1979, p. 607, quoting *In Re Roger S.*, 1977, p. 942).

5. *PARHAM* AND PATERNALISM

1. In *Planned Parenthood of Central Missouri v. Danforth* (1976), for example, Justice Blackmun described such a conflict of interests relative to abortion decision making as follows: "It is difficult . . . to conclude that providing a parent with absolute power to overrule a determination, made by the physician and his minor patient, to terminate the patient's pregnancy will serve to strengthen the family unit. Neither is it likely that such veto power will enhance parental authority or control where the minor and the nonconsenting parent are so fundamentally in conflict and the very existence of the [minor daughter's] pregnancy already has fractured the family structure" (p. 75).

6. TOWARD RESPECT FOR CHILDREN, YOUTH, AND FAMILIES

1. For example, Principle D mandates, in relevant part, that "[p]sychologists accord appropriate respect to the fundamental rights, dignity, and worth of all people." Principle E addresses psychologists' obligation "to contribute to the welfare of those with whom they interact professionally." Principle F goes further in its expanded definition of "professional and scientific responsibilities to the community and the society in which [psychologists] work and live" (American Psychological Association, 1992).

2. As we described in Chapter 4, *primary goods* are those goods that are recognized consensually as necessary for human dignity and welfare. Children and youth have an interest not only in contemporary primary goods but also in development of skills to facilitate their access to such goods as an adult.

3. By the same logic, minors' constitutional rights should be honored except when a compelling state interest outweighs minors' fundamental rights (see Melton, 1984a; Tribe, 1975. Cf. *San Antonio Independent School District v. Rodriguez*, 1973).

4. See, e.g., Model Act, §§ 102.A and 102.B (definitions of "competent" and "consent"), and §§ 103 and 115.D.

5. The inquiry about the necessary level of restrictiveness of treatment should be ongoing (see § 115.F.1).

6. In protracted litigation that resulted in a plethora of federal court decisions, *Pennhurst* concluded with closing of the institution after a holding that such services are inherently harmful. The court greeted this ultimate conclusion euphorically:

> This settlement is more than just a termination of litigation; it is the beginning of a new era for retarded persons. It is a confirmation that all parties to this litigation are now in complete agreement that the retarded citizens of this Commonwealth have a right to care, education and training in the community. It is a recognition by the Commonwealth and its Counties that retarded persons are not subjects to be warehoused in institutions, but that they are individuals, the great

majority of whom have a potential to become productive members of society. (610 F. Supp. at 1233–1234)

Also worth noting is the consistency of this latter approach with the evolving international standards of treatment by governments of citizens more generally and of children in particular. The position we have taken is consistent, for example, with the Convention (1978) in many respects (for a fuller discussion, see Melton, 1993b).

7. See, e.g., *Prince v. Massachusetts*, 321 U.S. 158, 166 (1944): "It is cardinal with us that the custody, care and nurture of the child reside first in the parents, whose primary function and freedom include preparation for obligations the state can neither supply nor hinder. . . . And it is in recognition of this that these decisions have respected the private realm of family life which the state cannot enter."

8. As has been recognized in the case of institutionalized mentally disabled adults, such a duty is embedded in the constitutional right to substantive due process, especially as it includes the right to personal security (e.g., *O'Connor v. Donaldson*, 1975; *Youngberg v. Romeo*, 1983).

9. The act includes a loophole that permits provision of treatment without incorporation into an educational plan when education officials appear unlikely to meet their responsibilities.

10. Additional Protections for Children Involved as Subjects in Research, 45 C.F.R. §§ 46.401 to 46.409 (1993) (see also Gray et al., 1995, pp. 58–62, for discussion of the permission-denial/assent-refusal dichotomies).

References

ABCAN (1993). *See* "United States Advisory Board on Child Abuse and Neglect."

Achenbach, T. M. (1974). *Developmental psychopathology.* New York: Ronald.

Achenbach, T. M. (1980). DSM-III in light of empirical research on the classification of child psychopathology. *Journal of the American Academy of Child Psychiatry, 19,* 395–412.

Achenbach, T. M., & Edelbrock, C. S. (1978). The classification of child psychopathology: A review and analysis of empirical efforts. *Psychological Bulletin, 85,* 1275–1301.

Addington v. Texas, 441 U.S. 418 (1979).

Additional Protections for Children Involved as Subjects in Research, 45 C.F.R. §§ 46.401–46.409 (1993).

Adelman, H. S., Lusk, R., Alvarez, V., & Acosta, N. (1985). Competence of minors to understand, evaluate, and communicate about their psychoeducational problems. *Professional Psychology: Research and Practice, 16,* 426–434.

Adelman, H. S., & Taylor, L. (1986). Children's reluctance regarding treatment: Incompetence, resistance, or an appropriate response? *School Psychology Review, 15*, 91–99.

Aden v. Younger, 57 Cal. App.3d 662 (1976).

Ahr, P. R., & Holcomb, W. R. (1985). State mental health directors' priorities for mental health care. *Hospital and Community Psychiatry, 36*, 39–45.

Allen, M. K. (1972). Persistent factors leading to application for admission to a residential institution. *Mental Retardation, 10*, 25–29.

Allen v. Illinois, 479 U.S. 1076 (1987).

Aman, M. G. (1983). Psychoactive drugs in mental retardation. In J. L. Matson & F. Andrasik (Eds.), *Treatment issues and innovations in mental retardation* (pp. 455–513). New York: Plenum.

Aman, M. G., & Singh, N. N. (1991). Pharmacological intervention. In J. L. Matson & J. H. Mulick (Eds.), *Handbook of mental retardation* (2nd ed.; pp. 347–372). New York: Pergamon.

Ambuel, B., & Rappaport, J. (1992). Developmental trends in adolescents' psychological and legal competence to consent to abortion. *Law and Human Behavior, 16*, 129–154.

American Bar Association. (1986). [Resolution on privatization of correctional facilities.] Summarized in *United States Law Week, 54*, 2416.

American Psychiatric Association. (1980). Diagnostic and statistical manual of mental disorders (3rd ed.). Washington DC: Author.

American Psychiatric Association. (1981, May). *Commentary: Guidelines for psychiatric hospitalization of minors.* Approved by the Assembly. Washington DC: Author.

American Psychiatric Association. (1982a). Four alternatives to the guidelines for the psychiatric hospitalization of minors: Clinical and legal considerations. *American Journal of Psychiatry, 139*, 974–975.

American Psychiatric Association. (1982b). Guidelines for psychiatric hospitalization of minors. *American Journal of Psychiatry, 139*, 971–974.

American Psychiatric Association. (1994). *Diagnostic and statistical manual of mental disorders* (4th ed.). Washington DC: Author.

American Psychological Association. (1992). Ethical principles of psychologists and code of conduct. *American Psychologist, 47*, 1597–1611.

Andrulis, D. P., & Mazade, N. A. (1983). American mental health policy: Changing directions in the 80s. *Hospital and Community Psychiatry, 34*, 601–606.

Annas, G. (1979, October). Parents, children, and the Supreme Court. *Hastings Center Report*, pp. 21–23.

Appelbaum, P. S. (1988). The new preventive detention: Psychiatry's problematic responsibility for the control of violence. *American Journal of Psychiatry, 413*, 779–785.

Appelbaum, P. S., & Grisso, T. (1995). The MacArthur treatment competence study I: Mental illness and competence to consent to treatment. *Law and Human Behavior, 19*, 105–126.

Armstrong, M. I., & Evans, M. E. (1992). Three intensive community-based programs for children and youth with serious emotional disturbance and their families. *Journal of Child and Family Studies, 1*, 61–74.

AuClaire, P., & Schwartz, I. M. (1986, May). *Preliminary results: An evaluation of the effectiveness of intensive home-based services as an alternative to placement for adolescents and their families.* University of Minnesota, Hubert H. Humphrey Institute of Public Affairs, Center for Youth Policy.

Austin, J. (1995). The overrepresentation of minority youths in the California juvenile justice system: Perceptions and realities. In K. K. Leonard, C. E. Pope, & W. M. Feyerherm (Eds.), *Minorities in juvenile justice* (pp. 153–178). Thousand Oaks CA: Sage.

Baker, B. L., Seltzer, G. B., & Seltzer, M. N. (1977). *As close as possible: Community residences for retarded adults.* Boston: Little, Brown.

Barber, C. C., Rosenblatt, A., Harris, L., & Attkisson, C. C. (1992). Use of mental health services among severely emotionally disturbed children and adolescents in San Francisco. *Journal of Child and Family Studies, 1*, 183–207.

Bartley v. Kremens, 402 F. Supp. 1039 (E.D. Pa. 1975) *vacated and remanded* 431 U.S. 119 (1977).

Bastien, R., & Adelman, H. (1984). Noncompulsory versus legally mandated placement, perceived choice, and response to treatment among adolescents. *Journal of Consulting and Clinical Psychology, 52*, 171–179.

Bateman, B. (1995). The physician and the world of special education. *Journal of Child Neurology, 10* (Supp. 1), S114–S120.

Beauchamp, T. L., & Childress, J. F. (Eds.). (1983). *Principles of biomedical ethics* (2nd ed.). New York: Oxford University Press.

Behar, L. (1985). Changing patterns of state responsibility: A case study of North Carolina. *Journal of Clinical Child Psychology, 14,* 188–195.

Bellah, R. N. (1975). *The broken covenant: American civil religion in time of trial.* New York: Seabury.

Belter, R., & Grisso, T. (1984). Children's recognition of rights violations in counseling. *Professional Psychology: Research and Practice, 15,* 899–910.

Bersoff, D. N., & Glass, D. J. (1995). The not-so Weisman: The Supreme Court's continuing misuse of social science research. *University of Chicago Law School Roundtable, 2,* 279–302.

Billingsley, A. (1964). Bureaucratic and professional orientation patterns in casework. *Social Service Review, 38,* 400–407.

Blacher, J. (1994). Placement and its consequences for families with children who have mental retardation. In J. Blacher (Ed.), *When there's no place like home: Options for children living apart from their natural families* (pp. 213–243). Baltimore: Paul H. Brookes.

Blacher, J., & Baker, B. L. (1992). Family involvement in residential treatment of children with retardation: Is there evidence of detachment? *Journal of Child Psychology and Psychiatry, 35,* 505–520.

Blackstone, W. (1765–1769/1979). *Commentaries on the Laws of England* (Vols. 1–4). Chicago: University of Chicago Press.

Blinder, B. J., Young, W. M., Fineman, K. R., & Miller, S. J. (1978). The children's psychiatric hospital unit in the community: I. Concept and development. *American Journal of Psychiatry, 135,* 847–851.

Bloom, R. B., & Hopewell, L. R. (1982). Psychiatric hospitalization of adolescents and successful mainstream reentry. *Exceptional Children, 48,* 352–357.

Board of Education of Hendrick Hudson Central School District Board of Education Westchester County v. Rowley, 458 U.S 176 (1982).

Bowe, F. G. (1995). Population estimates: Birth-to-5 children with disabilities. *Journal of Special Education, 28,* 461–471.

Braginsky, B. M., Braginsky, D. D., & Ring, K. (1969). *Methods of madness: The mental hospital as a last resort.* New York: Holt, Rinehart & Winston.

Brehm, S. S. (1977). The effect of adult influence on children's preferences: Compliance versus opposition. *Journal of Abnormal Child Psychology, 5,* 31–41.

Brehm, S. S., & Weinraub, M. (1977). Physical barriers and psychological reactance: 2-year-olds' responses to threats to freedom. *Journal of Personality and Social Psychology, 35,* 830–836.

Brown, P. G. (1982). Human independence and parental proxy consent. In W. Gaylin & R. Macklin (Eds.), *Who speaks for the child? The problems of proxy consent* (pp. 209–222). New York: Plenum.

Buckley, P. F., & Meltzer, H. Y. (1995). Treatment of schizophrenia. In Alan F. Schatzberg & Charles B. Nemeroff (Eds.), *The American Psychiatric Press textbook of psychopharmacology* (pp. 615–639). Washington DC: American Psychiatric Press.

Burlingame, W. V., & Amaya, M. (1985). Psychiatric commitment of children and adolescents: Issues, current practices, and clinical impact. In D. N. Schetky & E. P. Benedek (Eds.), *Emerging issues in child psychiatry and the law* (pp. 229–249). New York: Brunner/Mazel.

Burns, B. J., & Friedman, R. M. (1990). Examining the research base for child mental health services and policy. *Journal of Mental Health Administration, 17,* 87–98.

Bush, M. (1980). Institutions for dependent and neglected children: Therapeutic option of choice or last resort? *American Journal of Orthopsychiatry, 50,* 239–255.

Bush, M., & Gordon, A. C. (1978). Client choice and bureaucratic accountability: Possibilities for responsiveness in a social welfare bureaucracy. *Journal of Social Issues, 34*(2), 22–43.

Campbell, M., & Gonzalez, N. M. (1996). Overview of neuroleptic use in child psychiatric disorders. In M. A. Richardson & G. Haugland (Eds.), *Use of neuroleptics in children* (pp. 1–22). Washington DC: American Psychiatric Press.

Carlson, G. A., & Cantwell, D P. (1980). Unmasking masked depression in children and adolescents. *American Journal of Psychiatry, 137,* 445–449.

Carey v. Population Services International, 431 U.S. 678 (1977).

Chambers, D. L. (1978). Community-based treatment and the Constitution: The principle of the least restrictive alternative. In L. I. Stein & M. A. Test (Eds.), *Alternatives to mental hospital treatment* (pp. 23–39). New York: Plenum.

Child and Adolescent Services System Program, 42 U.S.C. § 290cc-13 (1988 & Supp. II 1990), amended by ADAMHA Reorganization Act, Pub. L. No. 102-321 §§ 115, 116, 106 Stat. 323, 346–348 (1992) (codified at 42 U.S.C. §§ 290bb-32, 290bb-32).

Chiles, J. A., Miller, M. L., & Cox, G. B. (1980). Depression in an adolescent delinquent population. *Archives of General Psychiatry, 37,* 1179–1184.

City of Cleburne v. Cleburne Living Center, 473 U.S. 432 (1985).

Clark, H. B., & Clarke, R. T. (Eds.). (1996). Wraparound services [special issue]. *Journal of Child and Family Studies, 5*(1).

Clark, H. B., Lee, B., Prange, M. E., & McDonald, B. A. (1996). Children lost within the foster care system: Can wraparound service strategies improve placement outcomes? *Journal of Child and Family Studies, 5,* 39–54.

Cohen, R., Preiser, L., Gottlieb, S., Harris, R., Baker, J., & Sonenklar, N. (1993). Relinquishing custody as a prerequisite for receiving services for children with serious emotional disorders: A review. *Law and Human Behavior, 17,* 121–134.

Conger, J. J. (1981). Freedom and commitment: Families, youth, and social change. *American Psychologist, 36,* 1475–1484.

Conroy, J. W., & Bradley, V. J. (1985). *The Pennhurst longitudinal study: Combined report of five years of research and analysis.* Philadelphia: Temple University, Human Services Research Institute.

Convention (1978). *See* "United Nations Convention on the Rights of the Child."

Costello, J. C., & Worthington, N. L. (1981). Incarcerating status offenders: Attempts to circumvent the Juvenile Justice and Delinquency Prevention Act. *Harvard Civil Rights-Civil Liberties Law Review, 16,* 41–81.

Cruzan v. Director, Missouri Department of Health, 497 U.S. 261 (1990).

Cullen, C. (1991). Experimentation and planning in community care. *Disability, Handicap and Society, 6,* 115–128.

Cullinan, D., Epstein, M. H., & Quinn, K. P. (1996). Patterns and correlates of personal, family, and prior placement variables in an interagency community based system of care. *Journal of Child and Family Studies, 5,* 299–321.

Curry, J. F. (1991). Outcome research on residential treatment: Implications and suggested directions. *American Journal of Orthopsychiatry, 61,* 348–357.

David D. v. Dartmouth School Community, 775 F.2d 411 (1st Cir. 1985).

Davidson, D. (1991). Developmental differences in children's search of predecisional information. *Journal of Experimental Child Psychology, 52,* 239–255.

Davis, I. P., & Ellis-MacLeod, E. (1994). Temporary foster care: Separating and reunifying families. In J. Blacher (Ed.), *When there's no place like home: Options for children living apart from their natural families* (pp. 123–161). Baltimore: Paul H. Brookes.

Dawley, H. H., Jr. (1985, Winter). A commentary on advertising. *Public Service Psychology,* p. 2.

Dennis, D. L., & Monahan, J. (1996). *Coercion and aggressive community treatment.* New York: Plenum.

Dishion, T. J., Loeber, R., Stouthamer-Loeber, M., & Patterson, G. R. (1984). Skill deficits and male adolescent delinquency. *Journal of Abnormal Child Psychology, 12,* 37–54.

Donaldson v. O'Connor, 493 F.2d 507 (5th Cir. 1974) *vacated and remanded* O'Connor v. Donaldson, 422 U.S. 563 (1975).

Dore, M. M. (1993). Family-based services in children's mental health care. *Child and Adolescent Mental Health Care, 3,* 175–189.

Duchnowski, A. J., & Friedman, R. M. (1990). Children's mental health: Challenges for the nineties. *The Journal of Mental Health Administration, 17,* 3–12.

Duchnowski, A. J., Johnson, M. K., Hall, K. S., Kutash, K., & Friedman, R. M. (1993). The alternatives to residential treatment study: Initial findings. *Journal of Emotional and Behavioral Disorders, 1,* 17–26.

Dulcan, M. K., Bregman, J. D., Weller, E.B., & Weller, R. A. (1995). Treatment of childhood and adolescent disorders. In Alan F. Schatzberg & Charles B. Nemeroff (Eds.), *American Psychiatric Press textbook of psycho-*

pharmacology (pp. 669–706). Washington DC: American Psychiatric Press.

Dworkin, R. (1977). *Taking rights seriously.* Cambridge: Harvard University Press.

Eamon, M. K. (1994). Institutionalizing children and adolescents in private psychiatric hospitals. *Social Work, 39,* 588–594.

Earle, K. A., & Forquer, S. L. (1995). Use of seclusion with children and adolescents in public psychiatric hospitals. *American Journal of Orthopsychiatry, 65,* 238–244.

Earhart, E., & Sporakowski, M. J. (Eds.). (1984). The family with handicapped members [Special issue]. *Family Relations, 33.*

Edelman, M. W. (1981). Who is for children? *American Psychologist, 36,* 109–117.

Education for All Handicapped Children Act 20 U.S.C. §§ 1401–1485 (1988 & Supp. III 1991).

Eisenberg, L. (1984). The case against for-profit hospitals. *Hospital and Community Psychiatry, 35,* 1009–1013.

Ellis, J. W. (1974). Volunteering children: Parental commitment of minors to mental institutions. *California Law Review, 62,* 840–916.

Epstein, M. H., Quinn, K. P., & Cumblad, C. (1994). A scale to assess the restrictiveness of educational settings. *Journal of Child and Family Studies, 3,* 107–119.

Epstein, M. H., Cullinan, D., Quinn, K. P., & Cumblad, C. (1995). Personal, family, and service use characteristics of young people served by an interagency community-based system of care. *Journal of Emotional and Behavioral Disorders, 3,* 55–64.

Evans, M. E., Armstrong, M. I., Dollard, N., Kuppinger, A. D., Huz, S., & Wood, V. M. (1994). Development and evaluation of treatment foster care and family-centered intensive case management in New York. *Journal of Emotional and Behavioral Disorders, 2,* 228–239.

Evans, M. E., Armstrong, M. I., & Kuppinger, A. D. (1996). Family-centered intensive case management: A step toward understanding individualized care. *Journal of Child and Family Studies, 5,* 55–65.

Evans, M. E., Banks, S. M., Huz, S., & McNulty, T. L. (1994). Initial hospitalization and community tenure outcomes of intensive case management for children and youth with serious emotional disturbance. *Journal of Child and Family Studies, 3*, 225–234.

Eyman, R. K., Borthwick, S. A., & Tarjan, G. (1984). Current trends and changes in institutions for the mentally retarded. In N. R. Ellis & N. W. Bray (Eds.), *International review of research in mental retardation* (Vol. 12, pp. 178–203). Orlando: Academic.

Fagan, J. (1995). Separating the men from the boys: The comparative advantage of juvenile versus criminal court sanctions on recidivism among adolescent felony offenders. In J. C. Howell, B. Krisberg, J. D. Hawkins, & J. J. Wilson (Eds.), *A sourcebook: Serious, violent, and chronic juvenile offenders* (pp. 238–260). Thousand Oaks CA: Sage.

Farber, B. (1968). *Mental retardation: Its social context and social consequences.* Boston: Houghton.

Farrington, D. P. (1995). The challenge of teenage antisocial behavior. In M. Rutter (Ed.), *Psychosocial disturbances in young people: Challenges for prevention* (pp. 83–130). Cambridge, England: Cambridge University Press.

Fernald, C. D. (1986). Changing Medicaid and intermediate care facilities for the mentally retarded: Evaluation of alternatives. *Mental Retardation, 24*, 36–42.

Fineberg, B. L., Kettlewell, P. W., & Sowards, S. K. (1982). An evaluation of adolescent inpatient services. *American Journal of Orthopsychiatry, 52*, 337–345.

Flomenhaft, K. (1974). Outcome of treatment for adolescents. *Adolescence, 9*, 57–66.

Forness, S. R., & Knitzer, J. (1992). A new proposed definition and terminology to replace "serious emotional disturbance" in Individuals with Disabilities Education Act. *School Psychology Review, 21*, 12–20.

Fotheringham, J. B. (1970, January/February). Retardation, family adequacy and institutionalization. *Canada's Mental Health*, pp. 15–18.

Frank, R. G., & Dewa, C. S. (1992). Insurance, system structure, and the use of mental health services by children and adolescents. *Clinical Psychology Review, 12*, 829–840.

Frank, R. G., & Kamlet, M. S. (1985). Direct costs and expenditures for mental health care in the United States in 1980. *Hospital and Community Psychiatry, 36*, 165–168.

Friesen, B. J., & Koroloff, N. M. (1990). Family-centered services: Implications for mental health administration and research. *Journal of Mental Health Administration, 17*, 13–25.

Frohboese, R., & Sales, B. D. (1980). Parental opposition to deinstitutionalization: A challenge in need of attention and resolution. *Law and Human Behavior, 4*, 1–87.

GAO. (1977). *Returning the mentally disabled to the community: Government needs to do more* (Report No. GAO/HRD-76-152). Washington DC: Author.

GAO. (1985a). *Residential care: Patterns of child placement in three states* (Report No. GAO/PEMD-85-2). Washington DC: Author.

GAO. (1985b). *Review of certain aspects of group home care for children in California* (Report No. GAO/HRD-85-62). Washington DC: Author.

Garbarino, J. (1995). Growing up in a socially toxic environment: Life for children and families in the 1990s. In G. B. Melton (Ed.), *Nebraska Symposium on Motivation: Vol. 42. The individual, the family, and social good: Personal fulfillment in times of change* (pp. 1–20). Lincoln: University of Nebraska Press.

Gardner, W., Scherer, D., & Tester, M. (1989). Asserting scientific authority: Cognitive development and adolescent legal rights. *American Psychologist, 44*, 895–902.

Gardos, G., & Cole, J. O. (1980). Overview: Public health issues in tardive dyskinesia. *American Journal of Psychiatry, 137*, 776–781.

Garland, A. F., & Besinger, B. A. (1996). Adolescents' perceptions of outpatient mental health services. *Journal of Child and Family Studies, 5*, 355–375.

Gary W. v. State of Louisiana, 437 F. Supp. 1209 (E.D. La. 1976).

Geis v. Board of Education, 589 F. Supp. 269 (D.N.J. 1984).

Gilboy, J. A., & Schmidt, J. R. (1971). "Voluntary" hospitalization of the mentally ill. *Northwestern University Law Review, 66*, 429–453.

Ginsburg, K. R., Slap, G. B., Cnaan, A., Forke, C. M., Balsley, C. M., & Rouselle, D. M. (1995). Adolescents' perceptions of factors affecting their decisions to seek health care. *Journal of the American Medical Association, 273*, 1913–1918.

Goffman, E. (1961). *Asylums*. New York: Doubleday.

Golan, M. B. (1978). *Privacy, interaction, and self-esteem*. Unpublished doctoral dissertation, City University of New York.

Gold, L. J., Darley, J. M., Hilton, J. L., & Zanna, M. P. (1984). Children's perceptions of procedural justice. *Child Development, 55*, 1752–1759.

Goren, S., Singh, N. N., & Best, A. M. (1993). The Aggression-Coercion cycle: Use of seclusion and restraint in a child psychiatric hospital. *Journal of Child and Family Studies, 2*, 61–73.

Goss v. Lopez, 419 U.S. 565 (1975).

Gould, M. S., Wunsch-Hitzig, R., & Dohrenwend, B. (1981). Estimating the prevalence of childhood psychopathology: A critical review. *Journal of the American Academy of Child Psychiatry, 20*, 462–476.

Gray, J. N., Lyons, P. M., Jr., & Melton, G. B. (1995). *Ethical and legal issues in AIDS research*. Baltimore: Johns Hopkins University Press.

Grisso, T. (1993, November). *Developing challenges to a retributive legal response to adolescent homicide*. Browning Hoffman Lecture presented at the University of Virginia, Institute of Law, Psychiatry, and Public Policy.

Grisso, T., & Appelbaum, P. S. (1995). The MacArthur treatment competence study III: Abilities of patients to consent to psychiatric and medical treatments. *Law and Human Behavior, 19*, 149–174.

Grisso, T., Appelbaum, P. S., Mulvey, E. P., & Fletcher, K. (1995). The MacArthur treatment competence study II: Measures of abilities related to competence to consent to treatment. *Law and Human Behavior, 19*, 127–148.

Grisso, T., & Vierling, L. (1978). Minors' consent to treatment: A developmental perspective. *Professional Psychology: Research and Practice, 9*, 412–427.

Grossman, F. K. (1972). *Brothers and sisters of retarded children: An exploratory study*. Syracuse NY: Syracuse University Press.

Gualtieri, C. T., & Hawk, B. (1980). Tardive dyskinesia and other drug-induced movement disorders among handicapped children and youth. *Applied Research in Mental Retardation, 1,* 55–69.

Gualtieri, C. T., Schroeder, S. R., Hicks, R. E., & Quade, D. (1986). Tardive dyskinesia in young mentally retarded individuals. *Archives of General Psychiatry, 43,* 335–340.

Gualtieri, C. T., Quade, D., Hicks, R. E., Mayo, J. P., & Schroeder, S. R. (1984). Tardive dyskinesia and other clinical consequences of neuroleptic treatment in children and adolescents. *American Journal of Psychiatry, 141,* 20–23.

Gudeman, J. E., Dickey, B., Evans, A., & Shore, M. F. (1985). Four-year assessment of a day hospital-inn program as an alternative to inpatient hospitalization. *American Journal of Psychiatry, 142,* 1330–1333.

Gutkind, L. (1993). *Stuck in time: The tragedy of childhood mental illness.* New York: Henry Holt.

Halderman v. Pennhurst State School & Hospital, 610 F. Supp. 1221 (E.D. Pa. 1985).

Halpern, J., Sackett, K. L., Binner, P. R., & Mohr, C. B. (1980). *The myths of deinstitutionalization: Policies for the mentally disabled.* Boulder CO: Westview.

Hargrove, D. S., & Melton, G. B. (1987). Block grants and rural mental health services. *Journal of Rural Community Psychology, 8,* 4–11.

Hawkins, J. D., & Catalano, R. F., Jr. (1993). *Risk-focused prevention using the social development strategy.* Seattle WA: Development Research and Programs, Inc.

Hawkins, R. P., Meadowcroft, P., Trout, B. A., & Luster, W. C. (1985). Foster family-based treatment. *Journal of Clinical Child Psychology, 14,* 220–228.

Henggeler, S. W. (1989). *Delinquency in Adolescence.* Newbury Park CA: Sage.

Henggeler, S. W., & Borduin, C. M. (1995). Multisystemic treatment of serious juvenile offenders and their families. In I. M. Schwartz & P. AuClaire. (Eds.), *Home-based services for troubled children* (pp. 113–130). Lincoln: University of Nebraska Press.

Henggeler, S. W., Melton, G. B., & Smith, L. A. (1992). Family preservation using multisystemic therapy: An effective alternative to incarcerating serious juvenile offenders. *Journal of Consulting and Clinical Psychology, 60,* 953–961.

Henggeler, S. W., Melton, G. B., Smith, L. A., Schoenwald, S. K., & Hanley, J. H. (1993). Family preservation using multisystemic treatment: Long-term follow-up to a clinical trial with serious juvenile offenders. *Journal of Child and Family Studies, 2,* 283–293.

Henggeler, S. W., Schoenwald, S. K., Pickrel, S. G., Rowland, M. D., & Santos, A. B. (1994). The contribution of treatment outcome research to the reform of children's mental health services: Multisystemic therapy as an example. *Journal of Mental Health Administration, 21,* 229–239.

Herbsleb, J. (1980). Institutionalization of juveniles: What process is due? *Nebraska Law Review, 59,* 190–213.

Herskowitz, J. (1987). Developmental toxicology. In C. Popper (Ed.), *Psychiatric pharmacosciences of children and adolescents* (pp. 81–123). Washington DC: American Psychiatric Press.

Hetherington, E. M., & Martin, B. (1979). Family interaction. In H. C. Quay & J. S. Werry (Eds.), *Psychopathological disorders of childhood* (2nd ed., pp. 247–302). New York: Wiley.

Heying, K. R. (1985). Family-based in-home services for the severely emotionally disturbed child. *Child Welfare, 64,* 519–527.

Hinckley, E. C., & Ellis, W. F. (1985). An effective alternative to residential placement: Home-based services. *Journal of Clinical Child Psychology, 14,* 209–213.

Hoagwood, K., & Cunningham, M. (1992). Outcomes of children with emotional disturbance in residential treatment for educational purposes. *Journal of Child and Family Studies, 1,* 129–140.

Hobbs, N. (1975). *The futures of children: Categories, labels, and their consequences.* San Francisco: Jossey-Bass.

Hobbs, N. (1982). *The troubled and troubling child: Reeducation in mental health, education, and human services programs for children and youth.* San Francisco: Jossey-Bass.

Hoffman, P. B., & Foust, L. L. (1977). Least restrictive treatment of the mentally ill: A doctrine in search of its senses. *San Diego Law Review, 14,* 1100–1154.

Hoge, M. A., Davidson, L., Hill, W. L., Turner, V. E., et al. (1992). The promise of partial hospitalization: A reassessment. *Hospital and Community Psychiatry, 43*, 345–354.

Hoge, S., Lidz, C., Eisenberg, M., Gardner, W., Monahan, J., Mulvey, E., Roth, L., & Bennett, N. (1994). *Coercion in the admission of voluntary and involuntary psychiatric patients.* Unpublished manuscript. (Available from Western Psychiatric Institute and Clinic, Law and Psychiatry Research Program, 3501 Forbes Ave, 7th Floor, Pittsburgh PA 15213.)

Holmes, D. S., & Urie, R. G. (1975). Effects of preparing children for psychotherapy. *Journal of Consulting and Clinical Psychology, 43*, 311–318.

House Select Committee on Children, Youth, and Families. (1985, June 6). *Emerging trends in mental health care for adolescents.* Oversight hearing.

Howell, J. C., Krisberg, B., & Jones, M. (1995). Trends in juvenile crime and youth violence. In J. Howell, B. Krisberg, J. Hawkins, & John Wilson (Eds.), *A sourcebook on serious, violent, & chronic juvenile offenders* (pp. 1–35). Thousand Oaks CA: Sage.

Humphrey v. Cady, 405 U.S. 504 (1972).

Huxley, P. (1990–91). Effective case management for mentally ill people: The relevance of recent evidence from the USA for case management services in the United Kingdom. *Social Work and Social Sciences Review, 2*, 192–203.

Hyde, K. L., Burchard, J. D., & Woodworth, K. (1996). Wrapping services in an urban setting. *Journal of Child and Family Studies, 5*, 67–82.

In re Gault, 387 U.S. 1 (1967).

In re Roger S., 19 Cal. 921 (1977).

Individuals with Disabilities Education Act, Pub. L. No. 101-476 (1990), 20 U.S.C.A. 1400–1485 (West Supp. 1991). [Originally enacted as the Education of the Handicapped Act and subsequently known as the Education for All Handicapped Children Act, first enacted in 1975. Name change to IDEA was enacted by Pub. L. No. 101-476 and required no change in text.]

Irving Independent School District v. Tatro, 468 U.S. 883 (1984).

J. L. v. Parham, 412 F. Supp. 112 (M.D. Ga. 1976), *reversed sub. nom.* Parham v. J. R., 442 U.S. 584 (1979).

Jackson-Beeck, M., Schwartz, I. M., & Rutherford, A. (1987a). *Trends and issues in juvenile confinement for psychiatric and chemical dependency treatment in the U.S., England, and Wales.* Minneapolis: University of Minnesota, Center for the Study of Youth Policy.

Jackson-Beeck, M., Schwartz, I. M., & Rutherford, A. (1987b). Trends and isssues in juvenile confinement for psychiatric and chemical dependency treatment. *International Journal of Law and Psychiatry, 10*, 153–165.

Jacobson v. Massachusetts, 197 U.S. 11 (1905).

Joint Commission on the Mental Health of Children. (1969). *Crisis in child mental health: Challenge for the 1970's.* New York: Harper & Row.

Jones v. United States, 463 U.S. 354 (1983).

Joyner v. Dumpson, 712 F.2d 770 (2d. Cir. 1983).

Juvenile Justice and Delinquency Prevention Act of 1974, Pub. L. No. 93-415, 88 Stat. 1109 (1974), codified as amended at 42 U.S.C. § 5601 et. seq. (1988 & Supp. V 1994).

Kalachnik, J. E. (1984). Tardive dyskinesia and the mentally retarded: A review. In S. E. Breuning, J. L. Matson, & R. P. Barrett (Eds.), *Advances in mental retardation and developmental disabilities* (Vol. 2, pp. 329–356). Greenwich CT: JAI.

Kaser-Boyd, N., Adelman, H. S., & Taylor, L. (1985). Minors' ability to identify risks and benefits of therapy. *Professional Psychology Research and Practice, 16*, 411–417.

Kashani, J. H., & Cantwell, D. P. (1983). Characteristics of children admitted to inpatient community mental health center. *Archives of General Psychiatry, 40*, 397–400.

Katz, J. (1984). *The silent world of doctor and patient.* New York: Free Press.

Katz, M. B. (1986). *In the shadow of the poorhouse: A social history of welfare in America.* New York: Basic Books.

Kazdin, A. E. (1986). Acceptability of psychotherapy and hospitalization for disturbed children: Parent and child perspectives. *Journal of Clinical Child Psychology, 15*, 333–340.

Keiter, R. B. (1982). Privacy, children, and their parents: Reflections on and beyond the Supreme Court's approach. *Minnesota Law Review, 66*, 459–518.

Kettlewell, P. W., Jones, J. K., & Jones, R. H. (1985). Adolescent partial hospitalization: Some preliminary outcome data. *Journal of Clinical Child Psychology, 14,* 139–144.

Kiesler, C. A. (1980). Mental health policy as a field of inquiry for psychology. *American Psychologist, 35,* 1066–1080.

Kiesler, C. A. (1982a). Mental hospitals and alternative care: Noninstitutionalization as potential public policy for mental patients. *American Psychologist, 37,* 349–360.

Kiesler, C. A. (1982b). Public and professional myths about mental hospitalization: An empirical reassessment of policy related beliefs. *American Psychologist, 37,* 1323–1339.

Kiesler, C. A. (1993). Mental health policy and the psychiatric inpatient care of children. *Applied and Preventive Psychology, 2,* 91–99.

Kiesler, C. A. (1994). Mental health policy and the psychiatric inpatient care of children: Implications for families. In J. Blacher (Ed.), *When there's no place like home: Options for children living apart from their natural families* (pp. 101–120). Baltimore: Paul H. Brookes.

Kiesler, C. A., & Sibulkin, A. (1987). *Mental hospitalization: Myths and facts about a national crisis.* Newbury Park CA: Sage.

Kirk v. Thomas S., 476 U.S. 1124 (1986).

Klein, R. G. (1991). Parent-child agreement in clinical assessment of anxiety and other psychopathology: A review. *Journal of Anxiety Disorders, 5,* 187–198.

Knitzer, J. (1982). *Unclaimed children: The failure of public responsibility to children and adolescents in need of mental health services.* Washington DC: Children's Defense Fund.

Knitzer, J. (1984). Mental health services to children and adolescents: A national view of public policies. *American Psychologist, 39,* 905–911.

Knitzer, J., Allen, M. L., & McGowan, B. (1978). *Children without homes: An examination of public responsibility to children in out-of-home care.* Washington DC: Children's Defense Fund.

Kobrin, S., & Klein, M. W. (1983). *Community treatment of juvenile offenders: The DSO experiments.* Beverly Hills CA: Sage.

Koocher, G. P. (1983). Competence to consent: Psychotherapy. In G. B.

Melton, G. P. Koocher, & M. J. Saks (Eds.), *Children's competence to consent* (pp. 111–128). New York: Plenum.

Krisberg, B. A., Litsky, P., & Schwartz, I. M. (1984). Justice by geography. *Journal of Research in Crime and Delinquency, 21*, 153–181.

Krisberg, B. A., Onek, D., Jones, M., & Schwartz, I. M. (1993). *Juveniles in state custody: Prospects for community-based care of troubled adolescents.* San Francisco: National Council on Crime and Delinquency.

Krisberg, B. A., & Schwartz, I. M. (1983). Rethinking juvenile justice. *Crime and Delinquency, 29*, 333–364.

Krisberg, B. A., Schwartz, I. M., Litsky, P., & Austin, J. (1986). The watershed of juvenile justice reform. *Crime and Delinquency, 32*, 5–38.

Kugel, R. B., & Shearer, A. (1976). *Changing patterns in residential services for the mentally retarded* (rev. ed.). Washington DC: President's Commission on Mental Retardation.

Lahey, B. B., & Kupfer, D. L. (1979). Partial hospitalization programs for children and adolescents. In R. F. Luber (Ed.), *Partial hospitalization: A current perspective* (pp. 73–90). New York: Plenum.

Lake v. Cameron, 331 F.2d 771 (DC Cir. 1964).

Latib, A., Conroy, J., & Hess, C. M. (1984). Family attitudes toward deinstitutionalization. In N. R. Ells & N. W. Bray (Eds.), *International review of research in mental retardation* (Vol. 12, pp. 67–91). Orlando FL: Academic.

Lee, S. (1994). *Heller v. Doe:* Involuntary civil commitment and the "objective" language of probability, *American Journal of Law and Medicine, 20*, 457–477.

Lerman, P. (1980). Trends and issues in the deinstitutionalization of youths in trouble. *Crime and Delinquency, 26*, 281–298.

Lessard v. Schmidt, 349 F. Supp. 1078 (E.D. Wis. 1972), *vacated and remanded,* 414 U.S. 437 (1974), *on remand,* 379 F. Supp. 1376 (E.D. Wis. 1974), *vacated and remanded on appeal,* 421 U.S. 957 (1975).

Levenson, A. I. (1983). Issues surrounding the ownership of private psychiatric hospitals by investor-owned hospital chains. *Hospital and Community Psychiatry, 34*, 1127–1131.

Levine, M., & Levine, A. (1992). *Helping children: A social history.* New York: Oxford University Press.

Leviton, S. P., & Shuger, N. B. (1983). Maryland's exchangeable children: A critique of Maryland's system of providing services to mentally handicapped children, *Maryland Law Review, 42,* 823–863.

Levitt, E. E., (1971). Research on psychotherapy with children. In A. E. Bergin & S. L. Garfield (Eds.), *Handbook of psychotherapy and behavior change: An empirical analysis* (pp. 474–494). New York: Wiley.

Lewis, C. E. (1983). Decision making related to health: When could/should children act responsibly? In G. B. Melton, G. P. Koocher, & M. J. Saks (Eds.), *Children's competence to consent* (pp. 75–91). New York: Plenum.

Lewis, C. E., & Lewis, M. A. (1983). Improving the health of children: Must the children be involved? *Annual Review of Public Health, 4,* 259–283.

Lewis, D. O., & Shanok, S. S. (1981). Racial factors influencing the diagnosis, disposition, and treatment of deviant adolescents. In D. O. Lewis (Ed.), *Vulnerabilities to delinquency* (pp. 295–311). New York: Spectrum.

Lidz, C. W., Gross, E., Meisel, A., & Roth, L. H. (1980). The rights of juveniles in "voluntary" psychiatric commitments: Some empirical observations. *Bulletin of the American Academy of Psychiatry and the Law, 8,* 168–174.

Lidz, C. W., Meisel, A., Zerubavel, E., Carter, M., Sestak, R. M., & Roth, L. H. (1984). *Informed consent: A study of decisionmaking in psychiatry.* New York: Guilford.

Lind, E. A., & Tyler, T. (1988). *The social psychology of procedural justice.* New York: Plenum.

Lipman, R. S. (1982). Psychotropic drugs in mental retardation: The known and the unknown. In K. D. Gadow & I. Bialer (Eds.), *Advances in learning and behavioral disabilities* (Vol. 1, pp. 261–282). Greenwich CT: JAI.

Lipsey, M. W. (1992). Juvenile delinquency treatment: A meta-analytic inquiry into the variability of effects. In T. Cook, H. Cooper, D. Cordray, H. Hartmann, L. Hedges, R. Kight, T. Louis, & F. Mosteller (Eds.), *Meta-analysis for explanation* (pp. 83–127). New York: Sage.

Loeber, R., Green, S. M., Lahey, B. B., & Stouthamer-Loeber, M. (1990). Optimal informants on childhood disruptive behaviors. *Development and Psychopathology, 1,* 317–337.

Loeber, R., & Stouthamer-Loeber, M. (1986). Family factors as correlates and predictors of juvenile conduct problems and delinquency. In M. Tonry & N. Morris (Eds.), *Crime and justice* (Vol. 7, pp. 29–149). Chicago: University of Chicago Press.

Loff, C. D., Trigg, L. J., & Cassels, C. (1987). An evaluation of consumer satisfaction in a child psychiatric service: Viewpoints of patients and parents. *American Journal of Orthopsychiatry, 57*, 132–134.

Lora v. Board of Education, 74 F.R.D. 565 (E.D.N.Y. 1977).

Lundy, M., & Pumariega, A. J. (1993). Psychiatric hospitalization of children and adolescents: Treatment in search of a rationale. *Journal of Child and Family Studies, 2*, 1–4.

Lyman, R. D., Prentice-Dunn, S., Wilson, D. R., & Taylor, G. E., Jr. (1989). Issues in residential and inpatient treatment. In R. Lyman, S. Prentice-Dunn and S. Gabel (Eds.), *Residential and inpatient treatment of children and adolescents* (pp. 3–22). New York: Plenum.

Maluccio, A. N., & Marlow, W. D. (1972). Residential treatment of emotionally disturbed children: A review of the literature. *Social Service Review, 46*, 230–250.

Manchester School District v. Charles M. F. and Ellen P., 1994 W.L. 485754 (D.N.H. 1994).

Marder, S. R., & Van Putten, T. (1995). Antipsychotic medications. In Alan F. Schatzberg & Charles B. Nemeroff (Eds.), *The American Psychiatric Press textbook of psychopharmacology* (pp. 247–261). Washington DC: American Psychiatric Press.

Marsden, G., McDermott, J. F., & Minor, D. (1977). Selection of children for residential treatment: A study of evaluation procedures and decision making. *Journal of the American Academy of Child Psychiatry, 16*, 427–438.

Martin, J. E., & Agran, M. (1985). Psychotropic and anticonvulsant drug use by mentally retarded adults across community residential and vocational placements. *Applied Research in Mental Retardation, 6*, 33–49.

Mary and Crystal v. Ramsden, 635 F.2d 590 (7th Cir. 1980).

Mashaw, J. L. (1983). *Bureaucratic justice: Managing social security disability claims.* New Haven CT: Yale University Press.

Massimo, J. L., & Shore, M. F. (1963). The effectiveness of a vocationally oriented psychotherapy. *American Journal of Orthopsychiatry, 33*, 634–643.

Mathews v. Eldridge, 424 U.S. 319 (1976).

McCoy, S. A. (1976). Clinical judgments of normal childhood behavior. *Journal of Consulting and Clinical Psychology, 44*, 710–714.

McEwen, C. A. (1980). Continuities in the study of total and nontotal institutions. *Annual Review of Sociology, 6*, 143–185.

McKinney, J. P., Chin, R. J., Reinhart, M. A., & Trierweiler, G. (1985). Health values in early adolescence. *Journal of Clinical Child Psychology, 14*, 315–319.

Meeks, J. E. (1995). Hospitalization and inpatient treatment. In G. Pirooz Sholevar (Ed.), *Conduct disorders in children and adolescents* (pp. 299–317). Washington DC: American Psychiatric Press.

Meisel, A. (1979). The "exceptions" to the informed consent doctrine: Striking a balance between competing values in medical decisionmaking. *Wisconsin Law Review, 1979*, 413–488.

Meisel, A., & Roth, L. H. (1976). The child's right to object to hospitalization: Some empirical data. *Journal of Psychiatry and Law, 4*, 377–392.

Melton, G. B. (1977). The psychologist as clinician-advocate: Issues in practice and training. *Journal of Clinical Child Psychology, 6*, 27–29.

Melton, G. B. (1981). Children's participation in treatment planning: Psychological and legal issues. *Professional Psychology: Research and Practice, 12*, 246–252.

Melton, G. B. (1983a). *Child advocacy: Psychological issues and interventions.* New York: Plenum.

Melton, G. B. (1983b). Children's competence to consent: A problem in law and social science. In G. B. Melton, G. P. Koocher, & M. Saks (Eds.), *Children's competence to consent* (pp. 1–18). New York: Plenum.

Melton, G. B. (1983c). Decision making by children: Psychological risks and benefits. In G. B. Melton, G. P. Koocher, & M. Saks (Eds.), *Children's competence to consent* (pp. 21–40). New York: Plenum.

Melton, G. B. (1983d). Minors and privacy: Are legal and psychological concepts compatible? *Nebraska Law Review, 62*, 455–493.

Melton, G. B. (1983e). Toward "personhood" for adolescents: Autonomy and privacy as values in public policy. *American Psychologist, 38*, 99–103.

Melton, G. B. (1984a). Developmental psychology and the law: The state of the art. *Journal of Family Law, 22*, 445–482.

Melton, G. B. (1984b). Family and mental hospital as myths: Civil commitment of minors. In N. D. Reppucci, L. A. Weithorn, E. P. Mulvey, & J. Monahan (Eds.), *Children, mental health, and the law* (pp. 151–167). Beverly Hills CA: Sage.

Melton, G. B. (1987a). Children, politics, and morality: The ethics of child advocacy. *Journal of Clinical Child Psychology, 16*, 357–367.

Melton, G. B. (1987b). The clashing of symbols: Prelude to child and family policy. *American Psychologist, 42*, 345–354.

Melton, G. B. (1989). Are adolescents people? Problems of liberty, entitlement, and responsibility. In J. Worell & F. Danner (Eds.), *The adolescent as decision-maker: Applications to development and education* (pp. 281–306). San Diego CA: Academic Press.

Melton, G. B. (1993a). Children, families, and the courts in the twenty-first century. *Southern California Law Review, 66*, 1993–2047.

Melton, G. B. (1993b). Is there a place for children in the new world order? *Notre Dame Journal of Law, Ethics and Public Policy, 7*, 491–532.

Melton, G. B. (1995). Introduction: Personal satisfaction and the welfare of families, communities, and society. In G. B. Melton (Ed.), *Nebraska Symposium on Motivation: Vol. 42. The individual, the family, and social good: Personal fulfillment in times of change* (pp. ix–xxvii). Lincoln: University of Nebraska Press.

Melton, G. B. (1996). The child's right to a family environment: Why children's rights and family values are compatible. *American Psychologist, 51*, 1234–1238.

Melton, G. B., & Davidson, H. A. (1987). Child protection and society: When should the state intervene? *American Psychologist, 42*, 172–175.

Melton, G. B., Koocher, G. P., & Saks, M. J. (Eds.). (1983). *Children's competence to consent.* New York: Plenum.

Melton, G. B., & Lind, E. A. (1982). Procedural justice in family court: Does the adversary model make sense? In G. B. Melton (Ed.), *Legal reforms affecting child and youth services* (pp. 65–83). New York: Haworth.

Melton, G. B., Petrila, J., Poythress, N. G., & Slobogin, C. (1997). *Psychological evaluations for the courts: A handbook for mental health professionals and lawyers* (2nd ed.). New York: Guilford.

Melton, G. B., & Pagliocca, P. (1992). Treatment in the juvenile justice system: Directions for policy and practice. In J. J. Cocozza (Ed.), *Responding to the mental health needs of youth in the juvenile justice system* (pp. 107–139). Seattle WA: National Coalition for the Mentally Ill in the Criminal Justice System.

Melton, G. B., & Saks, M. J. (1985). The law as an instrument of socialization and social structure. In G. B. Melton (Ed.), *Nebraska Symposium on Motivation: Vol. 33. The law as a behavioral instrument* (pp. 235–277). Lincoln: University of Nebraska Press.

Merriken v. Cressman, 364 F. Supp. 913 (E.D. Pa. 1973).

Mill, J. S. (1947). *On liberty.* Arlington Heights IL: AHM. (Original work published 1859)

Milazzo-Sayre, L. J., Benson, P. R., Rosenthal, M. J., & Manderscheid, R. W. (1986). *Use of in-patient psychiatric facilities by children and youth under 18, United States, 1980.* Statistical Note No. 175. Rockville MD: National Institute of Mental Health.

Miller, R. B., & Kenney, E. (1966). Adolescent delinquency and the myth of hospital treatment. *Crime and Delinquency, 12,* 38–48.

Miller, W. R., & Hester, R. W. (1986). Inpatient alcoholism treatment: Who benefits? *American Psychologist, 41,* 794–805.

Mills v. Rogers, 457 U.S. 291 (1982), *vacating and remanding sub. nom.* Rogers v. Okin, 634 F.2d 650 (1st Cir. 1980).

Milonas v. Williams, 691 F.2d 931 (10th Cir. 1982).

Minkin, E. B., Stoline, A. M., & Sharfstein, S. S. (1994). An analysis of the two-class system of care in public and private psychiatric hospitals. *Hospital and Community Psychiatry, 45,* 975–977.

Mirin, S. M., & Sederer, L. I. (1994). Mental health care: Current realities, future expectations. *Psychiatric Quarterly, 65,* 161–175.

Mnookin, R. H. (1973). Foster care: In whose best interest? *Harvard Educational Review, 43,* 594–638.

Mnookin, R. H. (1978). *Child, family and state: Problems and materials on children and the law.* Boston: Little, Brown.

Monahan, J., Hoge, S. K., Lidz, C. W., Eisenberg, M. M., Bennett, N. S., Gardner, W. P., Mulvey, E. P., & Roth, L. H. (1996). Coercion to inpatient treatment: Initial results and implications for assertive treatment in the community. In Deborah L. Dennis & John Monahan (Eds.), *Coercion and aggressive community treatment* (pp. 13–28). New York: Plenum.

Mordock, J. B. (1990). Funding children's mental health services in an underfunded climate: Collaborative efforts. *Journal of Mental Health Administration, 17*, 108–114.

Morse, S. J. (1978). Crazy behavior, morals, and science: An analysis of mental health law. *Southern California Law Review, 51*, 527–653.

Morse, S. J. (1982). A preference for liberty: The case against involuntary commitment of the mentally disordered. *California Law Review, 70*, 54–106.

Morse, S. J. (1985). *Cases and materials on mental health law*. Unpublished manuscript, University of Southern California Law Center.

Mowbray, C. T. (1992). The role of evaluation in the restructuring of the public mental health system. *Evaluation and Program Planning, 15*, 403–415.

Mulvey, E. P., & Peeples, F. L. (1996). Are disturbed and normal adolescents equally competent to make decisions about mental health treatment? *Law and Human Behavior, 20*, 273–287.

Mulvey, E. P., & Pieffer, M. (1993). A comparison of perceptions regarding the process of institutional placement. *Journal of Mental Health Administration, 20*, 254–263.

Mulvey, E. P., Arthur, M., & Reppucci, N. D. (1993). The prevention and treatment of juvenile delinquency: A review of the research. *Clinical Psychology Review, 13*, 133–157.

Myers, J. E. B. (1990). The child sexual abuse literature: A call for greater objectivity, *Michigan Law Review, 88*, 1709–1733.

National Commission for the Protection of Human Subjects in Biomedical and Behavioral Research. (1979). *The Belmont Report: Ethical Principles and Guidelines for the Protection of Human Subjects of Research* (DHEW publication (OS) 78-0012). Washington DC: Department of Health, Education, and Welfare.

National Research Council, Panel on High-Risk Youth. (1993). *Losing generations: Adolescents in high-risk settings*. Washington DC: National Academy Press.

New York State Association for Retarded Children, Inc. v. Rockefeller, 357 F. Supp. 752 (E.D. N.Y. 1973).

Note. (1984). Assessing the scope of minors' fundamental rights: Juvenile curfews and the Constitution. *Harvard Law Review, 97,* 1163–1181.

Numbers of handicapped children cited. (1985). *Update: Improving Services for Emotionally Disturbed Children, 1,* 3.

O'Connor v. Donaldson, 422 U.S. 563 (1975), *vacating and remanding* Donaldson v. O'Connor 493 F.2d 507 (5th Cir. 1974).

Office of Human Development Services. (1985). FY 1986 coordinated discretionary funds program; availability of funds and request for applications. *Federal Register, 50,* 35, 906–35, 953.

Okin, R. L. (1984). *Brewster v. Dukakis:* Developing community services through use of a consent decree. *American Journal of Psychiatry, 141,* 786–789.

Okin, R. L. (1985a). Expand the community care system: Deinstitutionalization can work. *Hospital and Community Psychiatry, 36,* 742–745.

Okin, R. L. (1985b). Variation among state hospitals in use of seclusion and restraint. *Hospital and Community Psychiatry, 36,* 648–652.

Olsen, L. (1981). *A point in time study of children and adolescents in state hospitals.* Unpublished manuscript, Massachusetts Department of Mental Health.

Owens, M. J., & Risch, S. C. (1995). Atypical antipsychotics. In Alan F. Schatzberg & Charles B. Nemeroff (Eds.), *The American Psychiatric Press textbook of psychopharmacology* (pp. 263–280). Washington DC: American Psychiatric Press.

Pandiani, J. A., Maynard, A., & Schacht, L. (1994). Mathematical modeling of movement between residential placements: A systems analytic approach to understanding systems of care. *Journal of Child and Family Studies, 3,* 41–53.

Parham v. J. R., 442 U.S. 584 (1979), *reversing sub. nom.* J. L. v. Parham, 412 F. Supp. 112 (M.D. Ga. 1976).

Parmelee, D. X., Cohen, R., Nemil, M., Best, A. M., Casell, S., & Dyson, F. (1995). Children and adolescents discharged from public psychiatric hospitals: Evaluation of outcome in a continuum of care. *Journal of Child and Family Studies, 4,* 43–55.

Parratt v. Taylor, 451 U.S. 527 (1981).

Pattison, R. V., & Katz, H. M. (1983). Investor-owned and not-for-profit hospitals: A comparison based on California data. *New England Journal of Medicine, 309*, 347–353.

Perlin, M. (1981). An invitation to the dance: An empirical response to Chief Justice Warren Burger's "time-consuming procedural minuets" theory in *Parham v. J. R. Bulletin of the American Academy of Psychiatry and Law, 9*, 149–164.

Perlmuter, L. C., & Monty, R. A. (Eds.). (1979). *Choice and perceived control*. Hillsdale NJ: Erlbaum.

Perry, G. S., & Melton, G. B. (1984). Precedential value of judicial notice of social facts: *Parham* as an example. *Journal of Family Law, 22*, 633–676.

Piersma, H. L. (1986–1987). Patient comments concerning psychiatric hospitalization. *Psychiatric Quarterly, 58*, 32–41.

Pilewski, M. E., & Heal, L. W. (1980). Empirical support for deinstitutionalization. In A. R. Novak & L. W. Heal (Eds.), *Integration of developmentally disabled individuals into the community* (pp. 21–34). Baltimore: Paul H. Brookes.

Planned Parenthood of Cent. Mo. v. Danforth, 428 U.S 52 (1976).

Poulos, T. M., & Orchowsky, S. O. (1994). Serious juvenile offenders: Predicting the probability of transfer to criminal court. *Crime and Delinquency, 40*, 3–17.

Poythress, N. G., Jr. (1978). Psychiatric expertise in civil commitment: Training attorneys to cope with expert testimony. *Law and Human Behavior, 2*, 1–24.

Prentice-Dunn, S., Wilson, D. R., & Lyman, R. D. (1981). Client factors related to outcome in a residential and day treatment program for children. *Journal of Clinical Child Psychology, 10*, 188–191.

President's Commission on Mental Health. (1978). *Report of the sub-task panel on infants, children, and adolescents: Vol. 3. Reports to the President of the President's Commission on Mental Health* (PCMH Publication No. P-78/12). Washington DC: U.S. Government Printing Office.

Prince v. Massachusetts, 321 U.S. 158, 166 (1944).

Program update: Home-based services. (1985). *Update: Improving Services for Emotionally Disturbed Children, 1*, 6–7.

Quay, H. C. (1979). Classification. In H. C. Quay & J. S. Werry (Eds.), *Psychopathological disorders of childhood* (2nd ed., pp. 1–42). New York: Wiley.

Quay, H. C. (1984). The opinions of mental health facility administrators on the effects of children's rights and deinstitutionalization. *Journal of Early Adolescence, 4*, 11–23.

Quay, H. C. (1986). A critical analysis of DSM-III as a taxonomy of psychopathology in childhood and adolescence. In T. Millon & G. Klerman (Eds.), *Contemporary directions in psychopathology: Toward the DSM-IV* (pp. 151–165). New York: Guilford.

Ransohoff, P., Zachary, R. A., Gaynor, J., & Hargreaves, W. A. (1982). Measuring restrictiveness of psychiatric care. *Hospital and Community Psychiatry, 33*, 361–366.

Rapley, M., & Baldwin, S. (1995). Normalisation: Metatheory or metaphysics: A conceptual critique. *Australian and New Zealand Journal of Developmental Disabilities, 20*, 141–157.

Rawls, J. (1971). *A theory of justice.* Cambridge MA: Harvard University Press.

Redding, R. E. (1993). Children's competence to provide consent to mental health treatment. *Washington and Lee Law Review, 50*, 695–751.

Relman, A. S. (1983). Investor-owned hospitals and health-care costs. *New England Journal of Medicine, 309*, 370–372.

Rennie v. Klein, 653 F.2d 836 (3d Cir. 1981), *vacated and remanded* 458 U.S. 1119 (1982).

Reppucci, N. D., & Crosby, C. A. (1993). Law, psychology, and children: Overarching issues. *Law and Human Behavior, 17*, 1–10.

Reppucci, N. D., Woolard, J. L., & Redding, R. E. (Eds.). (1996). Children's capacities in legal contexts. *Law and Human Behavior, 20*(3).

Richards, D. A. J. (1980). The individual, the family and the Constitution: A jurisprudential perspective. *New York University Law Review, 55*, 1–62.

Richardson, M. A., & Haugland, G. (1996). Typicality and atypicality in the development of neuroleptic side effects in child and adolescent psychiatric patients. In M. A. Richardson & G. Haugland (Eds.), *Use of neuroleptics in children* (pp. 43–66). Washington DC: American Psychiatric Press.

Rivlin, L. G., & Wolfe, M. (1985). *Institutional settings in children's lives*. New York: Wiley.

Roe v. Wade, 410 U.S. 113, 152–153 (1973).

Rogers v. Okin, 634 F.2d 650 (1st Cir. 1980), *vacated and remanded sub. nom.* Mills v. Rogers, 457 U.S. 291 (1982).

Romeo v. Youngberg, 644 F.2d 147 (3d Cir. 1980), *vacated and remanded* 457 U.S. 307 (1982).

Rosen, C. E. (1977). The impact of an Open Campus program upon high school students' sense of control over their environment. *Psychology in the Schools, 14*, 216–219.

Rosen, L. D., Heckman, T., Carro, M. G., & Burchard, J. D. (1994). Satisfaction, involvement, and unconditional care: The perceptions of children and adolescents receiving wraparound services. *Journal of Child and Family Studies, 3*, 55–67.

Rosenblatt, A. (1996). Bows and ribbons, tape and twine: Wrapping the wraparound process for children with multi-system needs. *Journal of Child and Family Studies, 5*, 101–117.

Rosenblatt, A., & Attkisson, C. C. (1992). Integrating systems of care in California for youth with severe emotional disturbance, I: A descriptive overview of the California AB377 evaluation project. *Journal of Child and Family Studies, 1*, 93–113.

Rosenblatt, A., & Attkisson, C. C. (1993). Integrating systems of care in California for youth with severe emotional disturbance, III: Answers that lead to questions about out-of-home placements and the AB377 evaluation project. *Journal of Child and Family Studies, 2*, 119–141.

Rosenblatt, A., Attkisson, C. C., & Fernandez, A. J. (1992). Coordinating systems of care in California for youth with severe emotional disturbance, II: Initial group home expenditure and utilization findings from the California AB377 evaluation project. *Journal of Child and Family Studies, 1*, 263–286.

Ross, C. J. (1996). From vulnerability to voice: Appointing counsel for children in civil litigation. *Fordham Law Review, 64*, 1571–1620.

Rotegard, L. L., Hill, B. K., & Bruininks, R. H. (1983). Environmental characteristics of residential facilities for mentally retarded persons in the United States. *American Journal of Mental Deficiency, 83*, 49–56.

Roth, E. A., & Roth, L. H. (1984, April). *Children's feelings about psychiatric hospitalization: Legal and ethical implications.* Paper presented at the meeting of the American Orthopsychiatric Association, Toronto.

Rothman, D. J., & Rothman, S. M. (1980, June). The conflict over children's rights: Putting *Parham* in perspective. *Hastings Center Report,* pp. 7–10.

Ruggie, M. (1990). Retrenchment or realignment? U.S. Mental Health Policy and DRGS. *Journal of Health Politics, Policy and Law, 15,* 145–167.

Rutter, M., & Giller, H. (1984). *Juvenile delinquency: Trends and prospects.* New York: Guilford.

Sallee, F., Rock, C. M., & Head, L. A. (1996). Cognitive effects of neuroleptic use in children with Tourette's syndrome. In M. A. Richardson & G. Haugland (Eds.), *Use of neuroleptics in children* (pp. 171–184). Washington DC: American Psychiatric Press.

Salley v. St. Tammany Parish School Board, 1995 WL 148721 (E.D. La. 1994).

San Antonio Independent Community School District v. Rodriguez, 411 U.S. 1 (1973).

Santosky v. Kramer, 455 U.S. 745 (1982).

Scalora, M. J. (1986, March). *Proprietary hospitals and children's mental health care: The certificate-of-need process.* Paper presented at the meeting of the American Psychology-Law Society, Tucson.

Schain, R. J., Bushi, S., Gardella, D., & Guthrie, D. (1980). Characteristics of children admitted to a state mental hospital. *Hospital and Community Psychiatry, 31,* 49–51.

Schall v. Martin, 467 U.S. 253 (1984).

Scheerenberger, R. C. (1978). Public residential services for the mentally retarded. In N. R. Ellis (Ed.), *International review of research in mental retardation* (Vol. 9, pp. 187–208). New York: Academic.

Scherer, D. B., Brondino, M. J., Henggeler, S. W., Melton, G. B., & Hanley, J. H. (1994). Multisystemic family preservation therapy: Preliminary findings from a study of rural and minority serious adolescent offenders. *Journal of Emotional and Behavioral Disorders, 2,* 198–206.

Schoenberger, A. E. (1981). "Voluntary" commitment of mentally ill or retarded children: Child abuse by the Supreme Court. *University of Dayton Law Review, 7*, 1–31.

Schwartz, I. M. (1991). Out-of-home placements of children: Selected issues and prospects for the future. *Behavioral Sciences and the Law, 9*, 189–199.

Schwartz, I. M. (1989/1990). Hospitalization of adolescents for psychiatric and substance abuse. *Journal of Adolescent Health Care, 10*, 473–478.

Schwartz, I. M. (1995). The systemic impact of family preservation services: A case study. In I. Schwartz & P. AuClaire (Eds.), *Home-based services for troubled children* (pp. 157–171). Lincoln: University of Nebraska Press.

Schwartz, I. M., & AuClaire, P. (Eds.). (1995). *Home-based services for troubled children*. Lincoln: University of Nebraska Press.

Schwartz, I. M., AuClaire, P., & Harris, L. J. (1991). Family preservation services as an alternative to the out-of-home placement of adolescents: The Hennepin County Experience. In K. Wells & D. Biegel (Eds.), *Family preservation services: Research and evaluation* (pp. 33–46). Newbury Park CA: Sage.

Schwartz, I. M., & Willis, D. A. (1994). National trends in juvenile detention. In I. Schwartz & W. Barton (Eds.), *Reforming juvenile detention: No more hidden closets* (pp. 13–29). Columbus: Ohio State University Press.

Schwartz, S. J. (1989/1990). Damage actions as a strategy for enhancing the quality of care of persons with mental disabilities. *New York University Review of Law and Social Change, 17*, 651–687.

Scott, E. (1992). Judgment and reasoning in adolescent decision making. *Villanova Law Review, 37*, 1607–1669.

Scott, E., Reppucci, N. D., & Woolard, J. (1995). Evaluating adolescent decision making in legal contexts. *Law and Human Behavior, 19*, 221–244.

Secretary of Public Welfare of Pennsylvania v. Institutionalized Juveniles, 442 U.S. 640 (1979).

Shatz, S. F., Donovan, M., & Hong, A. (1991). The strip search of children and the Fourth Amendment. *University of San Francisco Law Review, 26*, 1–40.

Shelton v. Tucker, 364 U.S. 479, 488–490 (1960).

Sherman, B. R. (1988). Predictors of the decision to place developmentally disabled family members in residential care. *American Journal on Mental Retardation, 92*, 344–351.

Sherman, R. (1994, August 8). Juvenile judges say: Time to get tough. *National Law Journal*, pp. A1, A24, A25.

Sherman, B. R., & Cocozza, J. J. (1984). Stress in families of the developmentally disabled: A literature review of factors affecting the decision to seek out-of-home placements. *Family Relations, 33*, 95–103.

Shichor, D. (1993). The corporate context of private prisons. *Crime, Law and Social Change, 20*, 113–138.

Sholevar, G. P. (Ed.) (1995). *Conduct disorders in children and adolescents.* Washington DC: American Psychiatric Press.

Shore, M. F., & Massimo, J. (1979). Fifteen years after treatment: A follow-up study of comprehensive vocationally oriented psychotherapy. *American Journal of Orthopsychiatry, 49*, 240–245.

Silver, S. E., Duchnowski, A. J., Kutash, K., Friedman, R. M., Eisen, M., Prange, M. E., Brandenburg, N. A., & Greenbaum, P. E. (1992). A comparison of children with serious emotional disturbance served in residential and school settings. *Journal of Child and Family Studies, 1*, 43–59.

Silverstein, E. M. (1980). Civil commitment of minors: Due and undue process. *North Carolina Law Review, 58*, 1133–1159.

Simmonds, D. W. (1976). Children's rights and family dysfunction: "Daddy, why do I always have to be the crazy one?" In G. P. Koocher (Ed.), *Children's rights and the mental health professions* (pp. 33–39). New York: Wiley.

Skiba, R., & Grizzle, K. L. (1992). Qualifications v. logic and data: Excluding conduct disorders from the SED definition. *School Psychology Review, 21*, 23–28.

Slenkovich, J. E. (1992). Can the language "social maladjustment" in the SED definition be ignored? *School Psychology Review, 21*, 21–22.

Small, A. C., & Teagno, L. (1979, November). *A comparative study of children's and their parent's expectations of psychotherapy.* Paper presented at the meeting of the American Association of Psychiatric Services for Children, Chicago.

Spaulding, W. J. (1979). Post-*Parham* remedies: The involuntary commitment of minors in Virginia after *Parham v. J. R. University of Richmond Law Review, 13,* 695–741.

Stanilla, J. K., & Simpson, G. M. (1995). Drugs to treat extrapyramidal side effects. In Alan F. Schatzberg and Charles B. Nemeroff (Eds.), *The American Psychiatric Press textbook of psychopharmacology* (pp. 281–299). Washington DC: American Psychiatric Press.

State v. Werner, 242 S.E.2d 907 (W.Va. 1978).

Stein, L. I., & Test, M. A. (Eds.), (1978). *Alternatives to mental hospital treatment.* New York: Plenum.

Steinberg, L., & Cauffman, E. (1996). Maturity of judgment in adolescent decision making. *Law and Human Behavior, 20,* 249–272.

Stone, A. (1982). Psychiatric abuse and legal reform: Two ways to make a bad situation worse. *International Journal of Law and Psychiatry, 5,* 9–28.

Strober, M., Green, J., & Carlson, G. (1981). Reliability of psychiatric diagnosis in hospitalized adolescents: Interrater agreement using DSM-III. *Archives of General Psychiatry, 38,* 141–145.

Stroul, B. A., & Friedman, R. M. (1986). *A system of care for severely emotionally disturbed children and youth.* Washington DC: Georgetown University, CASSP Technical Assistance Center.

Subramanian, K. (1985). Reducing child abuse through respite center intervention. *Child Welfare, 64,* 501–509.

Sutnick, G. B. (1993). "Reasonable Efforts" revisited: Reforming federal financing of children's mental health services. *New York University Law Review, 68,* 136–184.

Sutton, J. R. (1985). The juvenile court and social welfare: Dynamics of progressive reform. *Law and Society Review, 19,* 107–145.

Szasz, T. (1977). The child as involuntary mental patient: The threat of child therapy to the child's dignity, privacy, and self-esteem. *San Diego Law Review, 14,* 1005–1027.

Talbott, J. A. (1980). The problems and potential roles of the state mental hospital. In J. A. Talbott (Ed.), *State mental hospitals: Problems and pitfalls* (pp. 21–29). New York: Human Sciences.

Talbott, J. A. (1985). The fate of the public psychiatric system. *Hospital and Community Psychiatry, 36,* 46–50.

von Talge, J. (1995). Overcoming courtroom challenges to the DSM-IV, II: Preparing for and overcoming courtroom challenges to DSM-IV. *American Journal of Forensic Psychology, 13,* 49–59.

Tapp, J. L., & Levine, F. J. (1974). Legal socialization: Strategies for an ethical legality. *Stanford Law Review, 27,* 1–72.

Tapp, J. L., & Melton, G. B. (1983). Preparing children for decision making: Implications of legal socialization research. In G. B. Melton, G. P. Koocher, & M. J. Saks (Eds.), *Children's competence to consent* (pp. 215–233). New York: Plenum.

Tate, D. C., Reppucci, N. D., & Mulvey, E. P. (1995). Violent juvenile delinquents: Treatment effectiveness and implications for future action. *American Psychologist, 50,* 777–781.

Taube, C. A., & Barrett, S. A. (1985). *Mental health, United States 1985.* Rockville MD: National Institute of Mental Health.

Taylor, L., & Adelman, H. S. (1986). Facilitating children's involvement in decisions that affect them: From concept to practice. *Journal of Clinical Child Psychology, 15,* 346–351.

Taylor, L., Adelman, H. S., & Kaser-Boyd, N. (1983). Perspectives of children regarding their participation in psychoeducational decisions. *Professional Psychology: Research and Practice, 14,* 882–894.

Taylor, L., Adelman, H. S., & Kaser-Boyd, N. (1985a). Exploring minors' reluctance and dissatisfaction with psychotherapy. *Professional Psychology: Research and Practice, 16,* 418–425.

Taylor, L., Adelman, H. S., & Kaser-Boyd, N. (1985b). Minors' attitudes and competence toward participation in psychoeducational decisions. *Professional Psychology: Research and Practice, 16,* 226–235.

Testimony focuses on increased private hospitalization. (1985). *Update: Improving Services for Emotionally Disturbed Children, 1,* 3.

Thibaut, J., & Walker, L. (1975). *Procedural justice.* Hillsdale NJ: Erlbaum.

Thibaut, J., & Walker, L. (1978). A theory of procedure. *California Law Review, 66,* 541–566.

Thomas S. v. Flaherty, 699 F. Supp. 1178 (W.D. N.C. 1988).

Thomas S. v. Morrow, 781 F.2d 367 (4th Cir. 1986), *cert. den. sub. nom.* Kirk v. Thomas S., 476 U.S. 1124 (1986).

Thompson, J. W., Rosenstein, M. J., Milazzo-Sayre, L. J., & MacAskill, R. L. (1986). Psychiatric services to adolescents: 1970–1980. *Hospital and Community Psychiatry, 37*, 584–590.

Thompson, R. A., & Wilcox, B. L. (1995). Child maltreatment research: Federal support and policy issues. *American Psychologist, 50*, 789–793.

Thornberry, T. P., Lizotte, A. J., Krohn, M. D., Farnworth, M., & Jang, S. J. (1991). Testing interactional theory: An examination of reciprocal causal relationships among family, school, and delinquency. *Journal of Criminal Law and Criminology, 82*, 3–35.

Thornberry, T. P., Lizotte, A. J., Krohn, M. D., Farnworth, M., & Jang, S. J. (1994). Delinquent peers, beliefs, and delinquent behavior: A longitudinal test of interactional theory. *Criminology, 32*, 601–637.

Tiano, L. V. (1980–1981). *Parham v. J. R.:* "Voluntary" commitment of minors to mental institutions. *American Journal of Law and Medicine, 6*, 125–149.

Tinker v. Des Moines Independent Community School District, 393 U.S. 503 (1969).

Tjosvold, D., & Tjosvold, M. A. (1983). Social psychological analysis of residences for retarded persons. *American Journal of Mental Deficiency, 88*, 28–40.

Tolmach, J. (1985). "There ain't nobody on my side": A new day treatment program for black urban youth. *Journal of Clinical Child Psychology, 14*, 214–219.

Tribe, L. (1975). Childhood, suspect classifications, and conclusive presumptions: Three linked riddles. *Law and Contemporary Problems, 39*, 118–143.

United Nations Convention on the Rights of the Child, U.N. Doc. A/Res/44/25 (1978).

United States Advisory Board on Child Abuse and Neglect. (1993). *Neighbors helping neighbors: A new national strategy for the protection of children.* Washington DC: U.S. Government Printing Office.

United States v. Salerno, 481 U.S. 739 (1987).

Upshur, C. C. (1983). Developing respite care: A support service for families with disabled members. *Family Relations, 32*, 13–20.

Van Dusen, K. T. (1981). Net widening and relabeling: Some consequences of deinstitutionalization. *American Behavioral Scientist, 24*, 801–810.

Vernonia School District v. Acton, 515 U.S. 646, 115 S.Ct. 2386 (1995).

Vitek v. Jones, 445 U.S. 480 (1980).

Wadlington, W. J., Whitebread, C. H., & Davis, S. B. (1983). *Children in the legal system*. Mineola NY: Foundation.

Warren, C. A. B. (1981). New forms of social control: The myth of de-institutionalization. *American Behavioral Scientist, 24*, 724–740.

Washington v. Harper, 494 U.S. 210 (1990).

Watson, A. S. (1980). Children, families, and courts: Before the best interests of the child and *Parham v. J. R. Virginia Law Review, 66*, 653–679.

Weicker, L. (1987). It is time to reform medicaid. *American Journal of Mental Deficiency, 92*, 139–140.

Weisbard, A. J. (1986). Informed consent: The law's uneasy compromise with ethical theory. *Nebraska Law Review, 65*, 749–767.

Weisz, J. R., & Weiss, B. (1993). *Effects of psychotherapy with children and adolescents*. Newbury Park CA: Sage.

Weithorn, L. A. (1982). Developmental factors and competence to make informed treatment decisions. In G. B. Melton (Ed.), *Legal reforms affecting child and youth services* (pp. 85–100). New York: Haworth.

Weithorn, L. A. (1983). Involving children in decisions affecting their own welfare: Guidelines for professionals. In G. B. Melton, G. P. Koocher, & M. J. Saks (Eds.), *Children's competence to consent* (pp. 235–260). New York: Plenum.

Weithorn, L. A. (1988). Mental hospitalization of troublesome youth: An analysis of skyrocketing admission rates. *Stanford Law Review, 40*, 773–838.

Weithorn, L. A., & Campbell, S. B. (1982). The competency of children and adolescents to make informed treatment decisions. *Child Development, 53*, 1589–1598.

Wells, K. (1991). Placement of emotionally disturbed children in residential treatment: A review of placement criteria. *American Journal of Orthopsychiatry, 61*, 339–347.

Wexler, D. B. (1981). *Mental health law: Major issues*. New York: Plenum.

Wilson, J. P. (1978). *The rights of adolescents in the mental health system*. Lexington MA: Lexington Books.

Wingo, H., & Freytag, S. N. (1982). Decisions within the family: A clash of constitutional rights. *Iowa Law Review, 67*, 401–441.

Winick, B. J. (1989). The right to refuse mental health treatment: A First Amendment Perspective. *University of Miami Law Review, 44*, 1–103.

Winsberg, B. G., Bialer, I., Kupietz, S., Botti, E., & Balka, E. B. (1980). Home versus hospital care of children with behavior disorders: A controlled investigation. *Archives of General Psychiatry, 37*, 413–418.

Winsberg, B. G., & Yepes, L. E. (1978). Antipsychotics (major tranquilizers, neuroleptics). In J. S. Werry (Ed.), *Pediatric psychopharmacology: The use of behavior modifying drugs in children* (pp. 234–273). New York: Brunner/Mazel.

Wolfe, M. (1978). Childhood and privacy. In I. Altman & J. Wohlwill (Eds.), *Human behavior and environment: Advances in theory and research* (Vol. 3, pp. 175–222). New York: Plenum.

Wolfensberger, W. (1970). The principle of normalization and its implications to psychiatric services. *American Journal of Psychiatry, 127*, 291–297.

Wolfensberger, W. (1971). Will there always be an institution? II. The impact of new service models. *Mental Retardation, 9*, 31–38.

Wolfensberger, W. (1975). *The origin and nature of our institutional models.* Syracuse NY: Human Policy.

Wolins, M. (1969). Group care: Friend or foe? *Social Work, 14*, 35–53.

Wooden, K. (1976). *Weeping in the playtime of others: America's incarcerated children.* New York: McGraw-Hill.

Woodward, H. L. (1993). One community's response to the multi-system service needs of individuals with mental illnesses and developmental disabilities. *Community Mental Health Journal, 29*, 347–359.

Worsfold, V. L. (1974). A philosophical justification for children's rights. *Harvard Educational Review, 44*, 142–157.

Wurtele, S. K., Wilson, D. R., & Prentice-Dunn, S. (1983). Characteristics of children in residential treatment programs: Findings and clinical implications. *Journal of Clinical Child Psychology, 12*, 137–144.

Yamomoto, K. (1979). Children's ratings of the stressfulness of experiences. *Developmental Psychology, 15*, 581–582.

Yoe, J. T., Santarcangelo, S., Atkins, M., & Burchard, J. D. (1996). Wraparound care in Vermont: Program development, implementation, and evaluation of a statewide system of individualized services. *Journal of Child and Family Studies, 5,* 23–39.

Yoshikawa, H. (1994). Prevention as cumulative protection: Effects of early family support and education on chronic delinquency and its risks. *Psychological Bulletin, 115,* 28–54.

Youngberg v. Romeo, 457 U.S. 307 (1982), *vacating and remanding* 644 F.2d 147 (3d Cir. 1980).

Zander, T. (1976). Civil commitment in Wisconsin: The impact of *Lessard v. Schmidt. Wisconsin Law Review, 1976,* 503–562.

Zigler, E. F., & Balla, D. A. (1978). Impact of institutional experience on the behavior and development of retarded persons. *Annual Progress in Child Psychiatry and Child Development, 1978,* 417–433.

Zimmerman, S. L. (1984). The Mental Retardation Family Subsidy Program: Its effects on families with a mentally handicapped child. *Family Relations, 33,* 105–118.

Zinermon v. Burch, 494 U.S. 113 (1990).

Zito, J. M., Craig, T. J., & Wanderling, J. A. (1996). Neuroleptic use in children and adolescents hospitalized for psychiatric disorders: Gender issues and implications. In M. A. Richardson & G. Haugland (Eds.), *Use of neuroleptics in children* (pp. 23–41). Washington DC: American Psychiatric Press.

Index